Beyond Space and Time

The Science and Spirit of Distance Healing in Reiki

Beyond Space and Time

The Science and Spirit of Distance Healing in Reiki

Robert T. Yarborough

Pranava Books

Publisher's Cataloging-in-Publication Data

Yarborough, Robert T., 1960-
Beyond Space and Time: The Science and Spirit of Distance Healing in Reiki / by Robert T. Yarborough.
—First edition.
p. cm.
Includes bibliographical references and index.
ISBN 979-8-9912582-3-4

    1. Reiki (Healing art). 2. Quantum theory—Miscellanea. 3. Energy medicine. 4. Spiritual healing. 5. Metaphysics. I. Title.
RZ403 .Y37 2024
615.852 — dc23

LCCN: 2024921030

Printed in theUnited States of America

10 9 8 7 6 5 4 3 2 1

Dedication

Sparrow, Sydney, and Sage,
You illuminate my path and fuel my every intention.

May the universe always reflect the same healing energy back to you
that you so effortlessly bring into my life.

Contents

Author's Preface

Energy has fascinated me since I was a teenager. It's invisible, yet we experience it every day. It flows through us, connects us to each other, and even the universe itself. The concept that energy can heal, especially across time and space, seems magical. When I began my journey as a Reiki practitioner, I was amazed by the power of touch and intention in facilitating healing. But it wasn't until I explored distance healing in Reiki that I truly understood energy's vast, limitless potential.

Distance healing has always been a profound mystery to those unfamiliar with it, and for many, the idea that healing could transcend physical proximity seems implausible. But as I dove deeper into the teachings of Reiki and explored its connections with quantum physics, sacred geometry, and metaphysical principles, I realized that the answers to how and why distance healing works are not hidden— they are all around us, woven into the very fabric of the universe.

In writing *Beyond Space and Time*, I sought to bring together the spiritual and scientific aspects of Reiki distance healing. My goal is not only to demystify the process for practitioners and those interested in the healing arts but also to offer a comprehensive, holistic understanding of the greater forces at play. Energy is not confined by the boundaries of space or time; it is fluid, universal, and responsive to intention. Whether you're healing someone across a room or the world, the same principles apply: we are all connected by an energetic web that transcends physicality.

Throughout the book, I will introduce you to powerful concepts—quantum mechanics, the unified field, karma, and even the Akashic Records—all of which contribute to the effectiveness and depth of distance healing. By understanding these principles, we can better grasp how healing works and how deeply interconnected we all are. I believe that as we gain more insight into the true nature of energy, we unlock the ability to heal ourselves, each other, and, ultimately, the world.

This book is intended for Reiki practitioners, energy healers, and anyone intrigued by the mysteries of healing beyond the physical realm. I have included practical guidance, scientific theories, spiritual philosophies, and case studies to help bring these abstract concepts into tangible reality. Whether you want to deepen your healing practice or explore the profound nature of energy, I hope that *Beyond Space and Time* will serve as both a guide and an inspiration on your journey.

Energy knows no limits. Healing knows no boundaries. And as you'll see, we are all infinitely capable of connecting, healing, and thriving—no matter where we are.

Thank you for joining me on this exploration of distance healing in Reiki. May this book expand your awareness, open your heart, and empower your ability to heal beyond space and time.

With gratitude and light…

Distance Healing Across Time and Space

Distance healing in Reiki is a profound practice that transcends the ordinary boundaries of time and space. At its core, Reiki is the transmission of universal life energy from the practitioner to the recipient, traditionally through physical touch. However, one of the most remarkable aspects of Reiki is that this healing energy can be sent and received without physical proximity. This ability to heal at a distance is rooted in the understanding that energy is not confined by the limitations of space and that all living things are connected through an unseen web of energy that spans the entire universe.

Distance healing in Reiki defies the conventional understanding of physical separation. It operates in non-locality, a concept familiar to ancient spiritual traditions and modern quantum physics. This suggests that particles—and, by extension, people—can be connected across vast distances.

This unique approach in Reiki allows practitioners to extend healing energy to someone who may be in another room, city, or even country. With specific Reiki symbols, particularly Hon Sha Ze Sho Nen, the practitioner can connect with the recipient's energy field, sending healing vibrations across the ether. This symbol is often called the "bridge of light" or "no past, no present, no future," as it facilitates healing across distance and time.

For those new to Reiki, this may seem like a daunting or mysterious idea. How can energy move through space without a direct, physical connection? Yet, this concept becomes easier to grasp when we begin considering the interconnectedness of all life. Reiki's foundation lies in the understanding that everything—every person, plant, and even inanimate object—is made up of energy, vibrating at different frequencies. Through focused intention and meditation, the practitioner can tune into these frequencies, and channel energy like one might turn a radio dial to find a specific station. The energy moves where it is needed, guided by the intentions of both the practitioner and the recipient.

What makes distance healing in Reiki truly special is its capacity to heal over space and its ability to transcend time. Many practitioners report using distance healing to address past traumas or future concerns, as Reiki energy is not bound by the linearity of time. In this way, distance healing operates both in the present moment and beyond it, reflecting the infinite potential of energy to move fluidly through all dimensions of existence.

As we explore this concept further, it becomes clear that distance healing is not a passive act but an intentional connection. This bridge allows the practitioner and recipient to unite in a shared, energetic space. This energetic space exists beyond the limits of physical reality, where healing, growth, and transformation are not only possible but profoundly powerful.

Whether experienced with Reiki or new to the practice, distance healing can be an invitation to broaden your understanding of how energy works. It reminds us that healing is not confined to what we can see or touch but is an expansive, universal force that connects us all, no matter where we are.

The Goal of this Book

This book aims to take you on a journey that explores the practice of distance healing and the deeper questions of how and why it works. While Reiki is often seen as a spiritual healing practice, there is much more to uncover beneath the surface. This book seeks to bridge the gap between science, metaphysics, and spirituality, offering a comprehensive understanding of how energy healing transcends space and time.

The convergence of science and spirituality has opened up new ways of thinking about the world around us. What once seemed like opposing viewpoints—scientific reason versus spiritual belief—are now seen as complementary forces that explain the mysteries of the universe. In particular, advances in quantum physics have illuminated how energy behaves in ways that align with the ancient spiritual teachings on which Reiki is based. Concepts such as quantum entanglement and the unified field suggest that everything in the universe is connected, regardless of distance. That energy can be transmitted instantaneously across these vast connections. In this way, the science of energy mirrors the spiritual principles that have guided healing practices for millennia.

However, understanding distance healing requires more than just a scientific lens. While physics provides a framework, the metaphysical principles that explore the nature of existence beyond the physical help us grasp the full depth of what happens during a Reiki healing session. At the heart of Reiki is the belief that everything is made up of energy, vibrating at different frequencies. This energy flows through and around us, connecting us to the universe in ways beyond our senses. When we engage in distance healing, we are tapping into this energetic field, accessing the vibrational patterns that make up our reality, and sending healing intentions to influence those vibrations positively.

But it doesn't stop there. Spirituality, with its rich tradition of wisdom and practice, offers profound insights into the mechanics of distance healing. Reiki is a spiritually guided life force energy—its name reflects this truth. This book will delve into the spiritual aspects of Reiki, such as the role of intention, the use of sacred symbols, and the importance of cultivating a deep, compassionate connection with the recipient, even from afar. These elements give Reiki its healing power, helping practitioners send energy and align with the recipient's higher self and universal consciousness.

Ultimately, the aim is to guide you through a multi-layered understanding of distance healing—how it works scientifically, metaphysically, and spiritually. Whether you are a seasoned Reiki practitioner looking to deepen your knowledge or someone new to energy healing, you will find value in exploring these themes. We will examine how the ancient principles of energy healing align with the latest scientific theories, how metaphysical laws such as the Law of Vibration govern our ability to heal at a distance, and how spirituality elevates Reiki beyond technique into a transformative practice of connection and compassion.

As we move through the following chapters, you will see that distance healing is not just an abstract idea but a real, tangible force that operates in our world. Each step will unpack the scientific theories, metaphysical principles, and spiritual practices that allow Reiki energy to move effortlessly across time and space. This exploration will deepen your understanding of Reiki and broaden your perspective on the nature of healing, life's interconnectedness, and energy's boundless potential.

This is an invitation to expand your mind, open your heart, and see the world through the lens of energy, where distance is no barrier to healing and where the science of the universe and the spirit of life converge in perfect harmony.

Science and Spirit in Distance Healing

As we embark on this journey together, we must understand that distance healing in Reiki does not exist in isolation. It is supported by a rich tapestry of interconnected concepts, both ancient and modern, spiritual and scientific. Throughout this book, we will explore these concepts to uncover the full depth of how and why distance healing works. From the universe's fundamental laws to the complexities of quantum theory, each chapter will guide you through the layers of understanding that contribute to the power of Reiki healing.

One of the most fascinating principles we will dive into is quantum theory, particularly the phenomenon of quantum entanglement. In simple terms, quantum entanglement refers to how particles, once connected, remain linked no matter how far apart. This mirrors how Reiki energy can be sent across vast distances as the healer and recipient become energetically entangled. What happens to one particle—or person—affects the other, even if they are worlds apart. This scientific discovery has profound implications for understanding energy flow in healing practices, showing that distance is no barrier when transferring energetic information.

We will also explore the laws of the universe—fundamental principles that govern how energy flows and interacts with everything around us. One of the most essential of these is the Law of Vibration, which states that everything in the universe, from the largest star to the smallest atom, is in constant motion, vibrating at its unique frequency. Reiki practitioners harness this vibrational energy to align themselves with the recipient, attuning to their frequency to deliver healing energy. Understanding the Law of Vibration helps explain why Reiki is so effective at bridging distance: it's not about physical proximity but matching and shifting energy frequencies.

Another key concept that ties into distance healing is the Law of Cause and Effect, often called karma. Karma is the idea that every action, thought, or intention creates ripples in the energetic fabric of the universe, leading to consequences that may manifest across time and space. In Reiki, we can work to heal present-day issues and the energetic imprints left by past actions, even those from previous lifetimes. Distance healing, in particular, can address these karmic patterns, allowing the recipient to release old energy blockages and move forward with greater clarity and well-being.

Additionally, we will delve into the fractal nature of the universe. A fractal is a repeating pattern that exists at every scale, from the microscopic to the cosmic. This concept reveals the interconnectedness of all things: the part reflects the whole, and every individual is a microcosm of the greater universe. Reiki healing taps into this fractal structure, as healing one person at a distance can have ripple effects on the collective consciousness. The fractal universe shows us that healing energy does not only affect the individual but resonates throughout the entire web of existence, further amplifying the power of distance Reiki.

We'll also explore the idea of sacred geometry, the universal language of creation that underlies everything from the growth of plants to the spiraling galaxies in the cosmos. Sacred geometric patterns, such as the Flower of Life, reveal the blueprint of the universe's energetic structure. Reiki, too, operates within this energetic matrix, drawing upon these geometric principles to channel healing energy. The more we understand these universal patterns, the more we see how distance healing follows the natural laws of energy flow.

This book will also touch on spiritual traditions such as the Akashic Records. This vast, energetic library holds the memories of every soul's journey through time and space. Distance healing can access these records, helping to heal not just the physical body but the spiritual and emotional imprints carried across lifetimes. By understanding how these records store energetic information, we can begin to see how healing can be directed toward past traumas and future intentions, further extending the reach of Reiki across time.

These are just a few powerful, interconnected concepts we will explore together. These ideas—quantum theory, the laws of the universe, karma, fractals, sacred geometry, and the Akashic Records—play a vital role in understanding the vast potential of distance healing. As we continue through the chapters, you will see how these principles weave together, creating a holistic understanding of how energy moves, heals, and transforms us, no matter where we are in time or space.

The Foundations of Energy Healing

The Essence of Reiki Energy

Basic Principles of Reiki

Reiki is the practice of channeling universal life energy for healing, balance, and spiritual growth. The word "Reiki" itself is derived from two Japanese characters: "Rei," meaning universal, and "Ki," meaning life energy. Together, they represent the vast, boundless energy that permeates all living things. Whether you're familiar with the practice or just beginning to explore the world of energy healing, understanding this foundational concept is crucial.

Reiki works on the premise that energy is the force that animates all life. This energy, known as "Ki" in Japanese, "Chi" in Chinese, and "Prana" in Sanskrit, flows through and around us constantly. We experience health, vitality, and emotional balance when this energy flows freely. But when the energy becomes blocked or stagnant—due to stress, trauma, negative thoughts, or illness—it can lead to physical discomfort, emotional unrest, or even disease.

At the heart of Reiki is the understanding that we are all energy beings and that energy can be consciously directed to promote healing. The practitioner acts as a conduit, channeling this universal life energy to the recipient through direct touch or, as we will explore in greater depth, over distance. Reiki's ability to transcend physical contact makes it unique, allowing the energy to flow wherever it is needed, regardless of proximity.

Central to the practice of Reiki is the principle of intention. The practitioner does not "create" the healing energy but directs and amplifies it with intention. This intention is critical, aligning the practitioner's focus and energy with the recipient's needs. In many ways, intention acts as a bridge between the physical and energetic worlds, guiding the flow of Reiki to promote healing on all levels—physical, emotional, mental, and spiritual.

Setting an intention in Reiki is much like planting a seed. When a practitioner focuses on the well-being of the recipient, they are planting the seed of healing in the recipient's energy field. Just as a gardener tends to a plant, nurturing it with water and sunlight, the practitioner nurtures this healing process with the focused energy of Reiki, allowing the recipient's body and spirit to take what it needs from the universal life force.

Moreover, Reiki operates on the understanding that energy is intelligent. The universal life energy knows where to go and how to assist the recipient, guided by both the practitioner's intention and the recipient's needs. This idea that energy is intuitive might seem foreign to those who approach healing from a purely physical or medical standpoint, but in the world of Reiki, it is foundational. The practitioner does not control the outcome; instead, they trust that the energy will naturally flow to where it is needed most, facilitating a healing process uniquely suited to the recipient's current state of being.

In this way, Reiki is not a forceful intervention but a gentle encouragement—an invitation for the body, mind, and spirit to return to balance. The practitioner holds space, trusting in the intelligence of the universal energy and allowing it to do its work. This focus on trust and non-attachment is one of the hallmarks of Reiki healing. Rather than imposing an outcome, the practitioner releases any need to control and surrenders to the flow of the energy.

The principles of energy and intention in Reiki are not only applicable to the practice of hands-on healing but also form the foundation for distance healing. Whether the practitioner is physically present with the recipient or separated by time and space, the same energy flows with the same intention, guided by the same universal principles. Reiki transcends the physical world's limitations because the energy it channels exists beyond those limitations, tapping into the infinite, ever-present field of life force that connects all things.

Understanding these foundational principles of energy and intention is the first step in grasping the power of Reiki. As we continue this book, we will build on these ideas, exploring how they extend into the practice of distance healing, where Reiki's potential truly shines.

Energy Transmission and Healing in Traditional Reiki Practice

To understand the magic and science behind Reiki, it's essential to first grasp how energy transmission occurs during a traditional Reiki session. In its most basic form, Reiki is a hands-on healing practice where the practitioner channels universal life energy into the recipient, allowing this energy to flow through them to restore balance and promote healing on all levels. The beauty of Reiki is that it is simple, yet incredibly profound—an exchange of energy that works without the need for manipulation, medication, or invasive techniques.

During a Reiki session, the practitioner uses their hands to direct this universal life energy into the recipient's energy field, also known as the aura, and physical body. The practitioner serves as a conduit, allowing the energy to pass through them, into the recipient. In this process, the practitioner's own energy remains separate; they are not giving their energy to the recipient, nor are they taking energy from them. Instead, they are channeling the energy from the source—this universal field of life force energy that surrounds and permeates all things.

Imagine the practitioner as a hollow vessel or a clear channel through which energy flows. The energy itself is not generated by the practitioner but is drawn from an infinite and abundant source, often referred to as the universal energy or divine consciousness. The practitioner opens themselves up to this energy, allowing it to move through their body and out through their hands, directing it into the recipient's energy field and physical body.

One of the key principles of Reiki is that energy is drawn, not pushed. The recipient's body and energy system will pull in exactly the amount of energy it needs to restore balance. This means that the practitioner doesn't need to force or direct the energy in a specific way—it goes where it is most needed. Whether the recipient is experiencing physical pain, emotional distress, mental exhaustion, or spiritual disconnection, the universal energy naturally flows to the areas that require healing, bringing balance and harmony.

In traditional Reiki practice, this transmission of energy typically happens through a series of hand positions. These positions correspond to the recipient's energy centers, known as chakras, which are believed to regulate the flow of energy throughout the body. By placing their hands over these centers, the practitioner helps to clear blockages and restore the free flow of energy. The hands may be placed directly on the body or hover just above it, depending on the recipient's comfort level and the practitioner's style. In either case, the energy moves fluidly, guided by both the practitioner's intention and the recipient's innate wisdom.

The process of energy transmission in Reiki is often described as deeply relaxing. Recipients frequently report feeling warmth or tingling in the areas where the practitioner's hands are placed. Others may experience a sense of deep calm, emotional release, or even a shift in their awareness as the energy flows through them. This response to energy transmission varies from person to person and from session to session, but the overall effect is one of balance, peace, and healing.

What's particularly fascinating about Reiki is that the energy doesn't just address the immediate symptoms—it works on a holistic level, addressing the root causes of imbalances. Reiki has the ability to penetrate beyond the physical body, working within the emotional, mental, and spiritual layers of the recipient's being. For example, a physical ailment might be rooted in unprocessed emotions or negative thought patterns. As the universal life energy flows, it helps to release these blockages, allowing the body's natural healing mechanisms to kick in.

This holistic approach to healing is what sets Reiki apart from many other energy-based practices. It acknowledges that healing is not just about alleviating physical symptoms but about addressing the entire energetic ecosystem of the person. Everything is interconnected—mind, body, emotions, and spirit—and Reiki works to bring harmony to all these levels simultaneously.

Energy transmission in traditional Reiki is not a rigid process; it is fluid, intuitive, and deeply personal. Each session is different, guided by the unique needs of the recipient at that moment. The practitioner remains open and receptive, trusting that the energy will flow exactly where it is needed. This trust is an essential part of the practice, as Reiki practitioners learn to release control and allow the universal life energy to guide the healing process.

The role of the practitioner is to hold space for the recipient, offering their presence and channeling the energy without judgment or expectation. This creates a safe, supportive environment where the recipient can relax, open up, and receive the healing energy. It is a practice that relies on compassion, trust, and the inherent wisdom of the energy itself.

In traditional Reiki practice, this energy transmission can be experienced in person, where the practitioner and recipient are physically present with one another.

However, as we will explore later, Reiki's unique approach to energy transcends physical boundaries, making distance healing not only possible but equally effective. Whether the practitioner is near or far, the same universal energy flows, guided by the same principles of intention, trust, and compassion.

Distance Healing Enhanced by Non-Locality

The same universal life energy that flows through a practitioner's hands in traditional Reiki healing also flows when healing is conducted across distance. While it may seem counterintuitive at first—that one can send energy to someone who is not physically present—the principles that guide Reiki remain unchanged. The key to understanding how distance healing operates lies in non-locality, a term in quantum physics that describes how particles (or energies) can influence each other across great distances without any physical connection.

In traditional Reiki, the practitioner and recipient share the same physical space, allowing the energy to be directed immediately into the recipient's energy field. However, distance healing demonstrates that Reiki is not bound by physical proximity. Instead, it operates on a universal energy grid, where time and space are not limiting factors. Just as energy can be transferred directly through hands-on healing, it can also be transmitted across time and space, reaching a recipient wherever they may be.

Non-locality is a concept that helps explain this phenomenon. In the quantum world, non-locality suggests that two particles can be entangled, meaning their states are linked, regardless of the distance between them. This connection allows changes to one particle to affect the other instantly, even if they are light-years apart. This principle has been observed in quantum experiments. While Reiki operates on a spiritual and metaphysical level, the parallels to non-locality are clear: distance does not diminish the connection between a practitioner and a recipient, and energy can flow freely between them without regard for space.

Distance healing in Reiki is possible because the energy being channeled—universal life energy—is not confined to the physical plane. It exists within the larger, interconnected web of the universe, flowing through and around everything. When a Reiki practitioner focuses on sending healing energy to someone far away, they tap into this universal network, drawing on the same energy they would in person and directing it to the recipient's energy field.

One of the tools used to facilitate distance healing in Reiki is the Hon Sha Ze Sho Nen symbol, often referred to as the "distance symbol." This symbol bridges the practitioner and the recipient, allowing the energy to flow beyond physical boundaries. Its name is often translated to mean "no past, no present, no future," reflecting the timeless and spaceless nature of Reiki energy. With this symbol, the practitioner can connect with the recipient's energy field no matter where they are, transcending both time and space.

In practice, a distance healing session is like an in-person session regarding its intention and the energy being channeled. The practitioner sets the intention to send healing energy to the recipient and, through meditation and focus, connects to the recipient's energy field. Just as in a hands-on session, the practitioner allows the energy to flow through them and into the recipient, trusting that the universal energy knows where to go and what is needed.

Though the recipient is not physically present, many report experiencing the same sensations during a distance healing session as they would during an in-person treatment. They may feel warmth, tingling, or a sense of peace as the energy flows into their body. These responses reflect that Reiki energy operates beyond the physical realm—interacting with the subtle energy bodies (or auras) that surround and permeate all of us. In this way, the physical distance between the practitioner and the recipient becomes irrelevant; the energy does not need to travel through space in the traditional sense because it already exists in the recipient's energy field, waiting to be activated and guided by the practitioner's intention.

Distance healing in Reiki can even be applied across time. This means that a practitioner can send healing energy to a past event or a future situation, helping to heal unresolved traumas or setting the stage for future well-being. This is because, from an energetic perspective, time is not linear. It exists as part of the same energetic web that connects all things. The practitioner can tap into this web and direct energy not only across physical distances but across the timeline of a person's life.

It's essential to recognize that distance healing in Reiki does not work because of the practitioner's personal power. Instead, it works because of the universal principles of energy, which remain the same whether the practitioner and recipient are in the same room or separated by continents. The practitioner serves as a conduit for the universal life energy, setting the intention and allowing the energy to flow to the recipient, trusting that the connection between them is already in place.

This ability to heal across distance is one of the most powerful aspects of Reiki, as it reflects the deep interconnectedness of all things. Whether the practitioner is near or far, the energy remains the same, flowing where it is needed and facilitating healing in ways that transcend the limitations of the physical world (Dauth, et al). Non-locality, the use of Reiki symbols, and the practitioner's intention all play a role in making distance healing as effective and meaningful as hands-on healing.

In the following chapters, we will explore the mechanics of how this works, exploring the scientific theories and spiritual principles that explain why energy healing can travel across time and space. Distance healing in Reiki opens up a world of possibilities, reminding us that energy is not bound by physicality and that healing can occur anytime, anywhere.

Section Summary
The Essence of Reiki Energy

In this section, we explored the foundational concepts of Reiki energy and how it operates both in traditional hands-on healing and distance healing. Reiki, derived from the Japanese words "Rei" (universal) and "Ki" (life energy), is the practice of channeling universal life energy to promote healing, balance, and spiritual growth. This energy flows through all living things and is key to maintaining physical, emotional, mental, and spiritual well-being. Blockages in this flow can lead to discomfort or illness, and Reiki works to restore balance by clearing these blockages.

Energy Transmission in Traditional Reiki Practice

Energy transmission in a traditional Reiki session occurs when the practitioner channels universal life energy through their hands into the recipient's energy field and physical body. Acting as a conduit, the practitioner does not give their own energy but directs the universal life force to the recipient. The recipient naturally draws this energy to the areas where it is most needed. The process is deeply relaxing and intuitive, addressing physical symptoms and the emotional, mental, and spiritual roots of imbalance. Reiki's holistic approach restores harmony across all levels of the recipient's being.

Distance Healing Enhanced by Non-Locality

Reiki's power extends beyond physical proximity, as distance healing operates on the same energetic principles as hands-on Reiki. This ability is enhanced by the concept of non-locality, borrowed from quantum physics, which explains how energy can be transmitted across space and time. Practitioners use the Hon Sha Ze Sho Nen symbol to bridge the physical distance between themselves and the recipient, facilitating the flow of universal life energy wherever it is needed. Distance healing reflects Reiki's timeless and spaceless nature, allowing practitioners to send healing energy across great distances and to past and future events.

Reiki energy flows where it is needed through direct contact or across vast distances, guided by the practitioner's intention and the recipient's innate wisdom. This interconnected web of energy transcends physical limitations, offering profound healing on all levels of existence.

§

Beyond Space and Time

The Principle of Non-Locality in Energy Healing

One of the most fascinating and often challenging concepts for those new to energy healing is that Reiki can be transmitted across time and space, reaching its recipient without physical contact. To understand this, we must look beyond the physical world as we know it and delve into the realm of quantum physics and non-locality.

Non-locality, as understood in quantum mechanics, is the phenomenon where two particles, once connected, continue to affect each other no matter how far apart. Albert Einstein first proposed this idea as "spooky action at a distance," a term that reflected his skepticism about the concept. Yet, experiments have shown that once particles become entangled, a change in one particle is immediately reflected in the other, even if they are separated by great distances (Einstein, Podolsky, & Rosen, 1935).

For practitioners of Reiki and other energy healing modalities, non-locality provides a compelling framework for understanding how healing energy can be sent across vast distances. Just as particles can be connected across space in the quantum realm, people's energy fields can be entangled through the universal life force. This concept of non-locality in Reiki is not bound by physical proximity because it operates in a dimension of energy that transcends the limitations of time and space (Goswami, 1995).

Reiki practitioners use this principle to connect energetically with a recipient, regardless of location. During a distance healing session, the practitioner sets the intention to connect with the recipient's energy, creating a bridge through which healing can flow. This process is similar to the phenomenon of quantum entanglement, where the practitioner's energy field and the recipient's energy field become linked, allowing the flow of energy to pass between them (McTaggart, 2008).

Non-locality helps explain how energy can be transmitted and received even when the practitioner and the recipient are not in the same physical space. By tapping into the universal energy grid, the practitioner sends healing energy to the recipient, trusting that the energy will arrive precisely where needed, regardless of distance (Lipton, 2005). This is why many recipients of distance Reiki report sensations similar to those they experience in hands-on Reiki sessions, such as warmth, tingling, or a deep sense of relaxation.

Distance healing works because Reiki energy is not confined to the physical plane. It exists in the realm of the unified field, a concept described in both quantum physics and metaphysics. The unified field suggests that all things in the universe are interconnected, existing within a vast web of energy (Laszlo, 2007). Reiki practitioners tap into this field, drawing on the universal life energy that permeates everything and sending it to the recipient with focused intention. The universal energy is intelligent and intuitive, meaning it will flow to the areas where healing is most needed, even if the practitioner and recipient are miles apart (Brennan, 1988).

One of the most essential tools used in distance Reiki is the *Hon Sha Ze Sho Nen* symbol, which helps create this energetic bridge between practitioner and recipient. Often translated as "no past, no present, no future," this symbol transcends time and space, allowing healing energy to flow freely across distance (Petter, 2000). Using this symbol in their practice, the Reiki practitioner can focus their intention and connect with the recipient's energy field, regardless of where the recipient is in the physical world.

This symbol and the understanding of non-locality invite us to embrace a broader perspective on time and space. In many ways, Reiki reminds us that our modern understanding of reality is limited by physical perception. Still, energy exists and interacts beyond what we can see or touch. Reiki's ability to heal at a distance exemplifies how energy transcends the boundaries of physical reality.

Healing Across Time

In addition to transcending physical space, Reiki has the remarkable ability to transcend time. This ability to work across time may seem even more mysterious than distance healing, but it operates under the same foundational principles of energy and intention. Much like the universe it flows through, Reiki energy is not constrained by the linear nature of time as we typically perceive it. Instead, it can move freely along the past, present, and future continuum, making it a powerful tool for healing past wounds and setting the stage for future well-being.

To understand how Reiki can be applied across time, it's important to remember that in the energetic realm, time is not viewed as a straight line. Instead, time is fluid, like a spiral or a web, where all moments are interconnected. This concept echoes ancient spiritual beliefs and is increasingly supported by modern theoretical physics, particularly through the work of quantum mechanics, which suggests that time is not a fixed, linear progression but an elastic dimension that can stretch, bend, and intertwine (Barbour, 1999).

Reiki's capacity to heal the past allows practitioners to address unresolved traumas or emotional blockages that continue to influence a person's energy in the present. These blockages, often called energetic imprints, can result from difficult experiences that have left a lasting mark on the individual's physical, emotional, or spiritual body. When such events are not fully processed, they can disrupt the flow of energy, leading to patterns of behavior or illness that persist for years or even lifetimes.

In a Reiki session focused on healing the past, the practitioner sets the intention to send healing energy to the specific moment or event where the trauma or blockage occurred. The Hon Sha Ze Sho Nen symbol, which allows energy to flow across time and space, is again used to bridge the gap between the present and the past (Petter, 2000). By doing this, the practitioner helps to release the energetic charge associated with the event, bringing the recipient a sense of closure and peace. This process not only heals the past but also has ripple effects into the present, as the individual's energy field becomes free of the old patterns that once held them back.

Karma is closely linked to Reiki's ability to heal the past. In many spiritual traditions, karma refers to the consequences of our actions, thoughts, and intentions, which can carry over from one lifetime to the next (Karma, 2012). In this sense, Reiki can help resolve karmic imbalances by addressing the energetic wounds from past lives or early childhood experiences that have not yet been healed. This allows the individual to break free from the cycle of karma, clearing the path for personal growth and spiritual evolution.

Equally powerful is Reiki's ability to work in the future. While we often think of the future as something that has not yet occurred, in the energetic realm, the future is simply another aspect of the present. By sending Reiki energy to a future event or situation, the practitioner can influence the energy surrounding that moment, helping to create conditions that are conducive to positive outcomes. This practice is beneficial when an individual is preparing for a significant life event, such as a medical procedure, a job interview, or a major transition. By sending Reiki energy ahead of time, the individual can walk into the future more confidently and easily, knowing that the energy has already been set in motion to support their well-being.

Just as with healing the past, the practitioner uses the Hon Sha Ze Sho Nen symbol to send Reiki into the future. This intention-based approach to influencing future events is not about controlling the outcome but rather about creating an energetic environment that supports the highest good for the recipient. The energy sent ahead of time works in harmony with the natural flow of life, aligning the recipient with the best possible outcomes based on their current circumstances (Brennan, 1988).

While Reiki can influence the past and future, it does not interfere with free will or the natural course of events. Reiki is always guided by the principle of non-attachment, meaning that the practitioner releases any specific expectations about the healing outcome. Instead, the energy is sent with the intention that it will align with the recipient's highest good, trusting that the universal life force knows where and how to act.

The ability to heal across time makes Reiki an incredibly versatile and expansive tool for personal transformation. Whether addressing unresolved issues from the past or preparing for a future event, Reiki works by tapping into the timeless nature of energy, allowing healing to occur in ways that transcend our ordinary understanding of time. This approach reminds us that our experiences are not isolated moments but are deeply interconnected, forming a web of energy that shapes our lives.

As we explore distance healing we will see that this ability to heal across time is just one of the many ways Reiki opens up new possibilities for transformation. By learning to work with the fluid nature of time and energy, practitioners can help their recipients heal on levels that extend far beyond the present moment, allowing for a more profound sense of peace, balance, and alignment with the flow of life.

Healing the Present Moment

While distance healing and healing across time allow us to address the past and future, it is important to remember that Reiki is also profoundly powerful in the present moment. The true transformation begins in the present, as it is the only time we can directly engage with our lives, emotions, and energy. Many spiritual traditions emphasize the importance of living in the now, as this is where life truly happens. By its very nature, Reiki's energy flows freely in the present, aligning us with our most authentic selves and helping clear the energy we hold in the here and now.

Healing the present moment begins with understanding mindfulness—becoming fully aware of your thoughts, feelings, and surroundings without judgment. Mindfulness invites us to connect deeply with our current state, observe our emotions, pain, and stress, and allow healing to flow without resistance. Reiki complements this practice beautifully by amplifying the energy in the present moment, supporting emotional release, and encouraging deep relaxation.

When Reiki practitioners send healing energy through hands-on or distance healing, they anchor their awareness in the present, offering themselves and the recipient a deep connection to the universal life force in real-time. As this energy flows, it moves through any blockages in the recipient's energy field, bringing harmony and balance to the body, mind, and spirit.

In the context of distance healing, this connection to the present moment remains strong. Even though the practitioner may not be physically present with the recipient, they are still working in the now, guiding the flow of energy to heal the recipient at the moment they are experiencing. The same principles of energy flow apply: the energy will go where it is needed, guided by the recipient's body and spirit.

One of the most significant benefits of Reiki is its ability to help us become more grounded in the present. In our modern world, we are often consumed by thoughts of the past or worries about the future, which can lead to stress, anxiety, and a sense of disconnection. Reiki helps to quiet the mind, bring clarity, and return our awareness to the present, where we can begin to release our energetic burdens. This grounding in the "now" is essential for healing, as it allows the body's natural healing processes to function without the interference of mental or emotional distractions (Kabat-Zinn, 1994).

The present moment is also where we can tap into our inner wisdom. Reiki facilitates this connection by clearing away the energetic noise that blocks us from hearing our inner voice. As we relax into the flow of Reiki energy, we gain access to deeper insights, feelings, and clarity. This can be particularly important in distance healing, where the recipient may experience a sense of revelation or understanding as the energy moves through them, bringing to light emotions or thoughts they were previously unaware of. These moments of clarity are often vital to the healing process, allowing the recipient to take conscious steps toward emotional or spiritual resolution.

Healing the present also means accepting where we are at this exact moment—physically, emotionally, and spiritually. Reiki invites both the practitioner and the recipient to surrender to the energy, trusting that it will provide what is needed. This trust in the universal life force and the present moment fosters a deep sense of peace and acceptance, essential for lasting healing.

Reiki's ability to heal the past and influence the future is indeed profound, but it is through healing in the present that we experience the most immediate and transformative effects. Whether working hands-on or through distance, Reiki reconnects us with the flow of life as it unfolds in the here and now, helping us to release what no longer serves us and embrace the possibilities.

Section Summary
Beyond Space and Time

While distance healing and healing past or future events are powerful aspects of Reiki, the most immediate and transformative healing occurs in the present. Reiki aligns us with the now, where life and energy are most accessible.

Non-Locality in Energy Healing

Non-locality explains how Reiki energy can transcend physical space. Drawing parallels from quantum physics, Reiki practitioners use this concept to connect energetically with recipients, even when great distances separate them. Non-locality allows for the free flow of energy, with Reiki transcending space to provide healing where it is needed most. The Hon Sha Ze Sho Nen symbol is crucial in bridging the gap between the practitioner and the recipient during distance healing sessions.

Healing Across Time

Reiki's ability to transcend the limitations of time further enhances its healing potential. Reiki can be sent to both the past and future, addressing unresolved traumas or preparing for significant events. Reiki operates under the belief that time is non-linear, interconnected in a web-like structure where healing energy can be sent to past moments to release energetic blockages or to future situations to set the stage for positive outcomes. Again, the Hon Sha Ze Sho Nen symbol facilitates this time-transcending healing.

Healing the Present Moment

Reiki is practiced in the present moment. Healing begins here. When practiced with mindfulness, Reiki helps individuals become more grounded, reducing stress and anxiety by focusing on the now. By bringing clarity and clearing energetic noise, Reiki facilitates deeper self-awareness, enabling recipients to connect with their inner wisdom and release emotional burdens. Healing in the present allows the body, mind, and spirit to achieve balance, creating an immediate sense of peace and transformation.

While Reiki's reach spans time and space, healing in the present moment is where individuals experience the most profound effects. They are guided to release what no longer serves them and embrace the potential of the now.

§

Knowledge Review
Chapter One

The Foundations of Energy Healing

1. What do the words "Rei" and "Ki" mean, and how do they relate to the concept of Reiki?

2. What happens when the flow of life energy becomes blocked, and what are some causes of these blockages?

3. How does a Reiki practitioner channel healing energy, and what is their role in the process?

4. Why is intention important in Reiki, and how does it influence the healing process?

5. How does the practitioner's trust in the intelligence of energy affect the outcome of a Reiki session?

6. How does a Reiki practitioner channel energy into a recipient's energy field during a session?

7. How does Reiki work on a holistic level to promote healing?

8. What is non-locality, and how does it explain the ability of Reiki energy to be transmitted across distance?

9. How does distance healing in Reiki operate under the same energetic principles as hands-on healing?

10. How can Reiki energy be sent across time, and what benefits does this offer in healing past or future events?

11. What is non-locality in quantum mechanics, and how does it apply to Reiki energy healing?

12. How does non-locality enable a Reiki practitioner to send healing energy over distance?

13. What role does the Hon Sha Ze Sho Nen symbol play in distance Reiki healing?

14. What is the unified field, and how does it relate to Reiki's ability to heal across distances?

15. How does Reiki view time differently from the typical linear perception, and how does this allow healing to transcend time?

16. How can Reiki be used to heal past traumas, and what effects does this have on the present?

17. How does sending Reiki energy to future events influence outcomes, and what is the intention behind this practice?

18. What is the purpose of the Hon Sha Ze Sho Nen symbol in Reiki healing, and how does it function when healing across time?

19. Why is the present moment so important in Reiki healing?

20. How does Reiki help recipients become more grounded and reduce stress in the present moment?

21. What role mindfulness play in Reiki, and how does Reiki support emotional awareness?

22. What is the impact of Reiki on mental and emotional blockages, and how does it provide clarity?

Scientific Foundations for Distance Healing

Quantum Mechanics and the Unified Field

Quantum Entanglement and Energy Healing

As we continue exploring the deeper mechanics behind distance healing in Reiki, we arrive at a topic that bridges science and spirituality—quantum mechanics. Though it might seem daunting, this field of study provides valuable insights into the nature of reality. It helps explain how energy healing can transcend the boundaries of time and space. Specifically, the concept of quantum entanglement offers a powerful framework for understanding how Reiki works at a distance.

Quantum mechanics, the study of the behavior of particles on the smallest scales, has reshaped our understanding of the universe in ways that align closely with the principles of Reiki and other energy-healing modalities. An intriguing aspect in this field is the phenomenon of entanglement. In basic terms, quantum entanglement refers to how two particles, once connected, remain linked regardless of how far apart they are. A change in one particle will instantaneously affect the other, even if they are separated by vast distances (Einstein, Podolsky, & Rosen, 1935).

This idea of entanglement can be applied to the practice of Reiki, particularly in the context of distance healing. When a Reiki practitioner connects with a recipient energetically, the two become "entangled" within the same energetic field. Just as two entangled particles can influence each other instantaneously, the energy transmitted by the practitioner can flow to the recipient, regardless of physical distance. This energetic connection is not bound by the traditional laws of time and space so that distance healing can be as effective as in-person healing (Goswami, 1995).

The process of quantum entanglement in energy healing works similarly to how the physical particles behave. The practitioner and recipient establish an energetic link through the universal life force during a Reiki session, whether hands-on or from a distance. This link allows energy to be shared instantly and seamlessly like entangled particles. Even though the practitioner and recipient may not be physically close, the energy can still flow between them as if they were in the same room. This energetic connection is a key reason distance healing can transcend the physical barriers that might otherwise limit it (McTaggart, 2008).

Energy healers have intuitively understood that everything in the universe is interconnected for centuries. While this idea has been a cornerstone of spiritual practices like Reiki, modern science is now catching up to this ancient wisdom. Quantum mechanics, through phenomena like entanglement, supports the notion that physical separation does not diminish the connection between two beings. The universe's interconnected nature allows energy to move freely and effortlessly across distances, even between people who are thousands of miles apart.

In energy healing, particularly in Reiki, setting an intention and focusing on a recipient creates this energetic link. Through focused meditation, visualization, and the use of Reiki symbols like Hon Sha Ze Sho Nen, the practitioner can connect their energy with the recipient's energy field. This process activates the flow of universal life energy, which, like entangled particles, is instantly shared between the practitioner and recipient. The practitioner does not need to physically be present to guide the energy—once the connection is made, the energy follows, guided by the recipient's needs and the practitioner's intention (Petter, 2000).

While quantum entanglement provides a scientific basis for understanding how energy healing can transcend distance, it's also important to remember that Reiki is deeply rooted in trust and intuition. Practitioners don't need to control or manipulate the energy; they create the conditions for it to flow. Quantum entanglement offers a framework to explain this process, but at its core, Reiki relies on the universal principles of energy flow, connection, and intention. The practitioner serves as a conduit, allowing the energy to move where needed most while trusting that the energetic link between themselves and the recipient will do the rest.

The idea that everything in the universe is interconnected, even at the smallest quantum level, is a powerful affirmation of Reiki's potential. It reflects the ancient spiritual wisdom that we are all part of a larger whole, connected by a universal energy that transcends our physical forms. Quantum entanglement shows us that this connection is spiritual and scientific, offering a profound glimpse into the nature of reality and how we can harness these principles for healing.

The Unified Field: Interconnectedness and the Flow of Reiki Energy

As we continue to investigate quantum mechanics and its relevance to Reiki, we move from the concept of quantum entanglement to a broader and more encompassing theory: the unified field theory. This theory posits that everything in the universe—every particle, atom, planet, and star—is part of one vast and interconnected energy field. While still largely theoretical in physics, the idea of a unified field provides an invaluable framework for understanding how Reiki operates as an energy-healing modality that transcends distance, time, and physical form.

In the unified field model, all things are fundamentally connected. There is no true separation between you, me, the Earth, or the furthest reaches of the universe. The interconnectedness described by this theory aligns perfectly with the spiritual understanding that Reiki is based on: that we are all made of energy and that energy flows through and between all things, connecting us on levels we cannot always see or comprehend. In Reiki, this universal energy is known as the universal life force, which the practitioner channels during a healing session (Laszlo, 2007).

Just as quantum entanglement illustrates how particles can influence each other across great distances, the unified field theory suggests that Reiki practitioners work within a vast network of interconnected energy. When practitioners perform distance healing, they tap into this unified field, sending healing energy through a web of connections that permeates the entire universe. This concept explains why Reiki does not require physical proximity. Since everything is connected in the unified field, the energy can flow freely between the practitioner and the recipient, regardless of the distance between them.

The unified field theory echoes the ancient spiritual teachings found in many traditions, including the foundations of Reiki. For centuries, healers and mystics have taught that the universe is not made up of isolated parts but is a holistic, interconnected web of energy. What affects one part of the whole will inevitably influence the rest. This belief underlies the principle of oneness, a central tenet of many spiritual practices, including Reiki. The notion that we are all part of the same energetic field also reinforces the idea that healing one person contributes to the healing of the collective (Goswami, 1995).

From a practical perspective, the unified field theory helps explain why Reiki energy can move through distance and time, as explored earlier. When the practitioner connects with the recipient's energy field, they engage with the same universal energy that flows through all things. The Reiki practitioner's intention is an energetic signal, guiding the universal life force to the recipient. Because the practitioner and recipient are part of the same field, this signal can travel instantly, regardless of physical distance.

This seamless energy transmission is why Reiki is often described as "intuitive." The practitioner doesn't need to force or direct the energy in a specific way. Once the connection is made, the universal life force energy knows where to go. The practitioner facilitates this connection, allowing the energy to flow freely and intuitively to where it is needed most (Lipton, 2005).

Reiki's alignment with the principles of the unified field also opens the door to a profound realization: healing is not limited to the individual recipient. When Reiki energy is channeled, it does not stop at the boundary of one person's energy field. Because we are all interconnected within the same universal energy, the healing sent to one individual inevitably resonates with the larger collective field. This ripple effect means that every act of healing, no matter how personal or specific, contributes to the overall balance and well-being of the world. This idea echoes the spiritual principle of wholeness—the understanding that healing ourselves contributes to the healing of all beings (Brennan, 1988).

In the unified field, every thought, action, and intention reverberates throughout the entire web of existence. This concept also aligns with the metaphysical law of cause and effect, where every action or intention we set forth has consequences that ripple outward, impacting us and the world around us. Through their focused intention and connection with the unified field, Reiki practitioners contribute to this universal flow of energy, sending out healing vibrations that can potentially influence the recipient and the collective energy field (McTaggart, 2008).

The unified field theory also helps explain why Reiki practitioners often feel a deep connection with the healing recipient and the universal energy itself. As the practitioner channels the universal life force energy, they become more attuned to the flow of energy that permeates the entire universe. Many practitioners experience a heightened sense of unity, peace, and clarity during Reiki sessions, reflecting their connection to the larger energetic field. This connection is one of the reasons why Reiki is often considered a spiritual practice as much as a healing modality (Laszlo, 2007).

The unified field theory, then, is not only a scientific concept but a profoundly spiritual one. It affirms that we are all part of a greater whole, interconnected in ways that transcend the physical world. By tapping into this universal field of energy, Reiki reminds us that healing is not an isolated event—it is a process of realigning with the greater flow of life, returning to a state of balance and harmony with the world around us.

As we continue exploring the deeper aspects of Reiki, keep in mind that the principles of quantum entanglement and the unified field provide more than just scientific explanations for how Reiki works. They offer us a glimpse into the true nature of reality—one that is deeply interconnected, compassionate, and whole. The energy that flows through us during Reiki sessions is the same energy that sustains the universe itself, and by working with this energy, we are participating in the ongoing dance of creation and healing.

Non-Local Reality: Reiki's Alignment with the Quantum Realm

In addition to quantum entanglement and the unified field, non-locality is another concept from quantum mechanics that helps explain Reiki's power to heal across time and space. Non-locality refers to the idea that once connected objects can instantly influence each other's behavior, regardless of distance. This concept, which has been observed in the behavior of subatomic particles, offers an intriguing explanation for how Reiki can operate in a non-physical, energetic realm and produce healing effects from a distance.

To grasp the essence of non-locality, imagine two particles that were once part of the same system. Even if great distances separate them, their properties remain interconnected. No matter how far apart they are, a change in one particle is immediately reflected in the other. This seemingly impossible connection is a well-documented phenomenon in quantum physics that defies the conventional understanding of time and space (Einstein, Podolsky, & Rosen, 1935).

Reiki, too, operates through this non-local reality. When Reiki practitioners send healing energy across distance, they tap into the same underlying principle that governs quantum entanglement. The practitioner and the recipient, although separated physically, are connected energetically through the universal life force. Just as in quantum physics, this connection is instantaneous, transcending the need for physical proximity. The energy flows through the non-local field, guided by the practitioner's intention, and reaches the recipient wherever they are.

Non-locality suggests that the universe is not made up of isolated, independent objects but an interconnected web where everything influences everything else. This idea is key to understanding the nature of Reiki healing. When a practitioner sets the intention to heal a recipient, they are essentially creating a link in this energetic web, allowing the healing energy to flow freely through the non-local field. The concept of non-locality reinforces the idea that energy is not bound by distance; it flows naturally and effortlessly through the connections at the quantum level (Bohm, 1980).

In this sense, Reiki practitioners are not bound by the physical world's limitations. They can connect with others across distances, time, and dimensions through the non-local energy field. This is why distance healing works so effectively in Reiki: the practitioner's focused intention creates a bridge in the non-local field, allowing the energy to flow as if the recipient were in the same room (Goswami, 1995).

Another insight from non-locality is that time, as we experience it in our everyday lives, is not an absolute, linear progression. Just as non-local connections exist across space, they also exist across time. This is why Reiki practitioners can send energy to heal the past or prepare the future. The non-local energy field is not constrained by time, allowing Reiki energy to address events from the past and set the stage for future well-being. From a quantum perspective, the past, present, and future are all intertwined, existing simultaneously in the same energetic field (Barbour, 1999).

This understanding of time as a fluid, interconnected dimension is essential to Reiki's ability to heal across the timeline of a person's life. When a practitioner sends Reiki to a past trauma or future event, they work within the non-local field, allowing the energy to flow to the point where it is most needed. This explains why distance healing can be so powerful in addressing unresolved emotional or energetic blockages that have persisted for years or even lifetimes. By tapping into the non-local field, Reiki helps release these energetic patterns and restore balance to the recipient's energy system.

Non-locality also emphasizes the importance of intention in Reiki healing. In quantum mechanics, the act of observation can influence the behavior of particles, a concept known as the observer effect (Heisenberg, 1927). This idea mirrors the role of intention in Reiki. When a practitioner focuses their attention on a recipient, they guide the flow of energy, influencing the outcome of the healing session. The practitioner's focused intention acts as a catalyst, directing the universal life energy to flow in the direction of the recipient, much like how observation in the quantum world influences the behavior of particles.

The observer effect in quantum mechanics demonstrates that consciousness and intention play a crucial role in shaping reality. In Reiki, the practitioner's conscious intention creates the conditions for healing, allowing the universal life force to flow through the non-local field and reach the recipient. This alignment between quantum theory and Reiki further reinforces the idea that energy healing is not just a mystical concept but is grounded in the very nature of reality itself (McTaggart, 2008).

Ultimately, the principles of non-locality, the observer effect, and quantum entanglement provide a scientific foundation for understanding how Reiki can transcend time and space. These concepts demonstrate that the boundaries we perceive in the physical world—boundaries of distance, time, and separation—are illusions. In the quantum realm, everything is connected, and this interconnectedness allows energy to move freely, guided by intention, through the universal life force.

As we move into the following chapters, we will explore how these scientific insights can be applied to the practical aspects of Reiki healing. Whether you are sending energy to someone on the other side of the world or working to heal a traumatic event from the past, the principles of non-locality and quantum connection remind us that the power of Reiki lies not in physical proximity but in the deep, universal connection that links us all.

Section Summary
Quantum Mechanics and the Unified Field

This section explored how concepts from quantum mechanics—non-locality, quantum entanglement, and the unified field—align with the principles of Reiki and provide a scientific framework for understanding Reiki's ability to heal across time and space. By examining these ideas, we gain deeper insight into how Reiki transcends physical limitations, allowing practitioners to send healing energy over vast distances and time.

Quantum Entanglement and Energy Healing

Quantum entanglement refers to the phenomenon where two particles, once connected, remain linked regardless of the distance between them, allowing changes in one particle to affect the other instantly. This principle aligns with the practice of distance healing in Reiki. When a practitioner connects energetically with a recipient, they become "entangled" within the same energetic field, enabling the flow of healing energy across any distance. Reiki practitioners use intention and symbols like Hon Sha Ze Sho Nen to establish this energetic connection, creating an instant energy flow between practitioner and recipient, even when physically separated.

The Unified Field: Interconnectedness and the Flow of Reiki Energy

The unified field theory posits that everything in the universe is part of one vast, interconnected energy field. This theory explains how Reiki practitioners tap into the universal life force during a session, connecting to the recipient through the unified field. Because all things are connected within this field, healing energy flows seamlessly between practitioner and recipient, transcending physical proximity. The unified field reinforces the spiritual concept of oneness, affirming that healing one individual can resonate with and positively impact the larger collective. In this context, Reiki serves the individual and the entire interconnected web of energy in the universe.

Non-Local Reality: Reiki's Alignment with the Quantum Realm

Non-locality in quantum mechanics describes how two objects, once connected, can instantly influence each other's behavior, regardless of distance. This concept mirrors how Reiki practitioners send healing energy across space and time, using focused intention to create a bridge in the non-local field. Non-locality also allows Reiki to heal the past or future, as time in the quantum realm is fluid and interconnected. The practitioner's intention plays a vital role in guiding the flow of Reiki energy, much like how the observer effect in quantum mechanics shapes the behavior of particles. Through this lens, Reiki healing is seen as a powerful expression of the universe's interconnectedness.

Quantum entanglement, the unified field, and non-locality provide a framework for understanding the seemingly mystical aspects of Reiki, such as distance healing and healing across time. These principles illustrate that Reiki is not bound by the traditional limitations of time and space but operates within a deeply interconnected reality where energy can flow freely, guided by intention. Examining Reiki's alignment with the quantum realm deepens our appreciation of how this ancient practice fits into the modern understanding of the universe.

§

The Observer Effect and Energy Healing

Understanding the Observer Effect and Its Role in Reiki

We've explored how quantum mechanics offers a scientific framework for understanding Reiki's ability to heal across time and space, focusing on concepts like non-locality and quantum entanglement. As we delve further into the nature of energy healing, one of the more intriguing phenomena we encounter is the observer effect. This concept, rooted in quantum physics, suggests that the very act of observation can influence the behavior of particles. In the context of Reiki, this principle illuminates the profound role that consciousness and intention play in guiding healing energy.

The observer effect was first identified in the early 20th century during experiments designed to measure the behavior of subatomic particles, such as electrons. Scientists found that these particles behaved differently when observed than when they were not. Specifically, when observed, electrons behaved like particles—solid, defined points in space. However, when not observed, they behaved more like waves, spreading out over space, indicating that their state was not fixed until measured (Heisenberg, 1927). This led to the realization that the very act of observation could influence the outcome of an experiment, an idea that seemed to defy traditional logic.

In quantum mechanics, the observer effect reveals that consciousness directly impacts the physical world. While this concept might seem abstract, its implications for Reiki and energy healing are profound. Reiki practitioners have long understood that the mind can influence energy flow through focused intention and awareness. The observer effect offers a scientific explanation: when a Reiki practitioner focuses their consciousness on a recipient, they essentially " observe" the recipient's energy, directing it with their intention in the same way that observing particles in an experiment influences their behavior.

During a Reiki session, whether hands-on or at a distance, the practitioner acts as the "observer," guiding the energy flow with focused attention. By setting an intention for the healing, the practitioner shapes the way the energy moves, much like how the observation of particles in a quantum experiment determines whether they behave as particles or waves. This conscious observation allows the practitioner to influence the recipient's energy field, directing the universal life force to the areas that most need healing. The practitioner's attention becomes a powerful tool for shaping the outcome of the healing session (Goswami, 1995).

The observer effect also reinforces the importance of intention in Reiki healing. When practitioners set an intention, they are not merely hoping for a specific outcome but actively participating in creating it. The practitioner's focused awareness aligns with the recipient's energy field, guiding the flow of Reiki energy toward the intended result. This intention bridges the practitioner's consciousness and the recipient's energy field, ensuring the energy flows where most needed. In this sense, the practitioner is not only a passive conduit for the energy but an active participant in its direction and flow (Lipton, 2005).

It's important to note that the observer effect does not mean that the practitioner controls the outcome of the Reiki session. Instead, the practitioner's role is to create the conditions for healing by holding a space of focused awareness and intention. The universal life force energy, which is intelligent and intuitive, will ultimately flow in the most beneficial direction for the recipient. The practitioner's intention serves as a guide, helping the energy align with the recipient's needs, but it does not dictate the outcome. This mirrors the findings in quantum mechanics, where observation influences the behavior of particles but does not determine their final state; it simply shapes the possibilities.

The observer effect also highlights the importance of presence in Reiki healing. When a practitioner is fully present and focused during a session, they create a more potent space for healing. This is because their consciousness actively engages with the recipient's energy field, amplifying universal life force energy flow. In contrast, if the practitioner's mind is distracted or unfocused, the connection with the recipient's energy field may weaken, leading to a less effective healing session. Therefore, the quality of the practitioner's presence is a crucial factor in the success of the healing process (Kabat-Zinn, 1994).

The implications of the observer effect extend beyond individual Reiki sessions. This principle suggests that consciousness itself is a powerful force that shapes reality. In the broader context of energy healing, the observer effect reinforces the idea that we are co-creators of our reality through the power of our thoughts, intentions, and focused awareness. Reiki practitioners can tap into this creative potential by cultivating mindfulness and presence, guiding energy flow to promote healing, balance, and transformation.

The observer effect offers a scientific basis for understanding the role of consciousness in Reiki healing. By focusing their awareness and intention, the practitioner actively shapes the energy flow, guiding it toward the recipient's highest good. The act of observation in Reiki is not passive; it is a dynamic process that allows the practitioner to engage with the recipient's energy field in a meaningful and transformative way. As we explore the deeper aspects of energy healing, we will see that consciousness, intention, and presence are vital to Reiki and fundamental to the nature of reality itself.

Intention as a Catalyst

As we continue exploring the relationship between the observer effect and Reiki, it becomes clear that intention plays a central role in guiding energy flow during a healing session. In both the scientific and spiritual realms, intention is recognized as a catalyst that shapes outcomes. Whether through the focused observation of particles in quantum experiments or the mindful direction of energy in Reiki, intention is the bridge between consciousness and reality.

In Reiki, the practitioner's intention acts as a guiding force for the universal life energy. Once the practitioner establishes a connection with the recipient's energy field, they consciously set an intention for the session. This intention could be as specific as relieving physical pain or as broad as promoting overall well-being.

Regardless of the focus, the practitioner's intention aligns with the recipient's energy, directing the healing energy toward the desired outcome (Brennan, 1988).

Intention is not just about thinking positive thoughts or visualizing a result. In the context of Reiki, intention is an act of conscious creation. It involves the practitioner focusing their awareness on the recipient's needs and holding space for healing. By doing so, the practitioner creates the conditions for the universal life energy to flow in the right direction. This process is similar to how a gardener plants seeds in fertile soil and nurtures them to grow, trusting that the plants will thrive with time, water, and sunlight. The practitioner's role is to create a space where healing can take root while the energy, like the plant, follows its natural course.

Intention is powerful in Reiki because it can focus and amplify energy flow. Without intention, the energy might still flow, but it would lack the direction needed to address specific areas of imbalance. Just as the observer in quantum experiments shapes the behavior of particles through focused observation, the Reiki practitioner shapes the movement of energy through focused intention (McTaggart, 2008). By setting a clear intention, the practitioner provides a framework within which the energy can operate, ensuring that the healing session is purposeful and aligned with the recipient's highest good.

It's important to note that the recipient's intention is equally significant in the healing process. While the practitioner sets their intention to guide the energy, the recipient also plays an active role by being open to receiving the healing energy. When the recipient is fully present and consciously open to the experience, the energy can flow more freely, and the healing can be more profound. This dynamic interplay between the practitioner's intention and the recipient's openness creates a powerful synergy, enhancing the effectiveness of the Reiki session (Lipton, 2005).

In many ways, the relationship between intention and energy healing mirrors the scientific concept of coherence. Coherence refers to the alignment and synchronization of energy patterns. When coherent energy flows harmoniously and is organized, producing a more robust and efficient result. In the context of Reiki, the practitioner's intention brings coherence to the healing session, aligning the practitioner's energy with the recipient's needs. This coherent energy flow allows the healing to penetrate deeply into the recipient's energy field, promoting balance, harmony, and transformation (Laszlo, 2007).

One of the unique aspects of Reiki is that it works on multiple levels—physical, emotional, mental, and spiritual. This means the practitioner's intention can address various issues simultaneously, depending on the recipient's needs. For example, a practitioner might set an intention to alleviate physical pain in the recipient. Still, the energy may also heal underlying emotional or spiritual imbalances during the session. The practitioner doesn't need to consciously direct the energy to each level; their intention creates the framework, and the universal life energy, with its intuitive intelligence, does the rest. This is a critical distinction in Reiki: the practitioner is not "doing" the healing but instead creating the conditions for healing by guiding the energy with their intention (Petter, 2000).

This approach to healing aligns with the principle of non-attachment, a core teaching in Reiki and many spiritual traditions. Non-attachment means that while the practitioner sets an intention for healing, they do not become attached to a specific outcome. Instead, they trust that the universal life energy will flow where needed most and that the recipient will receive exactly what they need. This trust in the process is essential to the practice of Reiki. It reflects the understanding that healing cannot be forced or controlled but is a natural process that unfolds in its own time and way (Goswami, 1995).

The principle of non-attachment also allows the practitioner to remain open to the full range of possibilities for healing. Often, the recipient may receive healing in unexpected ways. For example, a session intended to address physical pain might instead result in an emotional release, bringing to light unresolved feelings that were contributing to the pain. In such cases, the practitioner's ability to remain unattached to a specific outcome allows the healing to occur on the deeper levels where it is most needed.

This way, intention becomes a focused and flexible tool in Reiki healing. It guides the energy toward a specific goal while also allowing space for the universal life energy to work in its own way. The practitioner's role is to hold the intention lightly, trusting in the intelligence of the energy and remaining open to the possibilities for healing that may arise. This balance between focused intention and non-attachment is what makes Reiki such a powerful and versatile healing modality.

The Power of Intention in Distance Healing

Reiki is not bound by time and space constraints. When practitioners perform distance healing, they tap into the same universal energy field that connects all living things, allowing them to channel healing energy across vast distances. Intention plays an even more central role in distance Reiki, as the practitioner's focused intention establishes and maintains the energetic link between themselves and the recipient.

In distance healing, the practitioner's intention becomes the primary mechanism for guiding energy flow. Without physical proximity, the practitioner relies on their intention to create a bridge between themselves and the recipient, connecting them through the universal life force energy. This connection is established through focused meditation, visualization, and the use of Reiki symbols, particularly Hon Sha Ze Sho Nen, which is often referred to as the distance symbol. This symbol bridges the gap between practitioner and recipient, transcending time and space to allow the energy to flow freely between them (Petter, 2000).

At the beginning of a distance healing session, the practitioner will typically spend time meditating or visualizing the recipient. This visualization process is crucial, as it helps the practitioner focus their intention and create a clear mental image of the recipient. Even though the practitioner and recipient may be separated by miles—or even by time—the practitioner's intention helps to collapse that distance, making it feel like they are in the same energetic space. The Hon Sha Ze Sho Nen symbol anchors this intention, creating a conduit through which the Reiki energy can flow (Rand, 1991).

This use of intention in distance healing mirrors the principles of quantum mechanics, particularly the observer effect. As we explored earlier, the observer effect demonstrates that observation can influence an experiment's outcome. In the context of Reiki, the practitioner's focused observation of the recipient's energy field allows the energy to flow to where it is needed most. The practitioner's intention catalyzes this process, guiding the energy through the non-local field (Heisenberg, 1927).

A powerful aspects of distance healing is its ability to transcend time and space. A practitioner can send Reiki energy to past, present, or future events through intention and the Hon Sha Ze Sho Nen symbol. For instance, a practitioner may send healing energy to past trauma or unresolved emotional experience, helping the recipient release the energetic imprints of that event. This process allows the recipient to heal in the present and free themselves from patterns of behavior or emotional blockages that have persisted since that time (Brennan, 1988).

Similarly, a practitioner can send healing energy to a future event. This might be done to help the recipient prepare for a significant life transition, such as a job interview, surgery, or major decision. By sending Reiki energy ahead of time, the practitioner creates an energetic foundation for the recipient, ensuring that they are supported and aligned with the highest possible outcome when that event occurs. In both cases—whether healing the past or preparing for the future—the practitioner's intention is the driving force behind the connection, allowing the energy to flow to the exact point where it is most needed (Lipton, 2005).

The role of intention in distance healing also extends to the recipient. Like in an in-person session, the recipient's openness to the healing process is crucial for free energy flow. If the recipient is fully present and receptive, the energy will move through them more effectively, bringing more profound healing. Often, recipients of distance Reiki feel sensations of warmth, tingling, or deep relaxation during the session, even though they may be miles away from the practitioner. These sensations testify to the power of the energetic connection established through intention (McTaggart, 2008).

Another critical factor in the effectiveness of distance Reiki is the state of consciousness that the practitioner maintains during the session. When performing distance healing, the practitioner must cultivate a deep sense of presence and mindfulness, allowing their intention to guide the energy without becoming attached to the outcome. This is where the principle of non-attachment, mentioned earlier, plays a critical role. By setting the intention for healing and releasing any specific expectations about how that healing should unfold, the practitioner creates a space for the universal life energy to flow naturally and intuitively (Kabat-Zinn, 1994).

Non-attachment in distance healing is particularly important because the practitioner is not physically present with the recipient. This means they cannot directly observe the recipient's reactions or physical cues during the session. Instead, they must trust in the process, knowing that the energy will reach the recipient most beneficially, even if they cannot see or feel it themselves. This requires a deep level of trust in the universal life force energy and in the power of intention to guide the healing process (Goswami, 1995).

At the end of a distance healing session, many practitioners close the session by once again visualizing the recipient, offering gratitude for the healing that has taken place, and setting a final intention for the recipient's continued well-being. This practice of gratitude and closure helps to reinforce the energetic connection that has been established and ensures that the healing energy continues to flow even after the session has ended.

Ultimately, intention is the cornerstone of distance healing in Reiki. Through focused intention, the practitioner connects with the recipient, directs the energy, and facilitates healing. Whether working with physical, emotional, mental, or spiritual issues, the practitioner's intention serves as the guiding force that shapes the flow of energy and allows the recipient to receive the healing they need. As we move forward, we will explore more advanced techniques for working with intention in Reiki and practical tips for enhancing your distance healing practice.

Section Summary
The Observer Effect and Energy Healing

This section delved into the crucial role of intention in Reiki healing, particularly in distance healing. It explores how it guides energy flow, establishes connections, and supports healing across time and space.

Intention as a Catalyst

In Reiki, the practitioner's intention is a powerful catalyst that directs universal life energy toward the recipient's specific needs. Much like how focused observation influences quantum particles, the practitioner's intention shapes the movement of energy during a session, guiding it toward the desired outcome. This intention also creates coherence in the healing process, aligning the practitioner's energy with the recipient's needs. While the practitioner sets an intention, they practice non-attachment, allowing the universal life energy to flow freely and naturally, trusting it will guide the healing where it is needed most.

The Power of Intention in Distance Healing

In distance Reiki, intention becomes the primary mechanism for creating an energetic connection between practitioner and recipient. Through meditation, visualization, and the use of the Reiki symbol Hon Sha Ze Sho Nen, the practitioner bridges the physical gap, allowing healing energy to flow across time and space. Intention also enables the practitioner to send healing energy to past traumas or future events, helping recipients release emotional blockages from the past or prepare for significant life transitions. Non-attachment is critical in distance healing, as the practitioner must trust the process and the universal energy, even without directly observing the recipient's reactions.

Understanding the Observer Effect and Its Role in Reiki

The observer effect from quantum mechanics highlights how observation influences the behavior of particles. In Reiki, the practitioner's focused observation and intention guide the flow of healing energy, much like how quantum particles behave differently when observed. The practitioner's awareness during a session allows the energy to flow toward the recipient's needs, emphasizing the connection between consciousness and energy. Being fully present and focused strengthens the healing connection, making the practitioner's presence and mindfulness essential to successful Reiki practice.

Intention acts as a guiding force that shapes energy flow, while the principle of non-attachment ensures that healing unfolds naturally. By combining focused intention with trust in the universal life energy, Reiki practitioners create powerful conditions for healing that transcend time, space, and physical proximity.

§

Zero-Point Energy and Infinite Potential

Zero-Point Energy: The Quantum Vacuum and Universal Life Force

As we continue to explore the scientific and metaphysical principles behind Reiki healing, we encounter one of the most intriguing concepts in quantum physics: zero-point energy. Zero-point energy is the lowest possible energy a quantum mechanical system can have, even at absolute zero temperature. In other words, an underlying energy field is still at play even in a complete vacuum—where all conventional forms of energy are seemingly absent. This idea of a quantum vacuum filled with potential energy offers a fascinating parallel to the universal life force energy that Reiki practitioners channel during healing sessions.

At the quantum level, zero-point energy is the energy that exists in the very fabric of space itself, a background energy that permeates the entire universe. This energy is not created or destroyed, but it is always present, existing as an infinite reservoir of potential. Scientists have discovered that, even in a vacuum devoid of matter, a measurable amount of energy is still present due to the fluctuations of quantum fields. These fluctuations generate zero-point energy, an ever-present force filled with immense potential (Laszlo, 2007).

Zero-point energy mirrors the universal life force energy concept central to

Reiki in many ways. Reiki practitioners understand that the energy they channel is not something they create but rather something they tap into—a universal, ever-present force that permeates all things. This energy is often described as infinite and boundless, flowing through everything in the universe. Zero-point energy gives scientific backing to the notion that the universe is filled with vast energy that can be accessed for healing, transformation, and growth (McTaggart, 2008).

Just as zero-point energy is constantly present, even in the emptiest spaces of the universe, the universal life force energy is always available to be channeled by the Reiki practitioner. The practitioner doesn't need to "generate" the energy because it already exists in abundance. Instead, they serve as a conduit, allowing the energy to flow through them and into the recipient. The idea that energy is always present, waiting to be harnessed, aligns with both the quantum understanding of zero-point energy and the metaphysical principles of Reiki.

One of the most powerful aspects of zero-point energy is its infinite potential. Scientists believe that the energy contained within a single cubic centimeter of space is incredibly vast, far beyond anything we can harness with modern technology. This immense potential parallels Reiki energy, often described as limitless in its healing capacity. Reiki practitioners understand that when they channel the universal life force, they are tapping into an infinite reservoir of energy that can address physical ailments and emotional, mental, and spiritual imbalances. The potential of Reiki energy, like that of zero-point energy, is boundless (Brennan, 1988).

In Reiki healing, zero-point energy helps explain why the energy can flow so freely and is always available, no matter the circumstances. Whether the practitioner performs hands-on or distance healing, the universal life force is always accessible and channeled for the recipient's highest good. This ever-present energy makes Reiki such a powerful tool for transformation, as it connects the practitioner and recipient to the essence of life itself—the underlying energy that animates and sustains the universe.

Another important connection between zero-point energy and Reiki is the idea of coherence. In quantum mechanics, coherence refers to the alignment and synchronization of quantum states, which allows for the smooth and efficient flow of energy. When quantum systems are coherent, they function harmoniously, maximizing their potential. Similarly, Reiki achieves coherence when the practitioner's energy is aligned with the universal life force, allowing the energy to flow smoothly and effectively to the recipient. The more coherent the practitioner's energy, the more powerful and transformative the healing session becomes (Goswami, 1995).

Achieving coherence in Reiki requires the practitioner to be fully present and focused during the healing session. This means aligning their energy with the flow of the universal life force, allowing the energy to move through them without resistance or distraction. When the practitioner is in a state of coherence, the healing energy flows effortlessly, guided by the recipient's needs and the practitioner's intention. This state of coherence allows the practitioner to tap into the infinite potential of the universal life force, drawing from the boundless reservoir of zero-point energy within the quantum vacuum.

Zero-point energy also reinforces that Reiki healing is not limited by time or space. Just as zero-point energy exists everywhere in the universe, regardless of physical location, the universal life force can be channeled to anyone, anywhere, at any time. This is why distance healing works so effectively in Reiki—physical boundaries do not constrain the energy. Whether the practitioner and recipient are in the same room or thousands of miles apart, the universal life force flows through the quantum vacuum, reaching the recipient with the same power and potential (Lipton, 2005).

Tapping into Infinite Potential: Techniques for Aligning with Universal Energy

Understanding zero-point energy as the foundation of the universe's boundless energy field gives us insight into the immense potential for healing through Reiki. However, harnessing this infinite potential requires more than just an intellectual understanding—it involves practical techniques that help Reiki practitioners align themselves with the universal life force and allow this energy to flow freely. This section will explore how practitioners can deepen their connection to this energy and enhance their ability to channel it effectively for both hands-on and distance healing.

Grounding

An essential techniques for tapping into Reiki's infinite potential is the practice of grounding and centering. Grounding refers to connecting one's energy to the Earth, while centering involves bringing the practitioner's attention to the present moment, aligning the mind, body, and spirit. These practices are crucial for creating the energetic conditions needed to channel Reiki effectively. By grounding, practitioners ensure their energy is stable and balanced, allowing them to serve as a clear conduit for the universal life force. Centering, on the other hand, helps practitioners focus their intention and bring their awareness fully into the present, where healing occurs (Kornfield, 1993).

Grounding can be achieved through various techniques, including deep breathing, visualization, and physical connection with nature. Many practitioners begin their Reiki sessions by visualizing roots extending from their feet into the Earth, anchoring them in the present moment and stabilizing their energy. This practice helps clear any energetic blockages within the practitioner and ensures they remain firmly connected to the Earth's energy throughout the session. Grounding creates a stable foundation for channeling Reiki energy, much like zero-point energy, which is the foundation for the universe's energy field.

Once grounded, the practitioner can move into a state of coherence, where their energy is aligned and synchronized with the universal life force. Achieving coherence requires the practitioner to quiet the mind and enter a state of deep relaxation. This state is often described as the "flow state," where the practitioner feels fully attuned to the energy around them, and the healing process feels effortless. In Reiki, coherence allows the practitioner to tap into the infinite potential of the universal life force, channeling energy smoothly and effectively to the recipient (Brennan, 1988).

Medication

A powerful tool for achieving coherence is meditation. Meditation helps practitioners quiet the mind, release distractions, and bring their awareness fully into the present moment. By cultivating mindfulness, Reiki practitioners can deepen their connection to the universal life force and enhance their ability to channel energy. Meditation also helps to clear the practitioner's energy field, ensuring they are a clear and open vessel for the healing energy to flow through. In this way, meditation is both a preparatory practice and an integral part of the Reiki session (Kabat-Zinn, 1994).

In addition to grounding, centering, and meditation, Reiki practitioners can enhance their ability to tap into infinite potential by using Reiki symbols. These symbols are powerful tools that help focus and direct energy flow. The most commonly used symbols in Reiki is the Cho Ku Rei, also known as the power symbol. Cho Ku Rei is often used at the beginning of a session to amplify the energy flow, acting like a switch that "turns on" the energy or increases its intensity. By incorporating this symbol into their practice, practitioners can draw more deeply from the universal energy field, channeling a stronger, more focused stream of Reiki energy to the recipient (Rand, 1991).

Another important symbol in Reiki is the Sei He Ki, which brings harmony and balance to the recipient's energy field. Sei He Ki is particularly effective in addressing emotional imbalances and is often used in conjunction with the Cho Ku Rei to ensure that the energy being channeled is powerful, balanced, and aligned with the recipient's highest good. When practitioners use these symbols with focused intention, they can tap into the deeper layers of the universal life force, drawing on the infinite potential of the energy field to facilitate profound healing (Petter, 2000).

Beyond symbols, practitioners can enhance their connection to the universal life force by cultivating an attitude of non-attachment. As we've discussed earlier, non-attachment is the practice of releasing expectations about the outcome of a healing session. Instead of focusing on a specific result, the practitioner trusts that the universal life energy will flow where needed most, aligning with the recipient's highest good. This attitude of trust and openness allows the practitioner to channel energy without interference, ensuring that the energy flows in its most pure and effective form (Goswami, 1995).

Non-attachment is particularly important when working with the concept of zero-point energy. Because zero-point energy is infinite and boundless, the practitioner's role is not to control or manipulate it but to allow it to flow. By releasing any need to direct the energy toward a specific outcome, the practitioner opens themselves to the full potential of the universal life force. This openness creates a more robust connection to the energy field, allowing the practitioner to channel deeper, more transformative healing (Lipton, 2005).

The final technique for aligning with infinite potential is the practice of gratitude. At the end of a Reiki session, many practitioners express gratitude for the energy that has flowed during the session and for the healing. Gratitude helps solidify the energetic connection between the practitioner and the recipient and between the practitioner and the universal life force. By offering gratitude, practitioners acknowledge the infinite potential of the energy they have worked with, reinforcing their connection to the limitless energy field that supports all healing (McTaggart, 2008).

Aligning with the infinite potential of zero-point energy and the universal life force requires a combination of grounding, coherence, intention, and non-attachment. By practicing these techniques, Reiki practitioners can deepen their connection to the boundless energy that flows through the universe, enhancing their ability to channel powerful healing energy to their recipients. As we move forward into the following chapters, we will explore additional practices for harnessing the full potential of Reiki energy and applying it in both hands-on and distance healing contexts.

Section Summary
Zero-Point Energy and Infinite Potential

By leveraging the vast, energetic reservoir of the quantum field, practitioners can access greater healing potential and amplify the flow of universal life energy in their sessions.

Tapping into Infinite Potential: Techniques for Aligning with Universal Energy

Reiki practitioners can enhance their connection to the universal life force by grounding, centering, and achieving coherence through meditation. These techniques help the practitioner become a clear conduit for the infinite energy present in the quantum field. Reiki symbols like Cho Ku Rei and Sei He Ki are also used to amplify and balance energy flow. Non-attachment and gratitude allow practitioners to align with the limitless potential of the universal life force, enhancing the effectiveness of healing sessions.

Integrating quantum-based techniques into Reiki practice provides access to an infinite reservoir of energy, allowing practitioners to channel healing on deeper, more profound levels. Whether working hands-on or remotely, using expanded visualization, attunement, resonance, and energetic expansion helps Reiki practitioners connect with the quantum field, increasing the potency and effectiveness of healing sessions. As they refine these techniques, practitioners can unlock the full potential of the universal life force, transcending physical boundaries to provide transformative healing.

§

Knowledge Review
Chapter Two

Scientific Foundations for Distance Healing

1. What is quantum entanglement, and how does it help explain Reiki distance healing?

2. How does a Reiki practitioner's and recipient's energetic connection mirror quantum entanglement?

3. How does quantum entanglement affirm the spiritual principle of universal interconnectedness in Reiki?

4. What is the unified field theory, and how does it relate to Reiki energy healing?

5. How does Reiki energy flow through the unified field, and why is physical proximity not necessary?

6. How does Reiki practice contribute to the healing of the collective, beyond just the individual recipient?

7. What is non-locality in quantum mechanics, and How do practitioners use the non-local field to send healing energy across distances?

8. How does non-locality enable Reiki to heal events from the past and influence the future?

9. How does the observer effect relate to the role of a Reiki practitioner during a healing session?

10. How does the practitioner's intention influence the flow of energy in a Reiki session?

11. How can a Reiki practitioner use intention to send healing energy to past or future events?

12. Why is the practitioner's presence and focus critical during a Reiki session?

13. Why is the recipient's openness important in the Reiki healing process, and how does it complement the practitioner's intention?

14. Why is visualization important in the distance healing?

15. How do zero-point energy and the universal life force energy share similar characteristics regarding availability and abundance?

16. How does the concept of zero-point energy help explain the limitless potential of Reiki healing?

17. What is coherence in quantum mechanics, and how does it enhance the flow of energy during a session?

18. Why are grounding and centering important in Reiki, and how do they help practitioners channel energy?

19. How does meditation help a Reiki practitioner achieve coherence and deepen their connection to the universal life force?

20. How do Reiki symbols like Cho Ku Rei and Sei He Ki enhance the flow of energy in a session?

21. Why are non-attachment and gratitude important in Reiki practice, and how do they influence energy flow?

Metaphysical and Spiritual Perspectives

The Laws of the Universe and Healing

The Law of Vibration: How Distance Healing Attunes to Energetic Frequencies

At the foundation of Reiki and other energy healing practices lies a profound understanding of the Law of Vibration, one of the universal laws that govern the energetic flow within and around all things. This law, central to metaphysical traditions and quantum physics, states that everything in the universe—physical or non-physical—vibrates at a specific frequency. This includes all living beings, thoughts, emotions, and even seemingly solid objects, all of which are essentially made up of energy vibrating at various rates. Understanding and attuning to these vibrations in Reiki and distance healing allows practitioners to channel healing energy effectively, no matter the distance between the healer and the recipient.

When a Reiki practitioner performs healing, whether in person or from afar, they work within this energetic field, aligning with the vibrations of the universal life force. As we've explored in previous chapters, Reiki energy is a subtle, high-frequency vibration attuned to the recipient's energy field to facilitate healing. The process of attunement—the alignment of the healer's vibration with that of the recipient—allows the practitioner to synchronize with the energetic frequency of the recipient's body, mind, and spirit, ensuring that the healing energy flows where it is needed most (McTaggart, 2008).

This principle is fundamental in distance healing, where the practitioner cannot rely on physical proximity to detect energy imbalances. Instead, they must tune in to the recipient's vibrational frequency through intention, visualization, and the use of Reiki symbols. The Law of Vibration teaches us that because everything is energy vibrating at different rates, connecting with someone's energy field is possible no matter where they are located. The healer can match their vibration to the recipient's and, through this resonance, transfer the universal life force to address any energetic blockages or imbalances in the recipient's system (Brennan, 1988).

Recognizing that the human body, emotions, and thoughts vibrate at different frequencies is essential. For example, positive emotions such as love, gratitude, and compassion tend to resonate at higher frequencies, while fear, anger, and sadness resonate at lower frequencies. In a Reiki session, the practitioner is working to raise the recipient's vibrational frequency, helping to dissolve lower-vibration energies and restore harmony to the body's energy field. The practitioner's energy vibration also plays a crucial role here—by maintaining a high-frequency vibration through mindfulness, meditation, and grounding practices, the healer becomes a clear and powerful conduit for the universal life force energy (Lipton, 2005).

Attuning to the Law of Vibration means that the practitioner must become highly sensitive to subtle energy shifts, both in themselves and the recipient. The practitioner tunes into the recipient's energy field through meditation, deep breathing, and visualization, adjusting their frequency to match. This vibrational alignment process makes Reiki effective at distance healing. Once the healer and recipient are "in sync," the energy flows seamlessly across space, guided by the universal law that all energy is interconnected (Goswami, 1995).

The Law of Vibration also shows how energy healing can address issues beyond the physical body. Because thoughts, emotions, and spiritual states are all forms of energy, they, too, can be healed through vibrational attunement. When a Reiki practitioner works to raise the recipient's vibration, they are addressing physical symptoms and helping to balance the emotional and mental bodies. This holistic approach to healing makes Reiki a powerful tool for transformation, as it works on all levels of the recipient's being to restore balance and harmony.

Understanding and working with the Law of Vibration is key to mastering the art of Reiki and distance healing. Practitioners can facilitate profound healing across space and time by attuning to the recipient's vibrational frequency and maintaining a high vibration within themselves.

The Law of Attraction: Aligning Intentions for Effective Healing

The Law of Attraction, perhaps one of the most well-known universal laws, states that "like attracts like"—what we focus on and energetically align ourselves with is what we attract into our lives. While this concept is often applied to manifesting desires in relationships, career, or personal success, it is equally vital in energy healing, particularly Reiki. Understanding the Law of Attraction allows Reiki practitioners to consciously align their intentions with the highest vibrational outcomes, ensuring their energy work is as effective and beneficial as possible.

The Law of Attraction is about the power of intention. In the practice of Reiki, intention is the guiding force behind every healing session. Before the practitioner channels the universal life force, they set a clear intention for the session—whether that intention is to relieve physical pain, release emotional blockages, or promote overall balance and harmony. The key here is that the practitioner's intention must be in alignment with the desired outcome, which means the practitioner must energetically align themselves with the healing they wish to bring about (Hicks & Hicks, 2006).

When a Reiki practitioner sets an intention for healing, they put a vibrational request into the universe. According to the Law of Attraction, the vibrations we send out are matched by the vibrations we receive. In this way, the practitioner's focused intention creates a vibrational frequency that attracts the healing energy needed for the session. This is why it is so essential for practitioners to maintain a high vibrational state and remain mindful of their thoughts and emotions during a healing session. If the practitioner's energy is aligned with positive, high-frequency emotions such as love, compassion, and trust, the healing energy they channel will be amplified and more effective (Lipton, 2005).

The Law of Attraction also applies to the recipient's role in the healing process. Just as the practitioner sets an intention for healing, the recipient must also be open and willing to receive the healing energy. If the recipient is resistant or closed off, their energetic frequency may not align with the universal life force, making it more difficult for the healing energy to take root. On the other hand, if the recipient is in a state of openness and receptivity, their vibration aligns with the practitioner's intention, creating a powerful resonance that enhances the healing process (Brennan, 1988).

In distance healing, the Law of Attraction becomes even more pronounced, as both the practitioner and the recipient rely heavily on the power of intention to facilitate energy flow. Without physical contact, the practitioner must set a clear intention for the energy to reach the recipient and trust that the universal life force will follow the path of least resistance. This is where the Law of Attraction plays a crucial role—focusing on the desired outcome and holding that vibration in their mind and heart; the practitioner attracts the energy needed to bring about healing, regardless of the physical distance between themselves and the recipient (McTaggart, 2008).

It is important to note that the Law of Attraction is not about forcing or controlling outcomes. The practitioner must always approach the healing process with an attitude of non-attachment. This means that while the practitioner sets an intention and focuses their energy on the desired outcome, they must also trust that the universal life force will guide the healing in the best possible way for the recipient's highest good. The Law of Attraction aligns with this principle of non-attachment. When the practitioner focuses on healing with an open, trusting heart, they attract the highest vibrational energy available but do not impose their will on the outcome (Goswami, 1995).

In practical terms, aligning with the Law of Attraction during a Reiki session involves several steps. First, the practitioner must ground and center themselves, ensuring their energy is stable and balanced. Next, they set a clear, focused intention for the session, visualizing the recipient's health, balance, or emotional peace—whatever the desired outcome. The practitioner maintains this focus as the session progresses, sending positive, high-frequency vibrations that attract the universal life force needed for healing. Finally, the practitioner releases the intention with trust and non-attachment, allowing the healing energy to flow freely and naturally to the recipient (Hicks & Hicks, 2006).

The Law of Attraction also emphasizes the importance of positive thinking and emotional alignment in healing. Negative thoughts, doubts, or fears can lower the practitioner's vibration, making attracting the high-frequency energy needed for effective healing more difficult. By contrast, when the practitioner cultivates inner peace, gratitude, and love, they raise their vibration, aligning themselves with the highest possible outcome for the healing session. In this way, the Law of Attraction is a powerful tool for Reiki practitioners, helping them channel the universal life force with clarity, focus, and positive intention.

The Law of Cause and Effect (Karma): How Past Actions, Thoughts, and Experiences Affect the Healing Process Across Time

The Law of Cause and Effect, commonly called Karma, plays a profound role in understanding how our past actions, thoughts, and experiences continue to influence our present state. The Law of Cause and Effect teaches us that every action, thought, and intention we project into the universe has consequences—sometimes immediate and sometimes manifesting over time. This law is intricately tied to karma, which suggests that the energy we put into the world comes back to us, shaping our reality positively and negatively. For Reiki practitioners, an awareness of karma is essential for understanding how past energetic imprints can affect the healing process and how distance healing can address these deep-seated patterns across time.

The Law of Cause and Effect is based on the principle that every action generates an energetic ripple. Whether these actions are physical deeds, spoken words, or even unspoken thoughts, they all carry an energetic charge that imprints our personal energy field. Over time, these energetic imprints accumulate and influence our health, emotions, relationships, and overall well-being. Positive actions and thoughts generate high-frequency vibrations that enhance our energy field. In contrast, negative actions and unresolved emotional experiences can create blockages, leading to energy imbalances in our life force (Brennan, 1988).

For Reiki practitioners, understanding how karma influences the recipient's energy is critical to facilitating effective healing. In many cases, the physical, emotional, or spiritual issues a recipient presents may be linked to past actions or experiences that continue to influence their energy. These energetic imprints can come from various sources, including unresolved trauma, repressed emotions, or habitual thought patterns that generate negative energy over time. By becoming aware of these karmic patterns, Reiki practitioners can help recipients release the energetic baggage preventing them from achieving balance and harmony (Lipton, 2005).

The universal life force energy that Reiki practitioners channel is not limited by linear time constraints—it can address energy blockages from the past, present, and future. This ability to transcend time is beneficial when working with the effects of karma. Reiki can be used to heal the lingering energetic imprints from past actions, helping the recipient to release old patterns and break free from the cycle of cause and effect that keeps them stuck in states of imbalance or illness (Petter, 2000).

This might involve working with a recipient who has experienced significant emotional trauma in the past. Even though the event may have occurred years or even decades ago, its energetic impact may still affect the recipient's emotional or physical health. During a Reiki session, the practitioner can set the intention to send healing energy to the past, targeting the original event where the trauma occurred. Doing so helps the recipient release the energetic blockages associated with that trauma, allowing the life force energy to flow freely once again and bringing the recipient into greater balance and peace (McTaggart, 2008).

Similarly, the Law of Cause and Effect teaches us that our actions and intentions shape our future. Reiki practitioners can use this understanding to help recipients align their energy with the highest possible outcomes for the future. Addressing current imbalances and clearing energetic blockages, the practitioner sets the stage for the recipient's future well-being. In some cases, practitioners may also use distance healing techniques to send Reiki energy to a future event, such as an upcoming surgery, a significant life transition, or a situation with potential stress or conflict. By doing so, they can help prepare the recipient energetically, ensuring that they enter the future event in a state of balance, peace, and alignment with their highest good (Brennan, 1988).

It's essential to recognize that the Law of Cause and Effect also applies to the practitioner's energy. Reiki practitioners are not immune to the influence of karma, and their ability to channel the universal life force can be impacted by their past actions, thoughts, and experiences. This is why self-care and energetic hygiene are essential for practitioners. By maintaining a balanced energy field and continually working to resolve their karmic imprints, practitioners ensure that they remain clear channels for healing energy, free from energetic blockages that could interfere with the flow of the universal life force (Kornfield, 1993).

The Law of Cause and Effect can be particularly powerful in distance healing. Because Reiki is not limited by time or space, practitioners can use distance healing to address karmic imprints from past lives or long-standing patterns that may have persisted over generations. By connecting with the recipient's energy field and attuning to the specific vibrational frequency of the karmic pattern, the practitioner can send healing energy to dissolve the energetic blockages and help the recipient break free from the cause-and-effect cycle holding them back. Deep karmic healing can lead to profound shifts in the recipient's energy, resulting in emotional, mental, and physical healing (Petter, 2000).

Finally, the Law of Cause and Effect reminds us of the importance of intentionality in Reiki practice. Just as our past actions and thoughts shape our present reality, the intentions we set in each healing session shape the outcome of the healing process. Reiki practitioners must always be mindful of their energy in the healing space, ensuring their thoughts, words, and actions align with the highest possible vibration. By cultivating love, compassion, and non-attachment, practitioners can align their energy with the universal life force, ensuring that their healing energy is pure, effective, and aligned with the recipient's highest good (Goswami, 1995).

The Law of Cause and Effect (Karma) is necessary in understanding how past actions, thoughts, and experiences influence healing. Reiki practitioners can use their awareness of this law to address karmic imprints, help recipients release old patterns, and align themselves and the recipient with positive energy that promotes healing and transformation. By working with the universal life force, practitioners can transcend the limitations of time and space, bringing healing to the past, present, and future.

Section Summary
The Laws of the Universe and Healing

This section explored how three key universal laws—the Law of Vibration, the Law of Attraction, and the Law of Cause and Effect (Karma)—influence Reiki healing and energy work. Understanding these laws allows Reiki practitioners to align their intentions, energy, and actions to facilitate deep, transformative healing in hands-on and distance sessions.

The Law of Vibration: How Distance Healing Attunes to Energetic Frequencies

The Law of Vibration states that everything in the universe vibrates at a specific frequency, including thoughts, emotions, and physical objects. In Reiki, practitioners work with the subtle, high-frequency vibrations of the universal life force to bring healing to recipients. Practitioners attune their vibration to the recipient's energy field through intention, visualization, and Reiki symbols, ensuring that the healing energy flows effectively, especially during distance healing.

Raising the recipient's vibration is central to clearing energetic blockages and restoring balance on all physical, emotional, mental, and spiritual levels.

The Law of Attraction: Aligning Intentions for Effective Healing

The Law of Attraction suggests that like attracts like; therefore, the energy we project aligns with what we receive. In Reiki, intention plays a crucial role in channeling the healing energy. Practitioners must align their intentions with high-frequency emotions such as love, compassion, and trust to attract positive energy during the healing session. This alignment enhances the effectiveness of Reiki, especially in distance healing, as the practitioner focuses on the desired outcome and trusts the universal life force to deliver the healing energy. The practitioner's and the recipient's openness and intention are vital to ensuring that the healing process aligns with the Law of Attraction.

The Law of Cause and Effect (Karma): How Past Actions, Thoughts, and Experiences Affect the Healing Process Across Time

The Law of Cause and Effect, commonly known as Karma, teaches that every action, thought, and intention has consequences, creating energetic imprints that shape an individual's present reality. Reiki practitioners can work with this law to help recipients release karmic imprints, clear energetic blockages, and break free from negative patterns caused by past actions or unresolved experiences. Reiki's ability to transcend time allows healing to occur in the present, past traumas, and future events. Practitioners can send healing energy to these times and situations, facilitating karmic healing that brings profound emotional, mental, and physical shifts.

Integrating the Laws of Vibration, Attraction, and Cause and Effect in Reiki healing provides a powerful framework for understanding how energy flows and interacts with intention and time. By attuning to these universal principles, Reiki practitioners can facilitate deep, holistic healing that addresses physical ailments and emotional, mental, and spiritual imbalances, creating lasting transformation for their recipients.

§

Sacred Geometric Patterns and Their Role in Understanding Universal Energy Structures

In the world of energy healing, sacred geometry provides a profound framework for understanding the structures of the universe and how energy flows through them. Sacred geometric patterns have been revered across ancient cultures as visual representations of the underlying order of the cosmos. These patterns—such as the Flower of Life, Metatron's Cube, and the Sri Yantra—are believed to encode the energetic blueprint of creation, illustrating how everything in the universe, from the smallest atom to the largest galaxy, is interconnected.

Sacred geometry shows us that energy moves in precise patterns and flows through the universe in harmonious, repetitive structures. These geometric forms offer a visual map of energy's natural flow, revealing how balance, harmony, and alignment can be achieved through energy work like Reiki. By tapping into the principles of sacred geometry, Reiki practitioners can align themselves more deeply with the universe's energetic design, enhancing the power of their healing sessions and connecting with the universal life force on a more profound level (Jain, 2013).

The Flower of Life: The Blueprint of Creation

One of the most well-known and revered symbols in sacred geometry is the Flower of Life, a pattern of overlapping circles arranged in a hexagonal grid. This symbol, found in ancient cultures worldwide, represents the interconnectedness of all life and the underlying energy that flows through the universe. Each circle in the Flower of Life can be seen as a ripple in the universal energy field, demonstrating how everything in existence is connected through a web of energy that is constantly in motion.

For Reiki practitioners, the Flower of Life is a powerful visual tool for understanding how energy moves through the universe and the human energy field. When visualizing this pattern during a healing session, practitioners can imagine energy moving in harmonious, flowing circles, interconnecting with every aspect of the recipient's energy body. The Flower of Life reminds us that the energy we channel during a Reiki session is part of a much larger whole, reflecting the universal life force at every level of creation (Stewart, 2009).

By incorporating the Flower of Life into their practice, Reiki healers can strengthen their connection to the recipient's energy field, seeing the energy as a continuous, interconnected flow that transcends time and space. This awareness of interconnectedness is particularly useful in distance healing, where the practitioner must rely on their intention to bridge physical separation and connect energetically with the recipient. The Flower of Life is a visual reminder that there is no true separation in the energy field—all things are connected through the same web of life.

Metatron's Cube: A Tool for Clearing and Balancing Energy

Another significant symbol in sacred geometry is Metatron's Cube, a complex figure of thirteen interconnected circles. Within the pattern of Metatron's Cube are the five Platonic solids—geometric shapes that are said to represent the building blocks of the universe. These shapes are associated with the elements—earth, water, fire, air, and spirit—and are thought to correspond to different aspects of the human body and energy field.

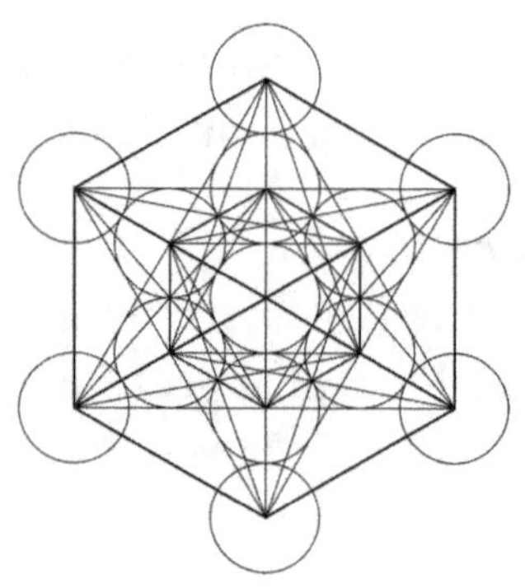

Metatron's Cube is often used in energy work to clear and balance energy. Its intricate geometric structure is believed to hold the key to unlocking higher states of consciousness, helping practitioners access more profound levels of healing energy. When working with Metatron's Cube in a Reiki session, practitioners can visualize the pattern spinning or expanding around the recipient's body, clearing out stagnant or blocked energy and bringing the energy field into balance (Melchizedek, 1999).

Metatron's Cube can be particularly powerful in distance healing, where the practitioner can visualize the geometric pattern surrounding the recipient's energy field. By imagining the cube as a protective and balancing force, the practitioner can help the recipient release old patterns of energy that no longer serve them and restore harmony to their physical, emotional, and spiritual bodies.

The Sri Yantra: Aligning with Higher Consciousness

The Sri Yantra, an ancient symbol from the Vedic tradition, is another powerful tool in sacred geometry. Composed of nine interlocking triangles, it represents the union of masculine and feminine energies and the soul's journey toward enlightenment. In energy healing, the Sri Yantra is often used as a symbol to align with higher states of consciousness and connect with the divine.

For Reiki practitioners, the Sri Yantra can serve as a visual guide for raising the recipient's vibrational frequency and helping them align with their higher self. By focusing on the geometric symmetry of the Sri Yantra during a healing session, practitioners can help the recipient clear lower vibrational energies and open themselves to higher frequencies of love, light, and wisdom. The Sri Yantra also reminds us that healing is about addressing physical symptoms and helping the recipient reconnect with their spiritual essence (Frawley, 2010).

These patterns help practitioners understand the universal energy structures that govern the flow of life force and offer powerful tools for deepening their connection to the recipient's energy field.

The Merkaba: Using Geometric Patterns for Distance Healing

The Merkaba is one of the most powerful symbols in sacred geometry and is often described as a vehicle for higher consciousness. Derived from ancient Egyptian and Hebrew traditions, the word "Merkaba" translates to "light, spirit, body," symbolizing the harmonious integration of these elements into one complete, unified system. In the context of energy healing, the Merkaba serves as a tool for accessing deeper levels of consciousness and is particularly useful in distance healing, where practitioners work within the recipient's energy field without being physically present.

The Merkaba is a three-dimensional geometric star tetrahedron composed of two interlocking tetrahedra—one pointing upward and the other downward. These two tetrahedra represent the balance between masculine and feminine energies, and their harmonious union is thought to create a powerful field of energy around the body. This field, often called the Merkaba field, extends beyond the physical body and acts as a conduit for higher-dimensional energy to flow through, facilitating healing, transformation, and spiritual awakening (Melchizedek, 1999).

Activating the Merkaba Field for Distance Healing

In distance healing, the Merkaba is a highly effective tool for establishing a robust, energetic connection between the practitioner and the recipient, regardless of physical location. By working with the Merkaba, practitioners can transcend the limitations of time and space, allowing the universal life force energy to flow seamlessly to the recipient. Activating the Merkaba field involves visualizing the star tetrahedron around the recipient's body and spinning the geometric shapes in opposite directions to generate a powerful, protective energy field.

When performing distance healing using the Merkaba, the practitioner can visualize the upward-pointing tetrahedrons spinning clockwise, symbolizing the activation of divine masculine energy, while the downward-pointing tetrahedron spins counterclockwise, representing the activation of sacred feminine energy. The intersection of these two energies creates a dynamic, balanced field that surrounds the recipient's energy body. This field protects the recipient from negative energies or external interference and serves as a conduit for the flow of healing energy from the practitioner (Frawley, 2010).

Activating the Merkaba allows the practitioner to connect with the recipient's higher self, facilitating deeper healing beyond the physical. By working with this geometric pattern, the practitioner can raise the vibrational frequency of the recipient's energy field, allowing them to release old patterns and blocks that may prevent healing. This technique is beneficial for addressing emotional or spiritual imbalances, as the Merkaba's energy can access higher dimensions of consciousness where these issues may be rooted (Jain, 2013).

Using the Merkaba to Balance and Align Energy

In addition to its use in distance healing, the Merkaba can also be employed to balance and align the recipient's energy field. When the Merkaba field is activated, it creates a symmetrical, harmonious structure around the body, which helps to align all aspects of the energy body. This is particularly useful for recipients experiencing energy imbalances, such as misaligned chakras or blocked energy channels.

During a Reiki session, the practitioner can visualize the Merkaba field surrounding the recipient and imagine the two tetrahedra spinning in harmony, helping to align the recipient's energy field with the universal life force. The practitioner can also use the Merkaba to clear stagnant or negative energy from the recipient's aura, allowing the energy to flow freely once again. By working with the Merkaba's geometric structure, the practitioner can facilitate deep healing at the physical, emotional, mental, and spiritual levels (Melchizedek, 1999).

Merkaba Meditation for Practitioners

Practitioners can also activate their Merkaba field to enhance their ability to channel healing energy. This involves using meditation and visualization techniques to activate the Merkaba field around their body, allowing them to access higher states of consciousness and strengthen their connection to the universal life force. By doing so, the practitioner can increase the effectiveness of their healing sessions, both in person and at a distance.

To activate the Merkaba through meditation, the practitioner can begin by sitting comfortably and focusing on their breath. After achieving a state of relaxation, the practitioner visualizes the two interlocking tetrahedra forming around their body. The upward-pointing tetrahedron is visualized as spinning clockwise, while the downward-pointing tetrahedron spins counterclockwise. As the tetrahedra spins, the practitioner imagines the Merkaba field expanding around them, creating a powerful energy field that extends beyond their physical body.

This meditation helps the practitioner align their energy with the universal life force, increasing their ability to act as a clear conduit for healing energy. It also helps to protect the practitioner's energy field from external interference, ensuring that they remain grounded and balanced throughout the healing session (Melchizedek, 1999). By regularly activating the Merkaba field through meditation, practitioners can deepen their connection to the higher dimensions of consciousness and enhance their ability to facilitate profound healing.

Integrating the Merkaba into Reiki Practice

The Merkaba is a versatile and powerful tool that can be integrated into hands-on and distance Reiki practice. Whether used to protect and balance the recipient's energy field, connect with their higher self, or facilitate deep emotional and spiritual healing, the Merkaba offers practitioners a way to work with sacred geometry to enhance their healing sessions. By tapping into the Merkaba's geometric structure and activating its energy field, Reiki practitioners can transcend the physical limitations of space and time, bringing powerful healing energy to the recipient from the higher dimensions of consciousness.

As we move forward, we will explore how these sacred geometric patterns, along with the principles of fractal geometry and holographic reality, help us understand the universe's interconnectedness and how healing occurs across time and space.

The Power of Sacred Geometry in Healing: Aligning Energy Fields with Universal Patterns

Sacred geometry in energy healing strengthens the practitioner's ability to facilitate transformation and tap into the deeper wisdom of the universe's structure. Understanding the principles of sacred geometric patterns allows Reiki practitioners to align the recipient's energy with these universal patterns, facilitating a more profound and lasting healing experience.

Sacred Geometry as a Blueprint for Healing

At its core, sacred geometry offers a visual and symbolic representation of how energy flows through the universe and within all living things. These geometric patterns, such as the Flower of Life, Metatron's Cube, and Merkaba, act as blueprints for understanding the fundamental principles that govern the cosmos. In Reiki, incorporating these geometric shapes into healing sessions helps practitioners work in harmony with the universe's natural order, aligning their healing intentions with the vibrational structure of life itself (Jain, 2013).

One key reason sacred geometry is so powerful in healing is that it reflects the harmonic balance inherent in the universe. Every shape in sacred geometry follows specific mathematical and vibrational principles, creating perfect harmony and symmetry. When energy becomes stagnant or blocked in the body, it is often due to the disruption of this natural harmony. By using sacred geometry as a guide, practitioners can restore balance to the recipient's energy field, helping the body, mind, and spirit realign with the natural flow of life force energy.

The Role of Symmetry and Proportions in Healing

Symmetry and proportion are two fundamental aspects of sacred geometry that offer powerful insights into the healing process. Like all natural forms, the human body follows the principles of sacred geometry. For example, the Golden Ratio—an important mathematical relationship found in many sacred geometric patterns—appears in the proportions of the human body, plants, animals, and galaxies. This ratio represents the ideal balance and harmony within the body and throughout the cosmos (Stewart, 2009).

In Reiki, restoring balance is often a key goal of healing sessions, and sacred geometry provides a natural framework for achieving this. When the practitioner visualizes sacred geometric patterns surrounding the recipient's body, they are helping to restore the natural symmetry and balance of the energy field. Whether the imbalance is physical, emotional, mental, or spiritual, sacred geometry guides the energy back into alignment with the universal blueprint of life (Brennan, 1988).

For instance, with its precise balance of masculine and feminine energies, the Sri Yantra can balance the energy flow between the different chakras, ensuring that no single chakra is overactive or under-active. By focusing on this geometric symbol during a Reiki session, practitioners can align the recipient's energy centers with one another, promoting overall harmony and balance within the body (Frawley, 2010).

Using Geometric Visualization in Reiki Healing

One practical way to integrate sacred geometry into Reiki healing is through geometric visualization. Visualization is already an essential tool in Reiki, as practitioners use their intention to guide the flow of energy toward specific areas of the recipient's body or energy field. By adding sacred geometric patterns into this visualization process, practitioners can enhance their ability to channel energy and direct it where it is needed most.

To incorporate sacred geometry into a healing session, the practitioner can begin by visualizing the recipient surrounded by a chosen geometric pattern, such as the Flower of Life or Metatron's Cube. The practitioner may imagine the energy flowing in harmonious circles or lines, following the sacred geometry pattern. This visualization helps to guide the energy through the recipient's energy field in a balanced, harmonious way, ensuring that no blockages or disruptions interfere with the healing process.

Practitioners can also use geometric visualization to clear energetic blockages. For example, suppose the practitioner senses that a particular area of the recipient's energy field is blocked. In that case, they can visualize a geometric shape, such as a spinning Merkaba, to clear the stagnation and restore energy flow. The spinning of the Merkaba or the movement of the Flower of Life creates a powerful energetic force that helps to dissolve blockages and allow energy to flow freely once again (Melchizedek, 1999).

Harmonizing Group Energy with Sacred Geometry

Another application of sacred geometry in Reiki is in group healing sessions. Whether working with a small group or leading a Reiki circle, practitioners can use sacred geometric patterns to harmonize the group's collective energy. By visualizing the group as surrounded by a geometric pattern, such as the Flower of Life, practitioners can create a unified energy field that allows the life force energy to flow freely between all participants. This is particularly useful in group distance healing, where sacred geometry can serve as a focal point for connecting the energies of multiple individuals across time and space (Stewart, 2009).

Sacred geometry can also be used to create a sacred space for healing. By incorporating geometric symbols into the physical space where the Reiki session takes place—such as placing images of the Flower of Life, Metatron's Cube, or the Sri Yantra around the room—practitioners can raise the vibration of the space, ensuring that it is aligned with the harmonious frequencies of the universe. This creates an optimal environment for healing and transformation, where both the practitioner and the recipient can connect more deeply with the universal life force energy.

Integrating Sacred Geometry for Long-Term Healing

The use of sacred geometry in healing is not limited to single sessions. Practitioners can help their recipients continue healing by encouraging them to meditate on sacred geometric patterns between sessions. By focusing on the Flower of Life, the Merkaba, or other sacred symbols during meditation, recipients can reinforce the balance and harmony established during the Reiki session, allowing them to maintain a high vibrational frequency over time.

Sacred geometry offers Reiki practitioners a powerful and effective way to align with the universal life force and guide healing energy through the recipient's body and energy field. Whether used for visualization, clearing blockages, or harmonizing group energy, these sacred patterns reflect the natural structure of the cosmos, allowing practitioners to work in alignment with the universe's inherent harmony. As we move forward, we will explore how the fractal nature of the universe and holographic reality provide further insight into the interconnectedness of all things and how distance healing operates within this framework.

Section Summary
Sacred Geometric Patterns and Their Role in Understanding Universal Energy Structures

In exploring sacred geometry and its application in Reiki healing, we uncover profound insights into how these geometric patterns serve as blueprints for understanding and manipulating the flow of universal energy. These patterns, like the Flower of Life, Metatron's Cube, and the Merkaba, reflect the natural order of the cosmos and can be harnessed by Reiki practitioners to align and balance energy fields during hands-on and distance healing sessions.

The Power of Sacred Geometry in Healing: Aligning Energy Fields with Universal Patterns

Sacred geometric patterns, such as the Flower of Life, Metatron's Cube, and Sri Yantra, are visual representations of the universal structure that governs the flow of energy. These patterns mirror the harmonic balance found in nature and the universe, illustrating the interconnectedness of all things. In Reiki healing, practitioners can use sacred geometry to restore balance in the recipient's energy field. Visualizing these patterns around the recipient helps guide energy to flow harmoniously, aligning with the universe's natural order. This section emphasizes the role of symmetry and proportion in achieving healing, as geometric patterns reflect the balance and harmony necessary for restoring physical, emotional, and spiritual well-being.

The Merkaba: Using Geometric Patterns for Distance Healing

The Merkaba is a powerful symbol in sacred geometry, composed of two interlocking tetrahedra that represent the balance of masculine and feminine energies. This three-dimensional star tetrahedron is a vehicle for higher consciousness and spiritual awakening. In distance healing, the Merkaba is a valuable tool for connecting with the recipient's energy field, transcending the limitations of time and space. By visualizing the Merkaba around the recipient, practitioners can create a dynamic, protective field that enhances the flow of healing energy. The Merkaba also balances and aligns the recipient's energy, helping to release blockages and raise their vibrational frequency. Practitioners can further activate their Merkaba through meditation to enhance their ability to channel healing energy.

Introduction to Sacred Geometric Patterns and Their Role in Understanding Universal Energy Structures

Sacred geometry provides a framework for comprehending the structures and flow of universal energy, which governs the interconnectedness of all living beings. Patterns like the Flower of Life, Metatron's Cube, and Sri Yantra reveal the underlying order of the cosmos, illustrating how energy moves in precise, harmonious ways. Reiki practitioners can incorporate these geometric shapes into their healing practice, using them as tools to align the recipient's energy with the natural flow of the universe. These patterns act as a visual guide for restoring balance in the recipient's energy field, facilitating deeper healing on physical, emotional, mental, and spiritual levels.

By integrating these geometric patterns into Reiki sessions, practitioners can align more deeply with the universal life force, guide healing energy more effectively, and support the recipient in achieving greater balance, harmony, and spiritual alignment.

§

The Fractal Nature of the Universe

The concept of the fractal nature of the universe offers a fascinating lens through which to understand the structure of reality and the mechanism of distance healing. In essence, fractals are infinitely repeating patterns that appear at every scale of the universe, from the vastness of galaxies to the intricacies of DNA. These patterns illustrate the fundamental idea that each part of a system contains the entire blueprint of the whole. In the context of Reiki and distance healing, the fractal nature of the universe helps explain how energy can be transmitted across time and space, as every part of the recipient's energy field reflects the greater whole of their being—and, by extension, the universe itself.

Fractals are more than just mathematical or visual phenomena; they are woven into the very fabric of reality. Fractal patterns permeate every level of existence, from the branching patterns of trees, rivers, and lightning to the spirals in galaxies and hurricanes. This continuous repetition of patterns across different scales mirrors the interconnectedness of all things. It shows that the same laws and structures that govern the universe also govern the human body and energy field (Briggs, 1992).

The fractal nature of the universe is a crucial principle that allows healing to occur locally and at a distance. Since every part of a person's energy field contains the entire pattern of their being, Reiki practitioners can access and influence the whole system through focused work on any one part. This idea is mirrored in the fractal pattern—no matter how small or large the segment you observe, it always reflects the same pattern in the larger system. This makes distance healing possible, as the energy a practitioner sends to a specific part of the recipient's energy field resonates through the entire being, creating healing effects at multiple levels (Gleick, 1987).

Fractals in the Human Energy Field

The human energy field, like the universe, is composed of intricate, repeating patterns that mirror the overall system of the body, mind, and spirit. Each chakra, meridian, and cell within the body reflects the entire system's energy. This understanding of fractal energy patterns allows practitioners to direct healing energy to a specific body area while knowing that the healing will resonate throughout the recipient's entire being.

For example, if a practitioner focuses on the recipient's heart chakra, the energy sent to that chakra will ripple out to the entire energetic system. In this case, the heart chakra reflects a smaller version of the whole energetic system, meaning that healing the heart chakra also affects the emotional, mental, and spiritual aspects of the recipient's energy. Similarly, working with the physical body through Reiki affects the emotional and mental bodies, as each aspect of the self contains the blueprint of the whole (Brennan, 1988).

This concept is particularly powerful in distance healing, where the practitioner may focus on a specific energetic imbalance but trust that the healing will spread throughout the recipient's entire being. When the practitioner visualizes sending energy to a particular part of the recipient's energy field, they are tapping into the fractal nature of the energy system. This allows the energy to move through the intricate web of patterns that comprise the recipient's body, mind, and spirit, creating a holistic healing experience regardless of physical distance.

The Part Reflects the Whole in Distance Healing

One of the most profound implications of the fractal nature of the universe is that every part of the system contains the blueprint of the whole. This principle applies to the recipient's energy field and the connection between the practitioner and the recipient during a Reiki session. When a practitioner connects with the recipient's energy, even from a distance, they connect to the whole of the recipient's being—every aspect of their physical, emotional, mental, and spiritual bodies.

This concept also extends to the relationship between the practitioner and the universe. As practitioners, we are not separate from the recipients we work with or the universal life force we channel. The fractal nature of the universe teaches us that each of us is a part of the greater whole and that healing one aspect of the system resonates throughout the entire web of life. By understanding this interconnectedness, Reiki practitioners can trust that the energy they send during a distance healing session will reach its intended destination, as both the practitioner and recipient are part of the same energetic fabric (Gleick, 1987).

Additionally, because the fractal nature of the universe demonstrates that the part reflects the whole, practitioners can use this principle to facilitate healing on multiple levels. For example, a physical ailment may reflect an emotional or spiritual imbalance, and vice versa. By working with the fractal structure of the energy field, practitioners can address the root cause of an issue by healing one aspect of the recipient's being, knowing that the effects will ripple out to the other elements.

Fractals as a Pathway for Universal Energy Flow

Fractals provide a powerful visual metaphor for how energy moves through the universe, illustrating that energy is infinite and interconnected across multiple dimensions. Each fractal pattern repeats itself endlessly, representing the flow of universal energy that Reiki practitioners channel during healing sessions. These infinite patterns echo how energy travels in a Reiki session—across physical boundaries, time, and space—because every part of the recipient's energy field is connected to the whole.

This understanding of fractal patterns offers a pathway for practitioners to access the universal life force in its most potent form. By visualizing the recipient's energy field as a fractal structure, the practitioner can more easily tap into the endless flow of energy that moves through the universe. This infinite energy source mirrors the patterns of nature, such as the spirals in galaxies or the veins in leaves, which all follow fractal geometry, demonstrating that the same life force flows through everything in existence (Briggs, 1992).

This concept reinforces the idea that healing can occur at any level of the recipient's being and that the energy they channel is part of a larger, more expansive flow that transcends the individual. The fractal nature of the universe ensures that healing one part of the energy field naturally leads to healing the whole, as each aspect is connected to the larger cosmic energy web. This fractal energy flow is significant in distance healing, where the practitioner relies on the universe's interconnectedness to guide the healing energy to the recipient, no matter where they are physically located (Gleick, 1987).

Fractal Healing: Working Beyond Physical Boundaries

Because each part of a system reflects the whole, practitioners can work with any part of the recipient's energy field—physical, emotional, or spiritual—and expect the healing effects to ripple throughout the entire being. This is especially relevant in distance healing, where the practitioner may never physically interact with the recipient but can still create profound healing effects through the fractal nature of the energy system.

This concept challenges the traditional notion that healing must occur through direct, hands-on contact. Instead, the fractal nature of the universe demonstrates that healing is holographic—meaning that the energy transmitted during a healing session resonates through the entire system, regardless of where the practitioner focuses their attention. When the practitioner channels energy to a specific area, such as the heart chakra or an emotional blockage, the fractal structure of the energy field ensures that the healing effects spread through the recipient's entire body, mind, and spirit (Brennan, 1988).

Distance Reiki sessions are just as effective as hands-on sessions, as the same universal principles of fractal geometry and interconnectedness apply. No matter how distant, the recipient's energy field is part of the larger universal system, and the practitioner's healing energy can easily flow through this web of connections. The fractal nature of the universe allows practitioners to trust that the energy will always reach the recipient and create healing effects at all levels of their being.

Holographic Reality: Every Part of the Universe Contains the Whole

While fractals provide a visual and structural understanding of the universe's interconnectedness, holographic reality takes this understanding to a deeper metaphysical level. The holographic principle asserts that every part of the universe contains the whole, much like how a hologram works. In a hologram, each small part contains the complete image of the whole, no matter how small the fragment is. In the same way, each part of the universe, including the human energy field, contains the entire blueprint of the larger universal structure. This holographic nature of reality explains how distance healing in Reiki is possible and effective.

In a holographic universe, every aspect of existence reflects the whole. This means that when a Reiki practitioner connects with the energy field of a recipient, they are not just interacting with a fragment or isolated part of that person's energy; they are connecting with the entirety of that person's being, which is intrinsically linked to the whole of the universe. This interconnectedness makes Reiki a powerful healing modality, especially when distance is involved (Bohm, 1980).

The holographic nature of reality explains how a practitioner can send healing energy across time and space, transcending physical limitations. In distance healing, the practitioner doesn't need to be physically present with the recipient because the recipient's entire energy system is accessible from any point in space. This reflects the holographic principle that the whole is present in every part. When a Reiki practitioner channels energy to the recipient, they work with the entire energetic matrix, allowing the healing to occur no matter where the recipient is located.

The Science Behind the Holographic Universe and Reiki

While the holographic principle has its roots in metaphysics, modern science, particularly quantum physics, supports this concept. Theories such as David Bohm's theory of implicate order and the holographic universe model developed by physicist Gerard 't Hooft suggest that the universe operates like a vast hologram, where every piece of information about the whole is encoded in each fragment of the universe. This means that when directed by a Reiki practitioner, healing energy can affect the recipient profoundly, as every part of the recipient's energy field contains the complete blueprint of their physical, emotional, and spiritual body (Bohm, 1980).

This concept is fundamental to how practitioners understand and facilitate healing in Reiki. When a practitioner sets the intention to send energy to the recipient, they are not simply targeting one isolated part of the recipient's body or mind—they are addressing the entire holographic matrix of the recipient's energy field. This allows the healing energy to move freely throughout the recipient's system, creating holistic and integrative healing effects that extend beyond the physical symptoms or immediate concerns the recipient may have (Talbot, 1991).

In a practical sense, the holographic nature of Reiki helps explain why distance healing sessions can have such profound effects on the recipient. Because the practitioner is working with the whole recipient's energy field, regardless of where they are located, the healing energy permeates every aspect of the recipient's being. This includes the physical body and the emotional, mental, and spiritual layers of the energy field, all of which are interconnected and contain the same holographic information.

Healing at Every Point in Space-Time

The universe's holographic nature also provides insight into how healing can occur across time and space. Just as every part of the universe contains the whole, each moment also includes the complete blueprint of the past, present, and future.

This concept is fundamental in Reiki, where practitioners often work to heal past traumas or prepare for future events. The holographic principle suggests that time, like space, is non-linear and interconnected, meaning that healing energy can be directed to a specific place and time (Laszlo, 2007).

For example, in a Reiki session focused on healing past trauma, the practitioner is not merely addressing the energetic imprints left behind by the trauma—they are working with the entire holographic structure of the recipient's past experiences, as well as how those experiences continue to influence the present and future. By sending healing energy to a past event, the practitioner helps the recipient shift their relationship to that moment, releasing the persistent, energetic blockages. This allows the recipient to move forward with greater ease, free from the energetic imprints of the past (Talbot, 1991).

Similarly, when a Reiki practitioner sends energy to a future event, such as an important life transition or a stressful situation, they are working with the holographic nature of time. Just as space is interconnected in the holographic universe, so is time. By setting the intention for healing and alignment, the practitioner helps the recipient energetically prepare for the future, ensuring that the event unfolds in the best possible way, aligned with the recipient's highest good.

Trusting in the Holographic Universe for Healing

One of the key lessons for Reiki practitioners when working with the holographic nature of reality is to trust in the interconnectedness of all things. This understanding allows practitioners to release any attachment to specific outcomes and focus on the broader picture of healing. The holographic principle teaches us that healing is not limited to the specific symptoms or challenges the recipient may face in the moment. Instead, healing energy addresses the entirety of the recipient's being, including aspects of their life and energy that may not be immediately visible.

This holistic approach to healing encourages practitioners and recipients to trust Reiki and the universal life force. By working with the holographic nature of reality, practitioners can tap into the full potential of the universe's healing energy, knowing that each part contains the whole. This means that no matter how distant or complex the healing session may seem, the energy will always flow to where it is needed most, creating profound and lasting effects at every level of the recipient's being.

Healing at Every Point in Space-Time: How Distance Healing Works Across Timelines

In addition to the holographic nature of reality, which reveals that every part of the universe contains the whole, the concept of healing across timelines extends the understanding of distance Reiki healing into the realm of time itself. This principle suggests that energy healing is effective across physical space and the continuum of time, meaning that past, present, and future events are interconnected and can all be influenced by the flow of healing energy.

The idea that healing can transcend the linear flow of time is rooted in the understanding that time, like space, is not a rigid, fixed dimension. Instead, time operates more like a fluid, interconnected web of experiences and energetic imprints. Events from the past are not isolated or detached from the present, but rather, they continue to influence our lives through the energetic patterns they have created. Similarly, future events, though yet to occur, are already beginning to take shape based on our present actions, thoughts, and intentions. By working with the universal life force, Reiki practitioners can influence these energetic imprints across time, creating healing and balance that reaches beyond the immediate moment (Brennan, 1988).

Healing Past Traumas and Energetic Imprints

Reiki has ability to heal past traumas and energetic imprints that continue to affect the present. When a person experiences a traumatic event, the energy of that event can become imprinted on their energy field, creating blockages or disruptions that persist long after the event has passed. These imprints can manifest as physical symptoms, emotional difficulties, or mental patterns that hinder personal growth and well-being.

By sending Reiki energy to the past, practitioners can help the recipient heal these lingering imprints, releasing the energy that has become stuck or stagnant in their energy field. This process allows the recipient to break free from the effects of past trauma and move forward with greater freedom and balance. In a distance healing session, the practitioner may visualize the recipient's energy field as existing in the present and the past, sending healing energy to the specific time when the trauma occurred. By addressing the root cause of the energetic imbalance, the practitioner can help the recipient release the past's hold on their current energy field (Bohm, 1980).

It's important to note that this healing across timelines does not change the past event itself; instead, it changes the recipient's energetic relationship to that event. By clearing the energetic imprint left by the trauma, the recipient can process the event's emotional, mental, and physical effects more effectively, allowing for a sense of closure and peace that may not have been possible. This type of healing is especially powerful for individuals who have carried unresolved trauma for many years, as it offers them the opportunity to release the energetic burden they have been carrying.

Preparing for Future Events

In addition to healing the past, Reiki practitioners can also use the principles of holographic reality and fractal time to influence future events. Just as past experiences leave energetic imprints that affect the present, future events are shaped by the energy generated in the present moment. By sending Reiki energy to a future event, practitioners can help the recipient align with the highest possible outcome, ensuring that the energy surrounding the event is balanced, harmonious, and supportive.

For example, a recipient preparing for a major life transition, such as a job interview, surgery, or a significant decision, can benefit from Reiki energy directed toward that future moment. The practitioner can visualize the event as though it has already occurred, sending healing energy to ensure that the recipient enters the experience in a calm, centeredness, and alignment with their highest good. This process helps the recipient prepare energetically for the event, creating a foundation of balance and positivity that increases the likelihood of a favorable outcome (Laszlo, 2007).

This approach to future-focused healing works because all moments—past, present, and future—are interconnected in the holographic and fractal view of time. By addressing the energy surrounding a future event in the present, practitioners can influence the flow of energy leading up to that event, helping to ensure that the recipient's future unfolds in alignment with their intentions and well-being.

Working with Parallel Timelines and Multiple Dimensions

Another intriguing aspect of healing across time is the possibility of working with parallel timelines or multiple dimensions. According to some metaphysics and quantum physics theories, every choice or action we take creates a branching path, leading to alternate timelines where different versions of ourselves experience different outcomes. These parallel timelines exist alongside our current experience, and in some cases, unresolved energetic imprints from these timelines can influence our present-day energy field.

Reiki practitioners skilled in advanced energy work may be able to access these parallel timelines during healing sessions, helping the recipient release any energetic residue from alternate versions of their life experience. This work benefits individuals who feel regret, guilt, or confusion about past decisions. By addressing the energy connected to these alternate paths, practitioners can help the recipient release the energetic influence of parallel timelines, allowing them to focus more fully on the present and move forward with clarity and purpose (Talbot, 1991).

Clearing Ancestral Energies

In addition to personal past traumas, Reiki can clear ancestral energies passed down through generations. Just as individuals carry the energetic imprints of their past experiences, they also inherit energetic patterns from their ancestors. These patterns can manifest as emotional or behavioral tendencies, physical health issues, or spiritual blockages. By sending Reiki energy to heal ancestral lines, practitioners can help recipients clear these inherited patterns, allowing them to break free from cycles of karma that may have persisted for generations.

During a distance healing session focused on ancestral healing, the practitioner may visualize the recipient's energy field as connected to their family line, extending back through generations. By sending healing energy to the entire lineage, the practitioner can help the recipient release the energetic burdens they have inherited, creating space for new, healthier patterns to emerge in the present and future.

Healing the Past, Present, and Future as a Unified Whole

Ultimately, the ability to heal across time—whether by addressing past traumas, preparing for future events, or clearing ancestral energies—highlights the deep interconnectedness of all things in the universe. In the holographic and fractal model, time is not a series of disconnected moments but a unified whole, where every moment influences every other. By working with the universal life force, Reiki practitioners can access and influence this interconnected web of time, helping recipients heal in the present and across their entire timeline.

By trusting in the principles of fractal and holographic reality, Reiki practitioners can facilitate healing that transcends the limitations of time and space. They offer recipients the opportunity to heal at every level of their being, across every dimension of their lives.

Section Summary
The Fractal Nature of the Universe

In the last section, we explored profound metaphysical and scientific concepts that underpin distance healing in Reiki, focusing on the fractal nature of the universe, holographic reality, and healing across timelines. These concepts provide a deeper understanding of how energy healing transcends physical boundaries and linear time, explaining how practitioners can influence the entire energy field of a recipient regardless of distance or time.

Fractal Nature of the Universe: How the Part Reflects the Whole

The fractal nature of the universe shows that every part of a system reflects the whole. This principle illustrates how healing one part of the body or energy field can affect the entire system. The human energy field, like the universe, is composed of intricate, repeating patterns that mirror the whole structure. This allows Reiki practitioners to send healing energy to a specific part of the recipient's body or energy field, knowing that the effects will resonate throughout the recipient's entire being. This is especially useful in distance healing, where energy sent to one aspect of the recipient's system influences their physical, emotional, and spiritual bodies.

Holographic Reality: Every Part of the Universe Contains the Whole

Holographic reality builds on the concept that every part of the universe contains the entire structure. Much like a hologram, where each fragment contains the whole image, each part of the human energy field mirrors the entirety of the recipient's being. This principle explains why distance healing works so effectively—when a Reiki practitioner connects with any part of the recipient's energy, they access the entire system, making it possible to send healing energy across space without physical proximity. The practitioner's energy interacts with the recipient's whole energy system, ensuring that the healing effects permeate all layers of the recipient's physical, emotional, and spiritual existence.

Time: How Distance Healing Works Across Timelines

The concept of healing across timelines extends the understanding of distance Reiki healing to time. Reiki can influence physical space and the continuum of time, including the past, present, and future. Practitioners can send healing energy to past traumas, helping recipients release energetic imprints that continue to affect their well-being. Reiki can also be directed toward future events, assisting recipients to align with the highest possible outcomes. This healing across timelines is possible because time, like space, is interconnected and non-linear. The practitioner works with the energetic imprints that connect all moments, enabling healing that spans an individual's life experiences, past, present, and future.

Reiki works through a unified and interconnected energy field, where every part contains the whole, and every moment in time is accessible. Through the principles of fractal geometry, holographic reality, and the ability to heal across timelines, Reiki practitioners are equipped to send healing energy that transcends physical and temporal boundaries, creating holistic and integrative healing effects that resonate through the recipient's entire being and timeline. These concepts deepen our understanding of how universal energy structures govern the flow of healing, offering practitioners tools for accessing infinite potential across space and time.

§

The Role of Karma and Past Lives

Understanding How Past Life Traumas and Karmic Imbalances Affect Present-Day Health

The concept of karma and past lives plays a significant role in understanding the deeper layers of healing in Reiki and other energy healing practices. Karma, which can be understood as the energy generated by our actions, thoughts, and emotions, follows us through our current life and across multiple lifetimes. When unresolved karmic patterns or traumas from past lives remain embedded in the energy field, they can manifest as physical, emotional, or mental imbalances in the present. Understanding how past life traumas and karmic imbalances affect present-day health allows Reiki practitioners to address deep-seated energetic issues and help recipients break free from cycles that may have persisted for centuries.

The Nature of Karma: Cause and Effect Across Lifetimes

In many spiritual traditions, karma is seen as the law of cause and effect—a universal principle that states that every action has a consequence. However, karma is not just about specific actions; it also involves the intentions, thoughts, and emotions behind those actions. These energetic imprints can accumulate throughout a lifetime, influencing a person's health, relationships, and overall well-being. When these karmic patterns are not resolved during a lifetime, they can carry over into future incarnations, where they continue to influence the person's energy field and life experience.

Karmic imbalances can be understood as energetic blockages that have persisted across multiple lifetimes. These blockages may manifest as recurring physical ailments, emotional struggles, or repeated patterns of behavior that seem to resist change. Often, these imbalances are tied to specific past life experiences where the individual may have experienced trauma, loss, or unresolved conflict. Without healing these karmic wounds, the energy of those experiences remains stuck, creating challenges in the present (Newton, 1994).

For example, a person who experienced betrayal or abandonment in a past life may carry the energetic imprint of that trauma into their current life. This unresolved karmic energy can manifest as trust issues, fear of intimacy, or a tendency to sabotage relationships. Similarly, someone who faced oppression or powerlessness in a past life may struggle with self-worth or empowerment in their current incarnation. By understanding the karmic roots of these patterns, Reiki practitioners can help recipients release these old energetic imprints and bring healing to both their present and past selves (Weiss, 1997).

How Past Life Traumas Manifest in the Present

Past life traumas can manifest in various ways, affecting the physical body and the subtle energy field. These imprints are often deeply embedded in the recipient's energy system, influencing everything from physical health to emotional reactions and thought patterns. In some cases, past life traumas may create specific physical symptoms that seem to have no apparent cause in the present lifetime. For example, a recipient who experienced injury or violence in a past life may suffer from chronic pain or tension in the corresponding area of their body in the present (Stevenson, 1974).

Past life experiences can also influence emotional and mental patterns. Individuals may carry fears, anxieties, or recurring emotional reactions that seem out of place in their current life circumstances. These emotional imprints are often tied to past life experiences where the person may have experienced similar emotions, such as fear, grief, or anger. By working with these energetic imprints, Reiki practitioners can help recipients heal their present-day emotional wounds and the deeper karmic patterns that drive these reactions (Weiss, 1997).

Karmic Lessons and Spiritual Growth

Karmic imbalances are not merely obstacles to be overcome—they also represent opportunities for spiritual growth and healing. The challenges from past life traumas and karmic imprints are often tied to the recipient's spiritual lessons in this lifetime. These lessons may involve learning forgiveness, compassion, self-empowerment, or unconditional love. By addressing these karmic imbalances through Reiki, practitioners can support recipients in their spiritual journey, helping them to resolve these old patterns and move toward greater alignment with their higher self.

In many cases, karmic healing involves forgiveness—not only of others but also of oneself. For example, a recipient who carries guilt or shame from a past life may need to release these emotions to heal fully. Reiki can help facilitate this process by bringing awareness to the old patterns and providing the required energetic support to let go of the past. Similarly, individuals who have experienced betrayal, loss, or harm in past lives may need to work through anger or resentment to release the karmic hold these emotions have on their energy field (Newton, 1994).

The Role of the Practitioner in Karmic Healing

When working with karmic imbalances and past life traumas, Reiki practitioners take on the role of facilitator and guide. It is not the practitioner's job to "fix" the recipient's karma but rather to create a space of healing where the recipient can become aware of the karmic patterns and begin releasing them. This may involve using specific Reiki symbols, such as Hon Sha Ze Sho Nen, which allows the practitioner to transcend time and space, facilitating healing across lifetimes. The practitioner's role is to support the recipient in accessing the universal life force energy, which can help clear these old energetic imprints and restore balance to the recipient's energy field (Petter, 2000).

In some cases, recipients may become aware of specific past life memories or experiences during a Reiki session, as the energy work helps to bring these memories to the surface. When this occurs, the practitioner can guide the recipient in processing these memories, helping them to understand the connection between their past life and their present-day challenges. This process of awareness and release is vital to resolving karmic imbalances, as it allows the recipient to consciously let go of the old patterns and embrace a new, more empowered way of being.

Healing the Present Through the Past

Ultimately, addressing karmic imbalances and past life traumas through Reiki is about healing the present by releasing the energetic hold that the past has on the recipient. By working with the universal life force energy, practitioners can help recipients dissolve the energetic blockages that have carried over from past lives, allowing them to step into a more balanced, harmonious, and empowered version of themselves in the present. This karmic healing benefits the individual and contributes to the healing of the greater collective, as each person's healing journey helps to raise the vibration of the whole (Weiss, 1997).

Distance Healing as a Tool to Address Past Life and Ancestral Wounds

Distance Reiki healing offers a unique and powerful method for addressing deep karmic imbalances, past life traumas, and even ancestral wounds. Because distance healing transcends the limitations of time and space, it allows practitioners to send healing energy to events and experiences from the past, whether in the recipient's lifetime, a past life, or within their ancestral lineage. By facilitating the flow of the universal life force energy to these distant times and places, practitioners can help recipients release the energetic imprints of unresolved pain, trauma, and inherited karmic patterns.

Healing Past Life Wounds Through Distance Reiki

In many cases, the energetic imprints left by past life traumas are deeply embedded in the recipient's energy field. These imprints may manifest as physical symptoms, emotional patterns, or spiritual challenges that resist traditional healing forms. Because distance Reiki works beyond the boundaries of the present moment, it is uniquely suited to help recipients heal these old wounds by addressing the energetic blockages that have carried over from past lives.

During a distance Reiki session focused on past life healing, the practitioner can use Hon Sha Ze Sho Nen, the Reiki symbol for transcending time and space, to connect with the recipient's energy at the time when the trauma occurred. By setting the intention to send healing energy to a specific past life, the practitioner can access the energetic imprint left by the experience and help to dissolve the blockages or unresolved emotions that have persisted across lifetimes. This allows the recipient to release the energetic ties to that experience and move forward without the weight of those old patterns affecting their present-day health and well-being (Petter, 2000).

Some recipients may be conscious of their past life experiences, while in others, the practitioner may intuitively sense the presence of past life energy that needs to be addressed. Either way, distance healing provides a safe and effective way to access these distant memories and traumas without requiring the recipient to relive them. Instead, the universal life force energy flows directly to the area of need, helping to release the energetic imprints and restore balance to the recipient's energy field.

Addressing Ancestral Healing Through Distance Reiki

In addition to healing past life wounds, distance Reiki is a powerful tool for ancestral healing. Just as individuals carry the energetic imprints of their past experiences, they can also inherit karmic patterns, emotional wounds, and unresolved trauma from their ancestors. These inherited energies can manifest as recurring patterns within a family, such as cycles of poverty, addiction, or emotional dysfunction. By addressing these ancestral imprints, Reiki practitioners can help recipients release the energy passed down through generations and clear the way for new, healthier patterns to emerge.

Ancestral healing with distance Reiki involves connecting with the family lineage—not just the immediate ancestors but also the energy that flows through the entire ancestral line. The practitioner can use distance healing techniques to send Reiki energy to specific ancestors or the lineage, helping to clear the unresolved energy that has been passed down. This process benefits the recipient and brings healing to the entire family system, creating positive ripple effects that extend beyond the individual (Brennan, 1988).

During a distance Reiki session focused on ancestral healing, the practitioner may visualize the recipient's family tree and set the intention to send healing energy to the root of the karmic patterns that have been inherited. This might involve sending energy to a particular ancestor who experienced significant trauma or hardship or working with the entire lineage to clear long-standing energetic imprints that have affected multiple generations. By releasing these ancestral wounds, the recipient is freed from the energetic patterns that have kept them stuck, allowing them to move forward with greater freedom and empowerment (Newton, 1994).

Healing Across Lifetimes and Lineages

Both past-life healing and ancestral healing share a common goal: to free the recipient from the energetic patterns that have carried over from previous generations or lifetimes, allowing them to live more fully in the present. Distance Reiki provides an effective means of doing this because it enables the practitioner to easily access these distant times and places, bringing the healing energy directly to where it is needed most.

The healing process across lifetimes and lineages involves releasing old patterns and integrating the lessons and wisdom that those experiences have provided. While past life traumas and ancestral wounds can create energetic blockages, they can also offer valuable insights into the recipient's spiritual journey. By working with these energies through distance Reiki, practitioners can help recipients reclaim the wisdom and strength that their ancestors or past selves may have developed, integrating those qualities into their current life in a healthy and balanced way (Weiss, 1997).

Sometimes, the recipient may experience a sense of release and resolution during a distance healing session focused on past life or ancestral energy. A feeling of emotional catharsis, spiritual clarity, or a deep sense of peace may accompany this. By releasing the energetic hold of the past, the recipient can move forward with greater alignment, free from the patterns that have kept them bound to old karmic imprints. This healing process allows new, positive energy to flow into their lives, creating space for growth, transformation, and spiritual evolution.

Using Intention to Guide Distance Healing Across Time and Space

As with all forms of distance Reiki, the practitioner's intention is crucial in guiding the healing energy to the appropriate place, whether that is a past life trauma, an ancestral wound, or a karmic imbalance. By setting a clear and focused intention, the practitioner helps to direct the flow of the universal life force energy to the specific time, place, or individual that needs healing. This allows the practitioner to work precisely, sending energy to the issue's root rather than merely addressing surface-level symptoms.

For practitioners working with past life or ancestral healing, it is essential to approach the session with an open heart and a sense of non-attachment to the outcome. These deep, energetic patterns can take time to heal fully, and it is essential to trust in the wisdom of the universal life force to guide the healing process in the most beneficial way for the recipient. By maintaining a state of mindfulness and presence, the practitioner allows the healing to unfold naturally without forcing or controlling the outcome.

The Holistic Impact of Distance Healing

Healing past life traumas and ancestral wounds through distance, Reiki benefits the recipient individually and contributes to the healing of the collective consciousness. Each person's healing journey is part of a larger web of interconnected energy. As individuals release old karmic patterns and ancestral imprints, they help raise the vibration of the collective. This collective healing can potentially transform individuals, families, communities, and even future generations.

Healing Across Timelines: Clearing Energetic Imprints from the Past

A wonderful aspects of Reiki, especially in the context of distance healing, is the ability to clear energetic imprints from the past. These imprints, whether from past lives, traumatic events, or ancestral experiences, can persist in a person's energy field and influence their present health, emotional state, and overall well-being. The ability to heal across timelines allows practitioners to reach into the energetic history of the recipient and release these imprints, creating a ripple effect of healing that transcends time and space.

Energetic Imprints and Their Influence on the Present

Energetic imprints are subtle, often invisible influences in the energy field due to unresolved past experiences. These imprints can come from various sources, such as trauma, emotional pain, karmic lessons, or ancestral patterns passed down through generations. Although the original event that created the imprint may be long over, the energy of that experience remains embedded in the individual's energy system, causing blockages or distortions in the flow of life force energy (Brennan, 1988).

For example, a person may have experienced intense grief in a past life or within their ancestral lineage, and this grief may manifest as a recurring emotional pattern in the present. This unresolved energy can create a range of issues, from chronic sadness to physical symptoms like tension in the chest or throat. Similarly, past experiences of abandonment, betrayal, or abuse can leave energetic scars that influence a person's ability to form healthy relationships, trust others, or feel secure in their environment (Newton, 1994).

By working with these energetic imprints, Reiki practitioners can help recipients free themselves from the energetic baggage of the past. This process involves identifying the source of the energetic blockage, often through intuitive guidance or tuning into the recipient's energy field, and then using the universal life force energy to dissolve the imprint. In doing so, the practitioner facilitates the release of old emotions, thoughts, and patterns, allowing the recipient to move forward without being held back by the unresolved energy of the past.

Healing Emotional and Physical Trauma from the Past

Reiki can assist in clearing energetic imprints is through healing emotional and physical trauma from the past. When a person experiences trauma—whether it is physical harm, emotional abuse, or intense fear—the energy of that experience can become lodged in their energy field. Over time, this trapped energy can create emotional imbalances, physical illness, or mental distress, even if the original trauma is not consciously remembered.

Through distance Reiki, practitioners can connect with the recipient's past timeline, sending healing energy to the moment when the trauma occurred. The practitioner helps unravel the energetic knot created in the recipient's energy field by addressing the trauma at its source. This healing often releases old emotions, such as fear, anger, or sadness, that have been suppressed for years. The recipient may feel a deep sense of emotional catharsis, followed by a newfound sense of freedom and peace (Weiss, 1997).

Sometimes, the recipient may be unaware of the trauma that caused the energetic imprint. These experiences may be buried in the subconscious or from a past life that the recipient does not consciously remember. However, distance Reiki can still reach these hidden layers of the energy field, offering healing even when the conscious mind is not fully aware of the source of the pain. The healing energy works subtly, gently clearing away the old wounds and restoring balance to the recipient's energy system.

Working with Karmic Patterns and Lessons

In addition to addressing trauma, Reiki can also be used to clear karmic patterns that have followed the recipient across multiple lifetimes. Karmic patterns are often repetitive cycles of behavior or emotional responses that arise from unresolved lessons from the past. These patterns may manifest in various ways, such as recurring relationship issues, chronic health problems, or feelings of being "stuck" in certain areas of life. By sending Reiki to these karmic imprints, practitioners can help the recipient break free from these cycles and integrate the lessons they need to learn (Newton, 1994).

For example, a recipient who has experienced repeated relationship betrayals may be dealing with a karmic lesson about trust and forgiveness. By using Reiki to clear the energetic imprints of these past experiences, the practitioner can help the recipient heal the emotional wounds associated with betrayal and open themselves to healthier, more balanced relationships in the future. Similarly, a person who struggles with chronic self-doubt or low self-esteem may be dealing with a karmic pattern related to self-worth. Reiki can help to release the old patterns of thought and behavior that have kept the recipient stuck in a cycle of self-criticism, allowing them to embrace a more empowered and positive self-image (Weiss, 1997).

Clearing Ancestral Energies from the Lineage

In addition to clearing personal and karmic imprints, distance Reiki can address ancestral energies passed down through the family lineage. Ancestral healing involves working with the energy of the recipient's ancestors, releasing unresolved trauma, pain, or karmic patterns that have affected the family for generations. These inherited energies can manifest as emotional or physical challenges that seem to "run in the family," such as cycles of addiction, abuse, or mental illness.

By sending Reiki energy to the recipient's family line, practitioners can help clear the energetic blockages passed down from generation to generation. This process benefits the recipient and brings healing to the entire family system, helping break the inherited trauma cycle and creating space for new, healthier patterns to emerge. As the recipient's energy field becomes clearer, they can escape the shadow of their family's past and create a new path forward, free from the burdens of ancestral karma (Brennan, 1988).

Integrating the Healing Across Timelines

Healing across timelines is about clearing away the old and integrating the lessons, wisdom, and growth that have come from past experiences. As the recipient releases the energetic imprints of the past, they can reclaim the strength, resilience, and spiritual wisdom that their past lives or ancestors may have developed. This integration process allows the recipient to move forward with a deeper understanding of their journey and a greater connection to their higher self.

This integration process is often accompanied by a sense of wholeness and spiritual alignment. As the old patterns are cleared away, the recipient can reconnect with their authentic self, free from the distortions of past trauma or karmic imprints. This sense of alignment allows the recipient to move forward on their spiritual path with greater clarity, purpose, and empowerment, knowing that the energetic ties of the past no longer bind them.

Section Summary
The Role of Karma and Past Lives

This section explores the powerful and transformative ability of Reiki to heal across timelines, addressing past life traumas, karmic imbalances, and ancestral wounds. By tapping into the universal life force, Reiki practitioners can transcend the limitations of time and space, accessing and clearing energetic imprints from past events, even those from previous lifetimes or inherited through familial lineage. The section outlines key principles and practices for understanding and facilitating healing in these contexts.

Healing Past Life Traumas and Karmic Imbalances

Karma, the energy generated by actions, thoughts, and emotions, follows individuals across multiple lifetimes. Unresolved karmic patterns or traumas from past lives can become deeply embedded in the energy field, manifesting as physical symptoms, emotional struggles, or behavioral patterns that continue into the present. Reiki practitioners can use distance healing to address these blockages by sending healing energy to past life experiences where trauma or imbalance occurred. By healing these old wounds, recipients can release the energetic burdens that influence their current health and well-being, allowing them to break free from recurring cycles and achieve spiritual growth.

Ancestral Healing and Clearing Lineage Imprints

Ancestral healing focuses on clearing inherited karmic patterns, emotional wounds, and unresolved trauma passed down through generations. These inherited energies can manifest as familial cycles of dysfunction, such as addiction, poverty, or mental illness. Distance Reiki enables practitioners to work with the recipient's family lineage, sending healing energy to ancestors or the entire ancestral line. By addressing and releasing these long-standing energetic imprints, recipients can free themselves from inherited burdens and create space for healthier patterns to emerge. This process often brings healing to the recipient and the entire family system.

Clearing Energetic Imprints from the Past and Across Timelines

Energetic imprints from past events, including trauma or emotional pain, can persist in the energy field and continue influencing a person's present life. These imprints may manifest as physical, emotional, or spiritual challenges that resist traditional forms of healing. Reiki practitioners can access these imprints through distance healing and dissolve the blockages or unresolved emotions that have persisted. This chapter emphasizes how clearing energetic imprints creates a ripple effect of healing, allowing recipients to move forward with greater clarity, balance, and freedom from the past's influence.

Addressing past life or ancestral wounds also helps recipients integrate the lessons and wisdom gained from these experiences, contributing to their spiritual evolution and empowerment.

§

Knowledge Review
Chapter Three

Metaphysical and Spiritual Perspectives

1. What is the Law of Vibration, and how does it relate to Reiki healing?

2. How do Reiki practitioners attune their vibration to the recipient's during distance healing?

3. How do different emotional states impact the vibrational frequency during a Reiki session?

4. How does raising the recipient's vibrational frequency during a Reiki session impact their physical, emotional, and spiritual well-being?

5. What is the Law of Attraction, and how does it relate to Reiki healing?

6. Why is aligning the practitioner's intention with the desired healing outcome crucial for effective Reiki healing?

7. How does the recipient's openness impact the effectiveness of a Reiki session based on the Law of Attraction?

8. Why is non-attachment important when applying the Law of Attraction in Reiki healing, and how does it support the process?

9. What is the Law of Cause and Effect (Karma), and how does it influence a person's energy in Reiki healing?

10. How can Reiki practitioners help release karmic imprints and energetic blockages from past experiences?

11. How does Reiki transcend time and space, and how can distance healing address karmic patterns or future events?

12. Why is self-care and energetic hygiene important for Reiki practitioners in the context of the Law of Cause and Effect?

13. How does sacred geometry provide a blueprint for understanding energy flow in the universe and its application in Reiki healing?

14. How does the Sri Yantra symbol assist in raising the recipient's vibrational frequency during Reiki healing?

15. What does the Merkaba represent in sacred geometry, and how is it relevant to energy healing?

16. How can a Reiki practitioner activate the Merkaba field for distance healing?

17. How does the Merkaba help balance and align the recipient's energy field during a Reiki session?

18. What is the purpose of Merkaba meditation for Reiki practitioners, and how is it performed?

19. What role does symmetry and proportion play in sacred geometry, and how does it apply to restoring balance in Reiki sessions?

20. How can sacred geometry be used to harmonize group energy and enhance the vibrational frequency of healing spaces?

21. What are fractals, and how do they relate to energy healing in the context of Reiki?

22. How does the fractal nature of the human energy field facilitate healing at both local and distance levels?

23. In what ways does the fractal nature of the universe challenge traditional notions of hands-on healing?

24. What is the holographic principle, and how does it apply to Reiki healing?

25. How does the holographic nature of the universe make distance healing effective?

26. How can Reiki practitioners use holographic visualization to enhance their healing sessions?

27. How does the concept of time as a fluid and interconnected web apply to Reiki healing?

28. How can Reiki help heal past traumas that continue to affect the present?

29. What role does Reiki play in preparing for future events, and why is it effective?

30. What is the significance of clearing ancestral energies in Reiki healing, and how is it done?

31. How does the holographic and fractal nature of reality explain Reiki's effectiveness across time and space?

32. What is karma, and how can unresolved karmic imbalances affect present-day health?

33. How can past life traumas manifest physically, emotionally, or mentally in the present?

34. Why is it essential to address karmic imbalances as part of spiritual growth and healing?

35. How can Reiki help in healing past life traumas and karmic imbalances?

36. What is the role of the Reiki practitioner in guiding recipients through karmic healing?

37. How does distance Reiki healing address past life traumas and karmic imbalances?

38. What are ancestral wounds, and how can they affect present-day health?

39. What are the holistic benefits of healing past life traumas and ancestral wounds through distance Reiki?

40. How do energetic imprints from past traumas or experiences influence a person's present-day health and emotional state?

41. How does distance Reiki help in clearing energetic imprints from past lives?

42. What are karmic patterns, and how can Reiki help clear them?

43. What is ancestral healing, and how can distance Reiki address inherited patterns within a family?

44. How does the process of integrating lessons from past experiences contribute to healing across timelines?

Tools for Enhancing Distance Healing

Symbols, Intentions, and Amplifying Distance Healing

The Power of Reiki Symbols

Another profound aspects of Reiki healing, especially in the context of distance healing, is the use of sacred symbols to focus and amplify the flow of energy. Reiki symbols are powerful tools that act as conduits for the universal life force, helping practitioners direct healing energy with precision, intention, and greater potency. Among these symbols, Hon Sha Ze Sho Nen plays a central role in distance healing, as it allows practitioners to transcend the limitations of time and space, connecting with the recipient's energy field regardless of where they are physically located.

Understanding Hon Sha Ze Sho Nen

Hon Sha Ze Sho Nen, often referred to as the "distance symbol" in Reiki, is a sacred geometric symbol that bridges the physical distance between the practitioner and the recipient. Its literal translation is "No past, no present, no future," or "The divine in me contacts the divine in you." This symbol helps to create an energetic connection that transcends time, space, and the physical body, allowing the healing energy to flow freely to the recipient, no matter how far away they may be.

In Reiki Level 2, practitioners are attuned to this symbol and learn how to use it in their distance healing sessions. Once invoked, Hon Sha Ze Sho Nen creates a bridge between the practitioner and the recipient, allowing the practitioner to access the recipient's energy field from afar. This connection bypasses the usual constraints of time and space, reinforcing that all energy is interconnected and that physical separation is an illusion regarding the flow of healing energy (Rand, 1991).

Hon Sha Ze Sho Nen is essential for healing across timelines, as it allows practitioners to send energy to a recipient's present circumstances and their past and future. This symbol will enable practitioners to work with energetic imprints from past lives, address ancestral wounds, and prepare recipients for future events. The symbol acts as a gateway, ensuring that the energy reaches its intended target and facilitates deep healing, regardless of the limitations of linear time.

How to Use Hon Sha Ze Sho Nen in Distance Healing

When performing distance healing, the practitioner invokes Hon Sha Ze Sho Nen at the beginning of the session to establish a strong, energetic connection with the recipient. The symbol can be visualized in the practitioner's mind, drawn in the air with the hands, or traced on paper as part of the healing process. Once the symbol is activated, the practitioner intends to send Reiki energy to the recipient, trusting that the energy will flow to the right place at the right time.

The intention behind the use of Hon Sha Ze Sho Nen is critical to its effectiveness. The practitioner's clear focus and intention help direct the energy to the recipient's energy field, no matter how far away they may be. Whether the recipient is on the other side of the world or in a different time zone, the energy flows seamlessly through the universal life force, guided by the practitioner's intention and the power of the symbol. This allows the practitioner to perform healing sessions across great distances as effectively as working with the recipient in person (Petter, 2000).

In addition to its use in distance healing, Hon Sha Ze Sho Nen can send energy to specific situations, events, or relationships. For example, a practitioner may use the symbol to send healing energy to a recipient's past trauma, helping to heal the emotional and energetic imprints left behind by that experience. Similarly, the practitioner can use the symbol to send energy to a future event, such as a surgery, exam, or life transition, ensuring the recipient is energetically prepared and supported.

Amplifying the Healing with Other Reiki Symbols

Hon Sha Ze Sho Nen is often used with other Reiki symbols to amplify the healing energy sent during a distance session. For example, the practitioner may use the Cho Ku Rei symbol, also known as the "power symbol," to increase the intensity of the transmitted healing energy. Cho Ku Rei is often drawn before or after invoking Hon Sha Ze Sho Nen to strengthen the flow of energy and ensure that the recipient receives the full benefit of the healing session (Rand, 1991).

Similarly, the Sei He Ki symbol, known as the "mental and emotional symbol," can be used alongside Hon Sha Ze Sho Nen to address specific emotional or mental imbalances. This combination is particularly powerful when healing trauma, anxiety, or other emotional challenges that have roots in the recipient's past experiences. By invoking both symbols, the practitioner creates a healing environment where the universal life force can flow more freely, dissolving energetic blockages and promoting emotional balance and clarity (Petter, 2000).

These symbols work together to enhance the healing process. Each serves a specific purpose while amplifying the overall flow of energy. By understanding how to combine the symbols, practitioners can create more focused, effective, and transformative healing sessions for their recipients.

Trusting in the Power of Symbols and Intention

Using Reiki symbols in distance healing highlights the importance of intention in the healing process. While the symbols hold sacred power, their effectiveness is amplified by the practitioner's focused intention and connection to the universal life force. In Reiki, the practitioner's role is to serve as a clear channel for this energy, directing it where it is needed most. The symbols act as tools to help guide the energy, but the practitioner's intention ultimately shapes the flow of healing.

In distance healing, practitioners must approach each session with a clear, focused mind and a heart full of compassion and openness. By setting a clear intention for healing, the practitioner aligns themselves with the recipient's highest good, allowing the energy to flow freely and effectively. Hon Sha Ze Sho Nen, along with the other symbols, is a powerful guide in this process, helping practitioners transcend time and space and facilitate healing on a deep, energetic level.

The Role of Focused Intention and Affirmations in Distance Healing

In Reiki, particularly in distance healing, intention plays a pivotal role in directing and amplifying the energy between the practitioner and the recipient. The principle that "energy follows thought" underscores the importance of the practitioner's mental focus and emotional clarity when conducting healing sessions. When used effectively, focused intention and affirmations can deepen the healing experience, aligning the practitioner's mind and energy with the universal life force, thereby enhancing the overall impact of the session.

Why Focused Intention is Key to Successful Distance Healing

Distance healing in Reiki works because the practitioner and recipient are connected through the universal energy field, transcending the physical boundaries of space and time. However, for this connection to be effective, the practitioner must have a clear and focused intention. This intention acts as a beacon, guiding the flow of energy from the practitioner to the recipient and ensuring that the healing energy reaches its intended destination.

When the practitioner sets an intention, they align their mental, emotional, and energetic focus with the healing goal. This focus creates a coherent energy field, allowing the universal life force to flow more freely and with greater potency. The clearer and more specific the intention, the more powerful the healing energy becomes. For instance, if the practitioner is working to alleviate physical pain or emotional distress in the recipient, setting a precise intention to heal that area or issue can amplify the flow of energy to that specific aspect of the recipient's being (McTaggart, 2008).

Setting an intention might involve mentally stating or visualizing the desired outcome before or during the healing session. The practitioner may focus on sending energy to a particular physical ailment, such as chronic back pain, or to an emotional challenge, such as anxiety or grief. By holding this intention throughout the session, the practitioner helps to shape the flow of energy, ensuring that it is directed where it is needed most.

How Affirmations Enhance the Power of Intention

While intention sets the direction of the healing energy, affirmations help to reinforce and amplify that intention. Affirmations are positive statements that align the practitioner's thoughts and emotions with the desired outcome of the healing session. When used during distance healing, affirmations are a powerful tool to focus the practitioner's mind and enhance the vibrational frequency of the energy being sent.

Affirmations work because they align the practitioner's energy with the universal life force in an intentional and supportive way. For example, suppose a practitioner is working to help a recipient overcome emotional trauma. In that case, they might use affirmations such as, "Healing flows effortlessly to release all past pain" or "The recipient is safe, loved, and free from emotional burdens." These affirmations not only shape the energy that the practitioner is sending but also raise the vibrational frequency of both the practitioner and the recipient, creating an environment of trust, healing, and empowerment (Emoto, 2005).

Affirmations can be used both by the practitioner during the session and by the recipient as part of their healing process. For instance, after a Reiki distance healing session, the practitioner may suggest specific affirmations for the recipient to repeat to continue reinforcing the healing energy. This practice helps align the recipient's energy field with the session's intention and fosters a deeper connection to their healing journey.

Creating Effective Affirmations for Healing

To create effective affirmations for Reiki healing, the practitioner should focus on positive, present-tense statements that reflect the desired outcome. Affirmations should always be stated as though the healing has already occurred, as this aligns with the universal principle that we attract what we believe and focus on. For instance, rather than saying, "The recipient will be healed," the practitioner should say, "The recipient is healed, whole, and at peace."

Here are some examples of affirmations that can be used during a Reiki distance healing session:

Physical Healing: "The recipient's body is strong, healthy, and full of vibrant energy."

Emotional Healing: "The recipient releases all fear and embraces peace, love, and harmony."

Mental Clarity: "The recipient's mind is calm, clear, and focused, free from worry and stress."

Spiritual Growth: "The recipient is aligned with their higher self and connected to the universe's infinite wisdom."

Incorporating affirmations like these into a healing session helps to anchor the practitioner's intention in a clear, positive framework, allowing the energy to flow with greater coherence and power. Whether consciously aware or not, the recipient benefits from the elevated vibrational frequency that these affirmations create in the energetic field.

Using Meditation to Support Intention and Affirmations

Meditation is another powerful tool that can be used to enhance focused intention and affirmations during distance healing. By calming the mind and entering a meditative state, the practitioner can maintain a state of mental clarity and emotional balance, which is essential for channeling Reiki energy effectively. Meditation also helps to dissolve any distractions or negative emotions that might interfere with the practitioner's ability to hold a strong intention.

Before a distance healing session, the practitioner may meditate, focusing on their breath and clearing their mind of any thoughts or worries. Once they are calm and centered, they can begin to set their intention for the session and visualize the healing energy flowing to the recipient. During the session, the practitioner can continue to use meditation techniques to stay present and focused, ensuring that the energy remains aligned with the intention and that the affirmations resonate throughout the recipient's energy field (McTaggart, 2008).

Meditation also allows the practitioner to connect more deeply with the recipient's energy, enhancing the flow of Reiki energy and allowing for a more intuitive understanding of the recipient's needs. By entering a meditative state, the practitioner can tune into the subtle shifts in the recipient's energy field, adjusting the energy flow as needed to ensure the healing is as effective as possible.

Maintaining a High Vibrational Frequency During Distance Healing

Maintaining a high vibrational frequency is one of the most important aspects of working with intention and affirmations in distance healing. The practitioner's vibrational frequency directly influences the effectiveness of the healing session, as the universal life force energy is more potent when the practitioner is aligned with positive, high-frequency emotions such as love, compassion, gratitude, and peace.

Focused intention, affirmations, and meditation can help the practitioner keep their vibrational frequency elevated throughout the session. This creates a powerful healing environment that amplifies the flow of energy, allowing the recipient to receive the maximum benefit of the session. In contrast, if negative emotions or distractions cloud the practitioner's energy, the healing energy may be less effective or diluted.

In addition to maintaining their vibrational frequency, the practitioner can help raise the recipient's vibration by setting the intention for the recipient to feel peace, joy, and balance during and after the session. The healing energy can flow more smoothly and create more profound, transformative results by aligning both the practitioner's and the recipient's energy fields with high-vibrational emotions.

In the next section, we will explore meditation and visualization as further tools to strengthen the healing process and help practitioners maintain focus and clarity during distance healing.

Using Meditation and Visualization to Strengthen the Healing Process

Meditation and visualization are two powerful techniques that can significantly enhance the effectiveness of Reiki distance healing. These practices help the practitioner maintain a deep state of focus and connection, allowing them to channel healing energy more effectively to the recipient. Combined with Reiki symbols, focused intention, affirmations, meditation, and visualization help create a powerful healing environment where the universal life force energy can flow freely and transformatively.

The Role of Meditation in Reiki Healing

Meditation is essential for Reiki practitioners because it helps calm the mind, balance emotions, and bring the practitioner into a heightened awareness and presence. In a Reiki session, whether hands-on or at a distance, maintaining this calm focus is crucial for effectively channeling energy. By meditating before and during the healing session, practitioners can enter a state of mental clarity where they can tune into both the recipient's energy field and the flow of the universal life force.

During distance healing, meditation bridges the practitioner's mind and the recipient's energy field, allowing the practitioner to hold the intention of healing with unwavering focus. This state of meditative awareness helps to quiet distractions, dissolve any negative or interfering thoughts, and bring the practitioner into a state of oneness with the energy being channeled. In this state, the practitioner can better sense the subtle shifts in the recipient's energy and adjust the flow of Reiki as needed (McTaggart, 2008).

Practicing Grounding Meditation Before Distance Healing

Grounding meditation is one of the most effective ways to prepare for a Reiki distance healing session. Grounding helps the practitioner center their energy and establish a solid connection to the Earth and the universal life force, creating a stable foundation for the healing session. This practice ensures the practitioner remains balanced, calm, and fully present throughout the session.

To perform a grounding meditation, the practitioner can begin by sitting or standing comfortably and focusing on their breath. As they inhale deeply, they visualize energy rising from the Earth, moving up through their body, and filling them with a sense of stability and strength. As they exhale, they release any tension, stress, or distracting thoughts, allowing them to dissolve into the ground. This grounding process prepares the practitioner for the healing session and helps clear their energy field, ensuring that they are a pure and clear conduit for Reiki energy (Petter, 2000).

By remaining grounded during the session, the practitioner can maintain a strong, energetic connection with the recipient, ensuring the healing energy flows steadily and without interruption. This is particularly important in distance healing, where practitioners must rely on their energetic connection to bridge the physical gap between themselves and the recipient.

Visualization Techniques for Distance Healing

Visualization is another critical tool in Reiki distance healing. It allows the practitioner to direct the energy flow with greater precision and intention, ensuring that the healing energy reaches the specific areas of the recipient's body, mind, or spirit that need attention. Visualization involves mentally picturing the desired outcome of the healing session, whether the recipient's body is bathed in healing light, the dissolution of an energetic blockage, or the restoration of emotional balance.

One effective visualization technique for distance healing is the golden light visualization. The practitioner visualizes the recipient surrounded by a warm, glowing light, representing the universal life force. This golden light envelops the recipient's body and energy field, gently dissolving any blockages, tension, or negative energy and filling the recipient with peace, healing, and vitality. As the practitioner maintains this visualization, they hold the intention that the recipient is fully receptive to the healing energy and that the energy flows precisely where it is needed.

Visualization can also direct healing energy to specific areas of the body. For example, suppose the practitioner knows the recipient is experiencing pain or illness in a particular part of their body. In that case, they can focus their intention on sending Reiki energy directly to that area. The practitioner might visualize the golden light concentrating on the recipient's heart, throat, or abdomen, wherever healing is needed most. This focused visualization helps intensify the energy flow to that area, creating a more targeted healing effect (Rand, 1991).

Using Symbols in Visualization for Distance Healing

Reiki symbols, such as Hon Sha Ze Sho Nen, Cho Ku Rei, and Sei He Ki, can be integrated into visualization practices to amplify the healing energy sent. The practitioner can visualize these symbols over the recipient's body or in the recipient's energy field, using the symbols to guide and enhance the energy flow. For instance, the practitioner might visualize the Hon Sha Ze Sho Nen symbol connecting them to the recipient. In contrast, Cho Ku Rei is visualized as a powerful light beam focusing energy into a specific part of the body (Petter, 2000).

In this way, Reiki symbols act as visual and energetic guides, helping direct the healing process with greater precision. By combining the power of visualization with the sacred geometry of Reiki symbols, practitioners can strengthen the energetic connection between themselves and the recipient, ensuring that the healing session is as effective as possible.

Maintaining Presence and Flow Through Meditation and Visualization

The combination of meditation and visualization allows the practitioner to maintain a state of presence and flow during the healing session. When the practitioner is fully present in the moment, focused on their breath, and aligned with the flow of Reiki energy, they can channel the universal life force with greater ease and effectiveness. Visualization strengthens this process by giving the practitioner a mental image or focal point to guide the healing energy. At the same time, meditation ensures that the practitioner remains clear, calm, and connected throughout the session.

Regularly practicing meditation and visualization techniques, Reiki practitioners can deepen their connection to the universal life force and refine their ability to direct energy in hands-on and distance healing sessions. These practices enhance the effectiveness of individual healing sessions and contribute to the practitioner's personal growth, spiritual alignment, and energetic balance.

Section Summary
Symbols, Intentions, and Amplifying Distance Healing

In the previous section, we explored the critical techniques of using focused intention, affirmations, meditation, and visualization to strengthen the effectiveness of Reiki distance healing. These tools enable Reiki practitioners to channel healing energy with greater clarity, precision, and depth, transcending physical and temporal boundaries.

The Power of Reiki Symbols: Hon Sha Ze Sho Nen for Transcending Time and Space

Reiki symbols are sacred tools that amplify the flow of energy and direct it with precision. Hon Sha Ze Sho Nen, the "distance symbol," plays a key role in Reiki distance healing by transcending the limitations of time and space. This symbol allows practitioners to connect with the recipient's energy field regardless of physical location, healing past traumas, present issues, or preparing for future events. The effectiveness of the symbol is guided by the practitioner's intention, which directs the energy flow. Combining Hon Sha Ze Sho Nen with other Reiki symbols like Cho Ku Rei and Sei He Ki enhances the potency of healing energy, allowing for a more powerful and transformative session.

The Role of Focused Intention and Affirmations in Distance Healing

Focused intention is the cornerstone of effective Reiki distance healing. The principle that "energy follows thought" emphasizes the importance of a clear, specific intention for directing energy flow. By setting focused intentions, practitioners guide the universal life force energy to areas needing healing. Affirmations further amplify the practitioner's intention by reinforcing positive, high-vibrational energy. Affirmations, whether spoken or mentally repeated, enhance the energy's vibrational frequency and strengthen the healing process. When the practitioner's intention is aligned with affirmations, healing energy flows with greater precision, potency, and clarity.

Using Meditation and Visualization to Strengthen the Healing Process

Meditation and visualization are powerful techniques that enhance the Reiki healing process by helping the practitioner maintain focus, calm, and a strong connection to the universal life force. Meditation ensures mental clarity and emotional balance, which are essential for directing healing energy effectively. Grounding meditation helps practitioners stabilize their energy before healing sessions, ensuring they remain centered throughout. Visualization, in combination with Reiki symbols, allows practitioners to guide energy flow with precision. Visualizing healing energy as light surrounding the recipient helps clear blockages and restore balance, making the healing process more targeted and effective.

Together, these techniques—Reiki symbols, focused intention, affirmations, meditation, and visualization—allow practitioners to harness the full potential of distance Reiki healing, creating a powerful, transformative experience for recipients, regardless of time and space.

§

Chakras and the Etheric Body

How Distance Healing Works on the Subtle Energy Bodies, Particularly the Etheric Field

In Reiki and other energy healing modalities, the subtle energy bodies play a crucial role in maintaining health, balance, and vitality. Beyond the physical body lies the etheric body, often referred to as the etheric field, which is the energetic double of the physical body. This field is the energetic blueprint for the physical body and is closely connected to our physical well-being and emotional, mental, and spiritual health. In distance healing, practitioners can work directly with this etheric field to clear blockages, restore balance, and facilitate deep healing, even when the recipient is not physically present.

The etheric body is just one layer of the human energy system, including the emotional, mental, and spiritual bodies. Together, these subtle bodies form the auric field, which extends beyond the physical body and interacts with the universal energy field. The etheric body is the closest of these layers to the physical body and is often described as a dense, vibrational energy that mirrors the physical form. It is through this layer that physical issues, as well as energetic imbalances, first manifest. By working on the etheric body during a distance healing session, Reiki practitioners can address these imbalances before they manifest more fully in the physical realm (Brennan, 1988).

Understanding the Etheric Field in Distance Healing

The etheric field is the energetic counterpart of the physical body and is essential for maintaining the body's health and vitality. In distance healing, practitioners can sense and work with this field by tuning into the vibrational patterns of the recipient's energy. Since the etheric field is directly connected to the physical body, any disruptions or blockages in this field can lead to physical symptoms, such as pain, illness, or fatigue. By sending Reiki energy to the etheric body, practitioners help clear these blockages and restore the flow of life force energy, supporting both the physical and energetic systems.

One of the key aspects of the etheric field is its ability to store energy and vibrate at different frequencies depending on the person's overall health and well-being. This field acts as a bridge between the physical and the non-physical aspects of the self, meaning that it is both influenced by physical conditions and shaped by thoughts, emotions, and spiritual experiences. When a Reiki practitioner works on the etheric body during a distance healing session, they address physical ailments and work with the subtle energy systems that influence the recipient's overall vitality (Judith, 2004).

Balancing Chakras and Clearing Blockages Through Distance Healing

At the heart of the etheric body lie the chakras, the spinning energy centers that regulate the flow of life force energy throughout the body. Seven main chakras are aligned along the spine, each corresponding to specific physical, emotional, mental, and spiritual functions. When the chakras are open and balanced, life force energy (ki or prana) flows freely through the body, supporting health, vitality, and emotional well-being. However, when one or more chakras become blocked or imbalanced, energy becomes stagnant, leading to physical symptoms, emotional distress, or spiritual disconnection.

During a Reiki distance healing session, the practitioner can work with the recipient's chakras using intention, visualization, and Reiki symbols to restore balance and clear blockages. For instance, if the recipient is experiencing emotional difficulty, the practitioner might focus on the heart chakra (Anahata), which governs love, compassion, and emotional healing. By sending Reiki energy to this chakra, the practitioner can help clear any emotional blockages, allowing the recipient to feel more open, balanced, and connected to their emotions.

The third eye chakra (Ajna) and crown chakra (Sahasrara) are also commonly addressed during distance healing, especially when the recipient is dealing with mental fog, confusion, or a lack of spiritual connection. By focusing on these higher chakras, practitioners can help the recipient gain clarity, strengthen their intuition, and deepen their connection to their higher self. Similarly, suppose the recipient struggles with stability, safety, or financial concerns. In that case, the practitioner may focus on the root chakra (Muladhara) to restore a sense of grounding and security (Judith, 2004).

Clearing Blockages in the Emotional, Mental, and Spiritual Layers

Beyond the physical and etheric bodies, distance healing can also address the emotional, mental, and spiritual layers of the recipient's energy field. Each of these layers corresponds to a different aspect of the person's overall well-being:

Emotional Body: The emotional body is closely linked to the heart chakra and governs our feelings, relationships, and capacity for love and compassion. The energy in this layer can become blocked or distorted when emotional imbalances, such as unresolved grief, anger, or sadness, occur. Distance healing can help clear these emotional blockages by sending loving, compassionate energy to the recipient's emotional body, promoting emotional release, healing, and balance.

Mental Body: The mental body is connected to the third eye and throat chakras and influences our thoughts, beliefs, and mental clarity. When the mental body is imbalanced, the recipient may experience overthinking, confusion, or limiting beliefs. By sending Reiki energy to the mental body, practitioners can help clear mental blockages, release limiting beliefs, and promote greater clarity and focus.

Spiritual Body: The spiritual body is associated with the higher chakras, particularly the crown chakra, and governs our connection to the divine and our sense of purpose in life. When the spiritual body is imbalanced, the recipient may feel disconnected from their spiritual path or experience a lack of meaning. Distance healing can help strengthen the recipient's connection to their higher self and the universal energy, allowing them to reconnect with their spiritual purpose and gain a deeper sense of peace and fulfillment (Brennan, 1988).

How Distance Healing Integrates All Layers of the Energy Field

The beauty of Reiki distance healing lies in its ability to work holistically across all layers of the energy field. By addressing the etheric body and the emotional, mental, and spiritual bodies, practitioners can facilitate deep, integrative healing that touches every aspect of the recipient's being. Whether the recipient is experiencing physical pain, emotional distress, or spiritual disconnection, Reiki energy works at the subtle levels of the energy field, restoring balance and harmony across all dimensions.

By focusing on the chakras and subtle energy bodies during a distance healing session, practitioners can help recipients clear energetic blockages, restore the flow of life force energy, and promote healing on all levels—physical, emotional, mental, and spiritual.

Balancing Chakras and Clearing Blockages Through Distance Healing

The chakra system maintains energy flow throughout the body and subtle energy fields in distance healing. The seven main chakras, aligned along the spine from the base to the crown of the head, act as energy centers that regulate physical, emotional, mental, and spiritual well-being. Each chakra governs specific aspects of the individual's experience. When these energy centers become blocked or imbalanced, it can lead to a wide range of issues, including physical discomfort, emotional instability, and spiritual disconnection. In Reiki, practitioners work with the chakras to restore balance and clear blockages, ensuring the free flow of life force energy.

During a distance Reiki session, the practitioner can use a combination of intention, visualization, and Reiki symbols to connect with the recipient's chakras and address any imbalances. By working with the chakras, the practitioner can influence the physical body and the emotional, mental, and spiritual layers of the recipient's energy field. Each chakra serves as a gateway for specific types of energy, and when this energy becomes stagnant or blocked, it can manifest as a disease in both the body and mind. The goal of balancing the chakras through distance healing is to remove these blockages and restore the harmonious flow of energy.

The Root Chakra: Grounding and Stability

The root chakra (Muladhara), located at the base of the spine, is responsible for grounding, stability, and feelings of safety. It is the foundation of the chakra system, and when it is blocked or imbalanced, the recipient may feel ungrounded, anxious, or disconnected from their body. In distance healing, the practitioner can focus on sending Reiki energy to the root chakra to restore stability and grounding.

To balance the root chakra, the practitioner may use the Cho Ku Rei symbol, which is known for increasing Reiki energy's power. By visualizing the Cho Ku Rei symbol at the base of the recipient's spine, the practitioner helps clear any blockages and strengthen the energy flow through the root chakra. This allows the recipient to feel more connected to the Earth, more secure, and more grounded in their physical experience (Judith, 2004).

The Sacral Chakra: Emotional Balance and Creativity

The sacral chakra (Svadhisthana), located just below the navel, governs emotions, creativity, and sensuality. When this chakra is blocked, the recipient may experience emotional imbalances, such as mood swings, numbness, or difficulty expressing creativity. A blocked sacral chakra can also lead to issues related to intimacy and relationships.

In a distance healing session, the practitioner can focus on restoring the free energy flow in the sacral chakra by visualizing a warm, orange light swirling around the recipient's lower abdomen. Using the Sei He Ki symbol, which is associated with emotional healing and balance, can further help dissolve any energetic blockages in this area. By balancing the sacral chakra, the practitioner helps the recipient reconnect with their emotions, creativity, and sense of joy (Judith, 2004).

The Solar Plexus Chakra: Personal Power and Confidence

The solar plexus chakra (Manipura), located in the upper abdomen, is the center of personal power, self-esteem, and confidence. When this chakra is blocked, the recipient may feel powerless, lack confidence, or struggle with self-doubt. Imbalances in the solar plexus chakra can also manifest as digestive issues or feelings of heaviness in the stomach.

In distance healing, the practitioner can visualize a bright, golden light radiating from the recipient's abdomen to balance the solar plexus chakra. The Cho Ku Rei symbol can also be used here, as it helps to increase the recipient's sense of personal empowerment and strengthen their connection to their inner strength. By restoring balance to the solar plexus chakra, the recipient can reclaim their confidence, make empowered decisions, and step into their power (Judith, 2004).

The Heart Chakra: Love, Compassion, and Emotional Healing

The heart chakra (Anahata), located at the center of the chest, governs love, compassion, and emotional healing. It serves as the bridge between the lower and upper chakras, connecting the physical and spiritual realms. When the heart chakra is blocked, the recipient may experience difficulty giving or receiving love, emotional pain, or a sense of disconnection from others.

In distance healing, the practitioner can send Reiki energy directly to the heart chakra by visualizing a vibrant, green light surrounding the recipient's chest. The Sei He Ki symbol promotes emotional healing and balance and can help dissolve heart-centered blockages. This energy work allows recipients to open their hearts, release emotional wounds, and cultivate deeper compassion for themselves and others (Brennan, 1988).

The Throat Chakra: Communication and Self-Expression

The throat chakra (Vishuddha), located at the throat, governs communication, self-expression, and truth. When this chakra is imbalanced, the recipient may struggle with speaking their truth, experience difficulty expressing themselves, or feel that others are not hearing them.

In distance healing, the practitioner can focus on the throat chakra by visualizing a bright, blue light at the recipient's throat. This helps to clear any blockages in communication and encourages the recipient to express themselves with clarity and confidence. The Hon Sha Ze Sho Nen symbol, which transcends time and space, can address any issues related to past experiences where the recipient may have felt silenced or unable to express their truth. Balancing the throat chakra allows the recipient to communicate more effectively and express their authentic self (Judith, 2004).

The Third Eye Chakra: Intuition and Mental Clarity

The third eye chakra (Ajna), located between the eyebrows, governs intuition, inner vision, and mental clarity. When this chakra is blocked, the recipient may feel disconnected from their intuition, experience a mental fog, or struggle to make decisions.

To balance the third eye chakra during a distance healing session, the practitioner can visualize a deep indigo light on the recipient's forehead. The Sei He Ki symbol can be used to clear any mental or emotional blockages clouding the recipient's judgment or intuition. By restoring balance to the third eye chakra, the recipient can experience greater mental clarity, enhanced intuition, and a deeper connection to their inner guidance (Brennan, 1988).

The Crown Chakra: Spiritual Connection and Higher Consciousness

The crown chakra (Sahasrara), located at the top of the head, governs spiritual connection and higher consciousness. When this chakra is blocked, the recipient may feel disconnected from their spiritual path or experience a lack of purpose or meaning in life.

In distance healing, the practitioner can focus on opening the crown chakra by visualizing a bright, violet, or white light at the top of the recipient's head. The Hon Sha Ze Sho Nen symbol can strengthen the recipient's connection to the divine and align them with their higher self. Balancing the crown chakra helps the recipient feel more spiritually connected and aligned with their life's purpose (Judith, 2004).

The Holistic Impact of Balancing the Chakras

Balancing the chakras through distance healing creates a holistic and integrative healing experience for the recipient. By addressing the flow of energy through each chakra, the practitioner helps restore balance and harmony in the physical body and the emotional, mental, and spiritual layers of the energy field. When the chakras are aligned and functioning optimally, the recipient is better able to experience health, vitality, emotional balance, and spiritual connection.

Healing the Emotional, Mental, and Spiritual Layers of the Recipient

In addition to balancing the chakras and clearing blockages in the etheric body, Reiki distance healing has the profound ability to address the deeper layers of the recipient's emotional, mental, and spiritual bodies. These layers are interconnected and reflect the overall state of the recipient's energy field, each playing a unique role in shaping physical, emotional, and spiritual health. By sending Reiki to these subtle layers, practitioners can create lasting change that supports the recipient's journey toward wholeness and well-being on every level.

Healing the Emotional Body: Releasing Emotional Wounds

The emotional body is the layer of the energy field that governs feelings, emotional experiences, and relationships. It is intimately connected to the heart chakra and influences how we experience love, compassion, joy, and sorrow. Emotional imbalances often manifest as energetic blockages in this layer, and they can stem from unresolved past traumas, suppressed emotions, or current stressors. When left unaddressed, these emotional blockages can eventually impact the physical body, leading to illness or discomfort.

During distance healing, practitioners can help the recipient release emotional wounds by sending Reiki energy directly to the emotional body. This process involves using symbols such as Sei He Ki, which are associated with emotional healing and balance. By visualizing the recipient's emotional body surrounded by a gentle, healing light, the practitioner facilitates the release of stuck emotions, such as grief, anger, or fear, allowing these energies to dissipate and heal (Judith, 2004).

As the emotional body begins to heal, the recipient may experience a sense of emotional release, manifesting as tears, relief, or inner peace. Reiki helps soften emotional blockages, creating space for recipients to process their feelings healthily. This emotional healing is particularly important for those who have been carrying unresolved grief, anger, or emotional trauma for an extended period.

Healing the Mental Body: Clearing Limiting Beliefs and Mental Patterns

The mental body governs our thoughts, beliefs, and perceptions. It is closely linked to the third eye and throat chakras, which influence mental clarity, intuition, and communication. When the mental body is out of balance, it can manifest as limiting beliefs, overthinking, confusion, or difficulty focusing. These mental blockages can create a negative loop in the recipient's thinking, leading to stress, anxiety, and even physical symptoms such as headaches or insomnia.

Reiki distance healing can clear these mental blockages by sending energy to the recipient's mental body, helping to dissolve patterns of negative thinking or limiting beliefs that no longer serve their highest good. Practitioners may use the Hon Sha Ze Sho Nen symbol to transcend time and space, addressing the root causes of these mental patterns, whether they originate in past experiences, childhood conditioning, or societal influences (Brennan, 1988).

By healing the mental body, Reiki supports the recipient in developing greater mental clarity, self-awareness, and an expanded perspective. The recipient may find themselves letting go of old beliefs that have kept them feeling stuck or limited, opening themselves to new ways of thinking that align with their higher self and spiritual path.

Healing the Spiritual Body: Strengthening Connection to Higher Self

The spiritual body is the highest layer of the energy field. It represents the recipient's connection to their higher self, the divine, and the universal energy that permeates all of existence. It is closely linked to the crown chakra and influences the recipient's sense of purpose, meaning, and spiritual growth. When the spiritual body is out of balance, the recipient may feel disconnected from their spiritual path, experience existential doubts, or struggle with a lack of purpose or fulfillment.

Distance healing offers a unique opportunity to work with the spiritual body, sending energy to strengthen the recipient's connection to the divine and align them with their spiritual essence. By visualizing the recipient's crown chakra and spiritual body bathed in a radiant violet or white light, the practitioner can help open the pathways for spiritual connection and growth. The Hon Sha Ze Sho Nen symbol is often used to transcend the limitations of the material world, allowing the recipient to reconnect with their higher self and the wisdom of the universal energy field (Judith, 2004).

As the recipient's spiritual body heals, they may experience a renewed sense of purpose, inner peace, and spiritual alignment. This healing can lead to a deeper understanding of their place in the universe and a greater connection to their spiritual path. For many recipients, healing the spiritual body is a transformative experience that allows them to step into a higher level of consciousness and live in greater alignment with their true selves.

Integrating Healing Across All Layers

The beauty of Reiki distance healing lies in its ability to work across all layers of the energy field—physical, etheric, emotional, mental, and spiritual. By addressing these interconnected layers, Reiki practitioners help the recipient achieve a state of holistic healing, where every aspect of their being is brought into balance and harmony. As the physical body heals, so do the emotional, mental, and spiritual bodies, creating a ripple effect of well-being that extends far beyond the immediate session.

The practitioner's role in this process is to serve as a clear and compassionate channel for the universal life force energy, directing it to the layers of the recipient's energy field that need attention. Whether the focus is on clearing emotional blockages, dissolving mental patterns, or deepening spiritual connection, the healing at one layer naturally influences the others. This interconnected approach allows for a more complete and transformative healing experience, supporting the recipient's journey toward greater health, balance, and spiritual growth (Brennan, 1988).

Section Summary
Chakras and the Etheric Body

The etheric body serves as the energetic blueprint for the physical body, mirroring its structure and influencing overall health and vitality. In distance healing practices like Reiki, practitioners work with the etheric body to clear blockages, restore balance, and support physical and energetic healing. By addressing the etheric field, energy healers can resolve imbalances before they manifest physically. This approach also impacts the emotional, mental, and spiritual bodies, all of which are interconnected layers within the auric field.

Understanding the Etheric Field in Distance Healing

The etheric field, closest to the physical body, is vital for maintaining health and wellness. Practitioners can tune into this field to detect blockages or disruptions that may lead to physical symptoms. Clearing these blockages through distance healing helps restore the flow of life force energy (ki) and maintains both physical and energetic well-being.

Balancing Chakras and Clearing Blockages Through Distance Healing

The chakras, the body's main energy centers, regulate the flow of life force energy. Imbalances or blockages in the chakras can disrupt this flow, causing physical, emotional, and spiritual problems. Distance healing works by using Reiki symbols, visualization, and intention to balance these chakras. Addressing specific chakras like the heart or root chakra can restore emotional well-being, confidence, or grounding, depending on the recipient's needs.

Clearing Blockages in the Emotional, Mental, and Spiritual Layers

Distance healing extends beyond the physical and etheric bodies, affecting the emotional, mental, and spiritual layers. Practitioners can help release emotional wounds, clear mental blockages, and enhance spiritual connections. Each layer corresponds to a different aspect of well-being, and healing one often creates positive effects in the others, resulting in holistic transformation.

By integrating healing across all these layers, distance Reiki supports comprehensive well-being, addressing physical ailments, emotional struggles, and spiritual disconnection simultaneously. Practitioners help restore balance across these energy bodies, facilitating a deeper and more harmonious state of health.

Meditation, Mindfulness, and Energy Attunement

Techniques for Attuning to Higher Frequencies for More Effective Distance Healing

As Reiki practitioners become more advanced, one of the most essential skills they develop is the ability to attune to higher energy frequencies. This ability allows practitioners to connect more deeply with the universal life force and channel healing energy in a more focused, potent way. In distance healing, attuning to these higher vibrational frequencies is particularly important because it strengthens the connection between the practitioner and the recipient, allowing healing energy to flow more smoothly and effectively across time and space.

Meditation, mindfulness, and specific energy attunement techniques can help practitioners access these higher frequencies, ensuring they are in the optimal energetic state for conducting powerful distance healing sessions. These practices benefit the practitioner's ability to channel energy and support their own spiritual growth and alignment, allowing them to become more effective conduits for the healing process.

The Role of Meditation in Raising Vibrational Frequency

Meditation is one of the most powerful tools for attuning to higher energy frequencies. By quieting the mind and entering a state of stillness, practitioners can connect more deeply with the subtle energies of the universal life force. Regular meditation helps raise the practitioner's vibrational frequency, enhancing their ability to channel Reiki energy with clarity and focus. The higher the practitioner's vibrational state, the more potent the healing energy they can channel.

For Reiki practitioners, a simple yet effective meditation technique involves focused breathing. By sitting comfortably and focusing on breathing, practitioners can quiet their minds and release any distractions or negative thoughts that may interfere with their connection to the universal life force. They can imagine drawing in pure, healing energy as they inhale, filling their body and energy field with light. As they exhale, they release tension, stress, or lower-vibrational energy. This breathing meditation helps to align the practitioner with the higher frequencies of the Reiki energy they will channel (Rand, 1991).

Another effective meditation technique for attuning to higher frequencies is light visualization. Practitioners can visualize themselves surrounded by a radiant white or golden light, representing the highest vibrational frequencies of the universal life force. As they sit in this light, they can imagine it infusing their entire being, raising their vibrational state and connecting them with the healing energy they will send during the distance session. This visualization raises the practitioner's frequency and strengthens their connection to the recipient.

Mindfulness and Energy Alignment

Mindfulness is the practice of being fully present in the moment and aware of one's thoughts, emotions, and physical sensations without judgment. For Reiki practitioners, cultivating mindfulness is essential for maintaining a clear, focused state of mind during healing sessions. When the practitioner is mindful, they can better tune into the subtle shifts in the recipient's energy field, respond precisely, and maintain a strong, energetic connection throughout the session.

In distance healing, mindfulness can be practiced by focusing on the intention of the session and being fully present with the recipient's energy. This means letting go of distractions, worries, or preconceived notions about the healing session's outcome. Instead, the practitioner remains open, receptive, and attuned to the flow of energy, allowing the universal life force to guide the process. Mindfulness enhances the practitioner's ability to channel energy effectively and creates a space of non-attachment where healing can unfold naturally and organically.

Practitioners can cultivate mindfulness by practicing body awareness during meditation. This involves scanning the body from head to toe, noticing any areas of tension, discomfort, or energetic imbalance. By bringing awareness to these sensations without judgment, the practitioner can release any resistance or blockages within their energy field, ensuring they are fully aligned and present for the healing session.

Attunement to Higher Energies: Deepening the Connection to the Universal Life Force

Attunement is aligning with higher energy frequencies, allowing practitioners to access the full potential of the Reiki energy they channel. In traditional Reiki practice, attunements are given by a Reiki Master during training, opening the practitioner's energy channels and enabling them to connect with the universal life force. However, attunement is also an ongoing process that can be deepened through regular practice, meditation, and intentional alignment with higher frequencies.

To enhance their attunement to the universal life force, practitioners can work with specific Reiki symbols, such as Cho Ku Rei (the power symbol) or Hon Sha Ze Sho Nen (the distance symbol). These symbols help to raise the practitioner's vibrational frequency and strengthen their connection to the energy they channel during a distance healing session. By visualizing these symbols and using them to activate the flow of energy, practitioners can amplify the healing power of the Reiki session and attune to the highest possible frequencies of energy (Petter, 2000).

Another powerful attunement technique is the practice of gratitude. Gratitude is one of the highest vibrational emotions, and by focusing on feelings of gratitude, practitioners can raise their frequency and align more fully with the universal life force. Before and during a distance healing session, practitioners can take a few moments to express gratitude for the opportunity to serve as a channel for healing, the energy they are working with, and the recipient's openness to receiving the healing. This simple practice can create a powerful, energetic shift, deepening the practitioner's attunement to higher energies and amplifying the overall healing experience.

Preparing for Distance Healing Through Attunement Practices

Before beginning a distance healing session, practitioners must prepare their energy field by attuning to higher frequencies. This preparation enhances the practitioner's ability to channel energy and ensures that the healing energy is delivered with clarity, purity, and focus. By engaging in meditation, mindfulness, and attunement practices before a session, practitioners create a sacred space within themselves, allowing them to serve as a clear and open conduit for the universal life force.

During the session, maintaining this state of alignment and presence allows the practitioner to stay connected with the recipient's energy field, respond intuitively to their needs, and direct the energy flow with precision. Attuning to higher frequencies benefits the practitioner's ability to channel healing energy and creates a more profound and transformative healing experience for the recipient.

Meditation and Mindfulness Practices to Enhance Focus and Intention

While distance Reiki healing is primarily about channeling the universal life force to promote healing, the practitioner's focus and intention are crucial in guiding this energy effectively. Meditation and mindfulness are instrumental in helping practitioners achieve a state of clarity, calm, and heightened awareness during healing sessions. These practices allow the practitioner to remain centered, prevent distractions, and maintain a continuous energy flow throughout the session.

Meditation is particularly valuable in developing the practitioner's ability to focus on a single point of intention. By training the mind through meditation, Reiki practitioners can cultivate a deeper presence and connection to the recipient's energy field, allowing for more targeted and effective healing.

Mindfulness Meditation: Staying Present with Energy

Mindfulness meditation is a practice that emphasizes being fully present in the current moment, observing thoughts, emotions, and sensations without attachment or judgment. For Reiki practitioners, this ability to stay fully present is critical during a distance healing session. When distractions, negative emotions, or mental clutter arise, they can interfere with the practitioner's focus and diminish the effectiveness of channeling the healing energy. Mindfulness helps practitioners become aware of these distractions as they arise and let them go, allowing the practitioner to return to the present moment.

To practice mindfulness meditation in preparation for a Reiki session, practitioners can start by sitting comfortably in a quiet space, focusing on their breath. As they breathe in, they allow themselves to notice the sensation of the air filling their lungs, and as they breathe out, they let go of any tension or distractions. If their minds wander, they gently bring their attention back to the breath without judgment. Returning to the breath trains the practitioner to stay present during healing sessions, focusing on the recipient's energy field and the flow of Reiki energy (Kabat-Zinn, 2003).

In a distance healing session, mindfulness can also be applied by continuously bringing awareness back to the recipient. Practitioners may mentally scan the recipient's energy field during the session, noticing any changes or subtle shifts in energy. This ongoing presence and awareness help practitioners stay in tune with the recipient's needs, adjusting the flow of Reiki energy in response to what they intuitively sense.

Guided Visualization: Enhancing Intention

Visualization is a powerful tool for enhancing the practitioner's intention during distance healing. It involves mentally creating an image or scenario that aligns with the desired outcome of the healing session. This practice strengthens the practitioner's focus and allows them to direct energy more effectively toward the recipient's specific needs. Visualization techniques can be used before and during the Reiki session to maintain the practitioner's clear intention and guide the energy flow.

One effective visualization technique involves imagining the recipient's energy field being bathed in healing light. The practitioner may visualize the recipient surrounded by a radiant golden or white light, representing the universal life force. This light can be seen flowing through the recipient's body, dissolving any blockages or imbalances and filling them with vibrant, healing energy. By holding this image throughout the session, the practitioner helps amplify the energy being sent and maintains a clear intention for the healing process.

Another visualization technique involves mentally projecting the Reiki symbols—such as Hon Sha Ze Sho Nen for distance healing—onto the recipient's energy field. Practitioners can imagine the symbol glowing brightly over the recipient as a gateway for energy flow across time and space. This visualization helps deepen the connection between the practitioner and the recipient, ensuring that the healing energy reaches its intended target with precision and strength (Petter, 2000).

Affirmation Meditation: Aligning with Healing Intentions

In addition to mindfulness and visualization, affirmation meditation can be valuable for aligning the practitioner's mind with their healing intention. Affirmations are positive, present-tense statements that reinforce the practitioner's focus and help elevate their vibrational frequency. During distance healing, affirmations can be used to affirm the desired outcome of the session and strengthen the practitioner's alignment with the healing energy.

For instance, a practitioner preparing for a distance healing session might meditate on affirmations such as:

"Healing flows effortlessly and reaches the recipient's highest good."
"I am a clear and open channel for Reiki energy, guiding it with love and compassion."
"The recipient is healthy, whole, and aligned with their highest self."

These affirmations help reinforce the practitioner's belief in the power of Reiki and their ability to facilitate healing. As the practitioner repeats these affirmations during meditation, they align their energy with the healing process, ensuring they remain focused and centered throughout the session (McTaggart, 2008).

Mindfulness Throughout the Session

Staying mindful during the entire Reiki session requires the practitioner to remain present with their breath, energy, and the recipient's energy field. Even as the session progresses, maintaining mindfulness helps the practitioner notice subtle changes in energy flow, areas of resistance, or shifts in the recipient's energy. This awareness enables the practitioner to intuitively adjust their focus, sending more energy to a specific location or simply allowing it to flow as needed.

One way to maintain mindfulness during the session is through the practice of body awareness. As the practitioner channels Reiki energy, they can periodically check in with their body, noticing any sensations, tension, or energetic shifts. By staying in tune with their own energy field, practitioners can ensure that they are grounded and centered and maintain a strong connection to the recipient.

Another technique for staying mindful is using gentle reminders during the session. The practitioner can mentally remind themselves to return to the present moment, stay focused on the recipient's energy, and trust in the flow of Reiki energy. These reminders can be as simple as silently repeating the words "presence" or "focus," helping to bring the mind back to the session whenever distractions arise.

Developing a Daily Practice for Long-Term Focus

For Reiki practitioners, developing a regular meditation and mindfulness practice outside of healing sessions is critical to long-term success. By meditating daily, even for just a few minutes, practitioners can build the mental clarity and focus required for distance healing. Over time, this regular practice strengthens the practitioner's ability to stay present, focused, and connected to the universal life force, enhancing the effectiveness of their Reiki sessions.

Daily practices such as mindful breathing, body scans, and visualization can help practitioners stay aligned with higher frequencies and maintain their ability to channel energy effectively. These practices also support the practitioner's well-being, ensuring they remain balanced, energized, and in tune with their spiritual path.

As we move forward, we will explore how expanding consciousness through meditation, mindfulness, and energy attunement allows practitioners to become more effective conduits for healing energy and deepen their connection to the universal life force.

Expanding Consciousness and Becoming a More Effective Conduit for Healing

Expanding consciousness is central to deepening a Reiki practitioner's ability to serve as a clear and powerful conduit for healing energy. As practitioners progress in their spiritual journey, they learn to connect with the recipient's energy and the broader universal energy field, which holds the infinite potential for healing. By expanding their consciousness through meditation, mindfulness, and spiritual attunement, practitioners can access higher energy frequencies, allowing them to facilitate deeper and more transformative healing experiences.

Expanding consciousness involves opening up to a broader awareness of the interconnectedness of all things. This process allows Reiki practitioners to transcend the limitations of the physical body and mind, tuning into the subtle energies that permeate the universe. As consciousness expands, practitioners develop a more profound connection with the universal life force and a deeper understanding of their role as healers within this vast, energetic web.

The Connection Between Consciousness and Energy Flow

Consciousness is intricately linked to the flow of energy. As practitioners expand their awareness and deepen their connection to the universal energy field, they can channel more potent healing energy to the recipient. This expanded consciousness allows practitioners to see beyond surface symptoms and address the deeper, underlying causes of imbalance within the recipient's energy field.

In Reiki distance healing, expanded consciousness enables practitioners to work across multiple dimensions of the recipient's energy field—physical, emotional, mental, and spiritual—while maintaining a clear focus on the recipient's highest good. Practitioners who have developed this expanded awareness are able to perceive subtle shifts in energy that may indicate areas of stagnation, blockages, or imbalance. This heightened sensitivity allows for more precise and effective healing, as the practitioner can direct energy exactly where it is needed most (Brennan, 1988).

To cultivate this expanded consciousness, practitioners can engage in regular meditative practices that encourage awareness of the interconnectedness of all things. By sitting in silence and focusing on the infinite nature of the universal life force, practitioners can move beyond the ego and access a state of pure awareness, where healing energy flows effortlessly and without interference.

Techniques for Expanding Consciousness in Reiki Practice

Several meditation techniques can help Reiki practitioners expand their consciousness and strengthen their ability to channel energy during distance healing sessions. These practices support the practitioner in deepening their connection to the recipient and the universal life force, allowing for more profound and transformative healing experiences.

Open-Heart Meditation: The heart chakra (Anahata) is often considered the gateway to higher states of consciousness and spiritual awareness. By focusing on the heart center during meditation, practitioners can expand their consciousness to include feelings of unconditional love, compassion, and connection to all beings. This practice enhances the practitioner's ability to send healing energy and elevates their vibrational frequency, allowing them to connect with the highest frequencies of the universal life force.

During an open-heart meditation, the practitioner can visualize their heart chakra glowing with a soft, green light, radiating love and compassion in all directions. As the heart opens, the practitioner can invite the universal life force to flow through them, using the energy of love as a powerful conduit for healing. This practice helps dissolve barriers between the practitioner and the recipient, creating a space of oneness where healing can occur effortlessly (Judith, 2004).

Cosmic Consciousness Meditation: Another technique for expanding consciousness is cosmic consciousness meditation, where the practitioner focuses on the vastness of the universe and their connection to the cosmic energy that flows through all things. This meditation helps practitioners move beyond their identity and ego, allowing them to perceive the recipient as part of the greater whole of the universe.

To practice cosmic consciousness meditation, practitioners can begin by sitting in a quiet space and closing their eyes. They may visualize themselves floating in the universe, surrounded by stars and galaxies. As they breathe deeply, they feel themselves merging with the cosmic energy that flows through the universe, becoming one with the infinite life force. This unity with the cosmos allows practitioners to channel powerful healing energy from a place of expanded awareness where time, space, and physical boundaries no longer exist.

Grounding in the Earth's Energy Field: While expanding consciousness is often associated with higher spiritual frequencies, it is equally important for practitioners to remain grounded in the physical realm. By connecting with the Earth's energy field, practitioners can ensure they act as clear, balanced conduits for the universal life force. Grounding helps stabilize the practitioner's energy and maintain a solid connection to the physical and spiritual planes.

Practitioners can ground themselves by visualizing roots extending from their feet deep into the Earth, anchoring them in its energy. This practice allows them to draw upon the stabilizing and nourishing energy of the Earth, ensuring that they remain centered and present throughout the healing session. By balancing the energy flow between the Earth and the cosmos, practitioners can create a harmonious, balanced space for healing to unfold (Judith, 2004).

Becoming a Clear and Open Conduit for Healing

As practitioners expand their consciousness and develop their ability to connect with higher energy frequencies, they become more effective conduits for healing. The more aligned the practitioner is with the universal life force, the more clearly and powerfully they can channel this energy to the recipient. This alignment requires the practitioner to maintain a state of non-attachment, where they trust in the flow of Reiki energy and allow the healing process to unfold naturally.

By letting go of any need to control the session's outcome, practitioners create space for the universal life force to work through them, guiding the healing energy to where it is needed most. This process of surrender allows the practitioner to serve as a pure channel for the healing energy without interference from personal desires, expectations, or fears. In this state, the practitioner's consciousness fully aligns with the recipient's highest good, ensuring that the healing energy is delivered with love, compassion, and clarity.

This expanded consciousness also allows practitioners to develop a deeper connection with their spiritual path. As they grow and evolve as healers, they become more attuned to the subtle energies that shape the universe, gaining greater insight into the nature of healing, energy, and consciousness. This spiritual growth benefits the practitioner and enhances the quality of the healing sessions they offer to others.

The Benefits of Expanded Consciousness for the Recipient

The benefits of working with a practitioner who has developed expanded consciousness are profound for the recipient. When practitioners can channel higher energy frequencies, recipients often experience deeper and more transformative healing sessions. This expanded energy addresses the surface-level symptoms and works on the deeper, underlying causes of imbalance within the recipient's energy field.

Recipients may feel a heightened sense of peace, clarity, and spiritual connection during and after the session. They may experience emotional or physical release as old blockages are dissolved and new levels of consciousness are accessed. Over time, working with a practitioner who operates from an expanded state of awareness can help recipients align more fully with their higher self, promoting lasting healing and spiritual growth.

Section Summary
Meditation, Mindfulness, and Energy Attunement

This section delved into the essential practices and techniques used in Reiki distance healing to expand consciousness, focus intention, and attune to higher frequencies for more effective healing. These practices help Reiki practitioners strengthen their connection with the universal life force and the recipient's energy field, facilitating more profound and transformative healing experiences. By cultivating mindfulness, engaging in meditation, and attuning to higher energy frequencies, practitioners become clear and powerful conduits for healing energy, capable of addressing imbalances across the physical, emotional, mental, and spiritual layers.

Techniques for Attuning to Higher Frequencies for More Effective Distance Healing

Attuning to higher vibrational frequencies is a critical skill for advanced Reiki practitioners. This process enhances the practitioner's ability to channel potent healing energy across time and space. Practices such as meditation, focused breathing, and the use of Reiki symbols—such as Cho Ku Rei and Hon Sha Ze Sho Nen—help practitioners align with the universal life force and raise their vibrational state. By working with higher frequencies, practitioners can create stronger energetic connections with recipients and facilitate more targeted and powerful healing sessions.

Meditation and Mindfulness Practices to Enhance Focus and Intention

Meditation and mindfulness are vital tools in enhancing a Reiki practitioner's focus and intention during healing sessions. Mindfulness meditation helps practitioners stay present with the recipient's energy field, allowing for more precise energy work. Visualization techniques, such as envisioning healing light surrounding the recipient or projecting Reiki symbols onto the recipient's energy field, further amplify the healing process. Affirmation meditation, where practitioners repeat positive statements to align their energy with the healing session, is another valuable practice for strengthening intention. These techniques allow practitioners to maintain a continuous flow of healing energy, ensuring they remain grounded, focused, and receptive to the needs of the recipient.

Expanding Consciousness and Becoming a More Effective Conduit for Healing

Expanding consciousness is crucial for Reiki practitioners who wish to become more effective conduits for healing energy. By expanding their awareness through practices like open-heart meditation, cosmic consciousness meditation, and grounding in the Earth's energy field, practitioners deepen their connection to the universal life force. This expanded consciousness allows them to perceive subtle shifts in the recipient's energy and direct healing energy where it is needed most. As practitioners continue to cultivate their spiritual growth and align with higher frequencies, they enhance their ability to facilitate deep, holistic healing for the recipient. The process also strengthens the practitioner's own spiritual evolution, contributing to both personal growth and the effectiveness of their healing sessions.

§

Knowledge Review
Chapter Four

Tools for Enhancing Distance Healing

1. What is the primary purpose of Hon Sha Ze Sho Nen in Reiki, and how does it transcend time and space?

2. How can a Reiki practitioner use Hon Sha Ze Sho Nen in a distance healing session?

3. What are the benefits of combining Hon Sha Ze Sho Nen with other Reiki symbols like Cho Ku Rei and Sei He Ki?

4. Why is intention important when using Reiki symbols, particularly in distance healing?

5. Why is focused intention important in Reiki distance healing, and how does it influence the energy flow?

6. How can affirmations support the practitioner's intention during distance healing?

7. What are effective affirmations for physical, emotional, and spiritual healing in Reiki sessions?

8. How does meditation help maintain focus and clarity during a Reiki healing session?

9. Why is maintaining a high vibrational frequency important in Reiki distance healing, and how can it be achieved?

10. How does meditation enhance a Reiki distance healing session?

11. What is the purpose of grounding meditation, and how can it be performed before a distance healing session?

12. How can visualization be used to direct Reiki energy during a distance healing session?

13. How can Reiki symbols be integrated into meditation and visualization to enhance the healing process?

14. Why is it important for Reiki practitioners to maintain a state of presence and flow during a healing session?

15. What is the etheric body, and how does it relate to physical health?

16. How can Reiki practitioners use distance healing to clear blockages in the etheric field?

17. What role do chakras play in distance healing, and how can clearing them support holistic well-being?

18. How does distance healing integrate across the etheric, emotional, mental, and spiritual bodies?

19. What is the main function of the chakra system, and why is it important to balance these energy centers during Reiki distance healing?

20. How can a practitioner use Reiki symbols and visualization to balance the recipient's root chakra during a distance healing session?

21. Which Reiki symbol is most commonly associated with emotional healing, and how can it be used to balance the sacral chakra during distance healing?

22. What are the typical signs of an imbalanced third eye chakra, and how can distance healing address these symptoms?

23. What is the role of the crown chakra in spiritual connection, and how can distance healing strengthen this connection?

24. How does the mental body influence thoughts and beliefs, and what techniques can a practitioner use to clear mental blockages during distance healing?

25. Describe how Reiki distance healing can strengthen the recipient's connection to their higher self through the spiritual body.

26. What are the benefits of integrating healing across the emotional, mental, and spiritual bodies during a distance healing session?

27. What Reiki symbol is associated with emotional healing, and how does it help in distance healing sessions?

28. Why is attuning to higher frequencies important for Reiki practitioners in distance healing?

29. Describe a simple meditation technique that can help raise a practitioner's vibrational frequency before a distance healing session.

30. How does mindfulness benefit Reiki practitioners during a distance healing session?

31. Which Reiki symbols are often used to enhance attunement to higher frequencies, and how do they function in a healing session?

32. How can gratitude be used as an attunement technique before a distance healing session?

33. How does visualization enhance the practitioner's intention during a Reiki distance healing session?

34. What are affirmations, and how can they be used during Reiki distance healing?

35. How can a practitioner maintain mindfulness throughout a distance healing session?

36. How does expanding consciousness enhance a Reiki practitioner's ability to channel healing energy?

37. What is open-heart meditation, and how does it help in expanding consciousness during distance healing?

38. Describe cosmic consciousness meditation and its role in Reiki distance healing.

39. How does grounding in the Earth's energy field support the practitioner in distance healing?

40. Why is non-attachment important in becoming an effective conduit for healing energy?

Advanced Concepts in Distance Healing

Multidimensionality and Parallel Universes

Multidimensional Beings and How Healing Can Occur Across Dimensions

The concept of multidimensionality suggests that each individual exists simultaneously on multiple planes of reality or dimensions. In energy healing, healing can occur within the physical body and across these multiple dimensions, affecting the subtle layers of the recipient's being that exist beyond the physical realm. Understanding multidimensionality expands the potential for distance Reiki healing, allowing practitioners to connect with the various aspects of the recipient's energy that exist in different dimensions and bring balance to the entire being.

Multidimensionality is based on the principle that the universe is far more complex than what we perceive through our physical senses. Just as we have an emotional, mental, and spiritual body in addition to our physical body, we also exist on multiple planes or dimensions that may be imperceptible to the ordinary mind. In these other dimensions, energy moves and operates in ways that transcend the limitations of time, space, and physical form. Distance Reiki healing allows practitioners to access these non-physical dimensions, bringing healing to the recipient at a deeper, more expansive level (Laszlo, 2007).

The Nature of Multidimensional Beings

Every person is a multidimensional being, meaning that we each exist not only in the third-dimensional world of physical matter but also in higher dimensions that correspond to our spiritual and energetic nature. These dimensions are interconnected, with each layer influencing the others. When one dimension experiences imbalance or disharmony, it can ripple through the other dimensions, affecting the person's overall well-being.

Healing the physical body is only one aspect of the overall healing process. The emotional, mental, and spiritual bodies also exist in different dimensions and require attention. For example, the emotional body might exist in the fourth dimension, where emotional energy is more fluid and dynamic than in the physical world. Likewise, the mental body may correspond to the fifth dimension, where thoughts and intentions shape reality more directly. The spiritual body may operate on even higher dimensions, where the connection to the universal life force is most potent.

By working with these multidimensional layers, Reiki practitioners can create healing that transcends the immediate physical symptoms and addresses the root causes of imbalance, whether they exist in the emotional, mental, or spiritual realms. This multidimensional approach allows for a more comprehensive healing experience, where the recipient's entire being is balanced across multiple planes of existence.

How Reiki Works Across Dimensions

The limitations of the physical dimension do not bind reiki energy. It is a form of universal life force energy that flows through all dimensions, making healing possible across these various planes. In distance healing, practitioners can access the recipient's energy field at multiple levels, including those outside the physical plane. By connecting with the recipient's higher dimensions, the practitioner can facilitate healing that affects the physical body and the recipient's emotional, mental, and spiritual aspects.

During a Reiki distance healing session, practitioners may use symbols like Hon Sha Ze Sho Nen to transcend time and space and connect with the recipient's energy at the multidimensional level. This symbol is a gateway that allows the practitioner to access the higher dimensions where the recipient's emotional, mental, and spiritual bodies reside. By sending healing energy to these dimensions, the practitioner can dissolve blockages, restore balance, and promote overall well-being in ways that may not be immediately visible on the physical level (Petter, 2000).

Sometimes, the practitioner may sense or intuitively perceive the recipient's multidimensional aspects, such as unresolved emotional trauma in the fourth dimension or mental blockages in the fifth dimension. These subtle energies can manifest as imbalances in the recipient's physical body, but they are often rooted in the higher dimensions where the recipient's thoughts, emotions, and spiritual energies reside. By working on these higher levels, the practitioner can bring about profound shifts in the recipient's overall state of being.

Healing in the Non-Physical Realms

An exciting aspect of multidimensional healing is the ability to work in the non-physical realms, where energy flows more freely and rapidly than in the dense physical world. Time and space do not operate in these higher dimensions as they do in the third-dimensional world. This allows Reiki practitioners to bypass the limitations of linear time and work directly with the energetic patterns that influence the recipient's physical and non-physical bodies.

For example, time is more fluid in the fourth dimension, where emotions and memories reside. This means that emotional wounds from the past can be accessed and healed even if they occurred many years ago. Similarly, the mental body in the fifth dimension may hold patterns of limiting beliefs or thought forms that can be cleared and restructured to align with the recipient's highest good. In these non-physical realms, healing is not constrained by the past or future; it occurs in the eternal present, where all possibilities exist simultaneously (Brennan, 1988).

By working in the non-physical realms, practitioners can address deep-seated issues that may have been resistant to healing on the physical plane alone. This approach allows for a more holistic healing experience, where the recipient's entire being is brought into alignment, not just their physical body. As the non-physical bodies heal, the changes ripple down to the physical level, creating lasting improvements in the recipient's health, emotional balance, and spiritual growth.

The Practitioner's Role in Multidimensional Healing

In multidimensional healing, the practitioner acts as a clear conduit for the universal life force energy, directing it to the dimensions and planes where it is needed most. This requires practitioners to expand their awareness beyond the physical body and attune to the subtle energies in higher dimensions. Through meditation, visualization, and intention, the practitioner can access the recipient's multidimensional aspects and facilitate healing across all layers of their being.

Practitioners who work in the multidimensional realms often rely on intuitive guidance to sense where blockages or imbalances occur. This intuitive awareness allows them to direct Reiki energy precisely, addressing the underlying causes of the recipient's challenges rather than just the symptoms. By holding a space of non-judgment and unconditional love, the practitioner helps the recipient release old patterns and energies that no longer serve them, promoting healing at the deepest levels.

Additionally, the practitioner must maintain a grounded presence while working in the multidimensional realms. The practitioner needs to stay connected to the physical plane, even while accessing higher dimensions, to ensure that the healing energy is fully integrated into the recipient's body. This balance between grounding and expanding consciousness allows the practitioner to create a stable and safe space for healing.

Impact of Healing in One Dimension Affecting Parallel Realities

The concept of parallel universes or realities suggests that multiple versions of reality exist simultaneously, each representing different possible outcomes or timelines. These parallel realities are shaped by the choices and actions we take and the energy we hold. In the context of distance Reiki healing, the fascinating possibility emerges that healing in one dimension or timeline can profoundly impact other parallel realities. By addressing blockages, imbalances, or trauma in one version of reality, the ripple effect can extend across multiple timelines, bringing healing and transformation to alternate versions of the recipient's experience.

The idea of parallel realities is rooted in both metaphysics and modern theories of quantum physics, where the concept of the multiverse suggests that every decision we make creates a new branch in the timeline, resulting in infinite possibilities coexisting. Reiki healing can influence these parallel realities because energy is not limited to a single timeline; it flows freely across dimensions and can affect the energy fields of other versions of the self. In other words, by sending healing energy to one aspect of the recipient's current timeline, we may also influence the energy of alternate selves that exist in parallel realities (Talbot, 1991).

How Parallel Realities Influence Our Current Experience

Parallel realities are not just abstract concepts—they actively influence our current experience in subtle but powerful ways. Every decision we make, and every action we take creates an energetic imprint that ripples across multiple timelines. In one reality, we may have taken a different career path, chosen different relationships, or made decisions that shaped our lives in different directions. These alternate versions of ourselves continue to exist in parallel, and the energy dynamics of those realities can influence our present experience.

For example, suppose a person in one reality is struggling with unresolved emotional trauma or limiting beliefs. In that case, that energy can resonate in parallel realities, influencing the person's energy field in their current timeline. Similarly, if a person experiences healing in one reality—physical, emotional, or spiritual—that healing can create positive shifts across other timelines, leading to a more harmonious and balanced energy in the present moment.

In Reiki, this concept means that healing the recipient in one timeline may also benefit their energy field in other dimensions or realities. This is particularly important when it comes to healing trauma or emotional wounds that have carried over from the past. By addressing the energetic imprint of those experiences in one dimension, practitioners can create healing that reverberates across multiple timelines, offering the recipient relief in their current life and the lives of their parallel selves.

Healing Across Timelines and Parallel Universes

Practitioners can access the recipient's parallel realities through symbols like Hon Sha Ze Sho Nen during a Reiki distance healing session. This symbol allows the practitioner to transcend the boundaries of time and space, creating a bridge between the current timeline and alternate dimensions. Once this connection is established, the practitioner can send healing energy to the recipient's alternate selves, addressing imbalances or blockages in parallel realities.

For instance, if a recipient is experiencing chronic anxiety or fear, the practitioner may sense that these emotions are not only rooted in the current timeline but are also present in alternate realities. By sending Reiki energy to these parallel versions of the recipient, the practitioner can help dissolve the energetic patterns contributing to the anxiety, creating healing that extends across multiple dimensions. As the energy of these alternate realities shifts, the recipient in the present timeline may experience a profound sense of relief, peace, and emotional balance (McTaggart, 2008).

Similarly, practitioners can use Reiki to influence future timelines by sending energy to alternate versions of the recipient who may face future challenges or difficulties. By healing these alternate realities, the practitioner helps to create a more harmonious and aligned future for the recipient in their current timeline. This healing process across timelines allows the recipient to step into a version of their future that is free from past blockages and aligned with their highest potential.

The Ripple Effect of Healing in Parallel Universes

When healing occurs in one dimension or reality, it creates a ripple effect that influences other dimensions. This is because all dimensions and timelines are interconnected at the energetic level. The energy shift in one reality can reverberate across the entire multiverse, affecting all versions of the self. This ripple effect can profoundly change the recipient's life as the healing energy flows freely across timelines and dimensions.

For example, a recipient who has been carrying the energy of past trauma may experience relief not only in their current life but also in the alternate realities where that trauma has also influenced their energy. As the trauma is healed in one dimension, the ripple effect brings healing to other versions of the recipient who the same energetic imprint may have impacted. This leads to a more balanced and harmonious experience across all timelines, allowing the recipient to move forward with greater freedom and alignment.

The ripple effect also works in reverse: challenges or unresolved energy in parallel realities can influence the recipient's current timeline. This is why addressing healing at the multidimensional level is so important. By clearing blockages and restoring balance in one dimension, practitioners help the recipient create a more aligned and harmonious experience across all aspects of their being, both in the present and alternate realities (Talbot, 1991).

The Practitioner's Role in Multidimensional and Parallel Reality Healing

When working with parallel realities, Reiki practitioners must approach the healing session with an open mind and a deep trust in energy flow. Because parallel universes and timelines exist beyond the linear concepts of time and space, practitioners must remain attuned to the subtle energies that guide the healing process. This requires the practitioner to enter a state of expanded consciousness, where they can sense the energetic dynamics of the recipient's parallel selves and direct healing energy accordingly.

One key aspect of working with parallel realities is the practitioner's ability to trust their intuition. Often, the practitioner may not consciously understand the details of the recipient's alternate timelines, but they can sense the energy that needs to be addressed. By following their intuitive guidance and allowing the Reiki energy to flow freely, the practitioner can create healing that transcends the current timeline and influences the recipient's experience across multiple realities.

Additionally, practitioners can use visualization techniques to connect with the recipient's parallel selves. This may involve visualizing the recipient's energy field as a series of overlapping layers or dimensions, each representing a different timeline or version of the recipient's experience. By sending Reiki energy to each of these layers, the practitioner helps to clear blockages and restore balance across all timelines, ensuring that the recipient's energy is aligned with their highest good in every reality.

Creating Lasting Change Across Dimensions

The ultimate goal of healing in parallel realities is to create lasting change that resonates across all dimensions of the recipient's being. By addressing the underlying energy patterns that influence the recipient's current timeline and alternate selves, practitioners help the recipient step into a version of reality that is free from old blockages and aligned with their highest potential. This process of multidimensional healing allows the recipient to experience profound shifts in their physical, emotional, mental, and spiritual well-being, both in the present moment and in their alternate realities.

As we move forward to the next chapter, we will explore how the collective consciousness and the Akashic Records play a role in distance healing, allowing practitioners to tap into the energetic repository of all experiences across lifetimes.

Healing in the Quantum Field: Bridging Science and Spirituality

The concept of healing across parallel universes and multidimensional realities is deeply connected to the idea of the quantum field—a space where all possibilities exist simultaneously and the boundaries of time and space dissolve. In science and spirituality, the quantum field is the underlying energetic framework connecting everything in the universe. In this field, Reiki healing, especially distance healing, finds a powerful foundation, allowing practitioners to affect energy beyond the constraints of the physical world and linear time.

In quantum physics, non-locality suggests that particles can be connected and communicate across vast distances, seemingly defying the conventional rules of space and time. This phenomenon is known as quantum entanglement and has intriguing parallels to how Reiki works in distance healing. Just as entangled particles remain connected regardless of physical separation, Reiki practitioners can connect with a recipient's energy field across time, space, and dimensions, facilitating healing no matter how far apart they are (Bohm, 1980).

This connection between Reiki and quantum theory provides a scientific framework for understanding how healing can occur across multiple realities. By working within the quantum field, Reiki practitioners tap into the unified energy that connects all things, allowing them to influence the recipient's current timeline and parallel dimensions, where alternate versions of the recipient exist. This multidimensional approach to healing mirrors the quantum potential in which all outcomes are possible, and energy shifts can influence not just one aspect of reality but many.

How the Quantum Field Supports Distance Healing

The quantum field is often described as a sea of infinite potential, where every possible outcome and reality coexists. In the context of Reiki distance healing, this field allows practitioners to connect with the recipient's energy, regardless of physical location, and send healing energy across dimensions. When a practitioner set the intention to send healing energy to the recipient, they are tapping into the quantum field, where time and space no longer present barriers. Instead, the healing energy flows instantly to where it is needed most.

This principle of non-locality is what makes distance healing so effective. It bypasses the need for the practitioner and recipient to be physically present with each other because, in the quantum field, the connection between their energy fields is instantaneous. As a result, the healing energy can move through the dimensions, reaching the recipient's alternate selves and creating ripple effects that extend far beyond the current moment (Laszlo, 2007).

Additionally, because the quantum field is a space of infinite possibility, Reiki practitioners are not limited to healing the recipient's present circumstances. They can also influence past experiences and future timelines, shifting energy to create lasting change across all aspects of the recipient's existence. By sending Reiki energy to a point in the recipient's past where trauma or emotional imbalance occurred, the practitioner helps clear the energetic imprint left by that experience, allowing healing to flow into the present and positively affect future timelines.

The Role of Intention in the Quantum Field

Intention is a critical component of working within the quantum field. When a Reiki practitioner sets a clear intention for healing, they are essentially "collapsing" the infinite possibilities in the quantum field into a specific outcome. This is similar to the concept of the observer effect in quantum physics, where observation influences the behavior of particles. In Reiki, the practitioner's intention acts as the guiding force that shapes how the healing energy flows through the quantum field.

For example, suppose a practitioner sets the intention to heal a recipient's emotional trauma. In that case, they are directing the energy in the quantum field to focus on the specific vibrational frequency associated with that trauma. The energy then flows through the quantum field, not just to the recipient's current emotional state but also to the alternate timelines and dimensions where that trauma may have left an imprint. In this way, intention bridges the practitioner, the recipient, and the quantum field, ensuring that the healing energy reaches all layers and dimensions of the recipient's being (McTaggart, 2008).

Through this process of intention, Reiki practitioners can create profound healing across multiple realities. By setting a focused, clear intention, practitioners guide the healing energy to where it is needed most, both within the recipient's current timeline and in parallel universes where alternate versions of the recipient may exist.

Visualizing the Quantum Field in Healing

In Reiki distance healing, visualization is powerful when working in the quantum field. Practitioners can use visualization techniques to strengthen their connection to the quantum field and direct healing energy to the recipient's multidimensional aspects. One effective visualization involves imagining the recipient's energy field existing within a vast web of light, each strand representing a different timeline or dimension. As the practitioner sends Reiki energy to the recipient, they can visualize it moving along the light strands, reaching the recipient in every timeline and dimension where healing is needed.

Another visualization involves imagining the quantum field as a sea of potential, with the recipient's energy field appearing as a glowing orb of light within this sea. The practitioner can then visualize the Reiki energy flowing into the recipient's orb, illuminating it and dissolving any blockages or imbalances. This imagery helps the practitioner focus on the recipient's multidimensional energy, ensuring the healing energy is delivered across all realities and dimensions.

By incorporating visualization techniques, practitioners can deepen their connection to the quantum field and enhance their ability to work across dimensions. This strengthens the flow of Reiki energy and expands the practitioner's awareness of the recipient's multidimensional nature, allowing for a more comprehensive and transformative healing experience.

Bridging Science and Spirituality Through Quantum Healing

Integrating quantum theory and Reiki healing represents a powerful bridge between science and spirituality. While Reiki has its roots in ancient spiritual traditions, modern science—especially the study of quantum mechanics—offers a framework for understanding how healing energy works across time, space, and dimensions. The concept of non-locality, for example, provides a scientific explanation for the effectiveness of distance healing. At the same time, the idea of the quantum field aligns with the spiritual belief in the interconnectedness of all things.

Understanding the relationship between the quantum field and healing can deepen Reiki practitioners' appreciation for the profound potential of their work. By recognizing that they are not just working with the recipient's physical body or energy field but also with the underlying quantum structure of the universe, practitioners can approach healing with a greater sense of responsibility and reverence. This expanded perspective allows them to tap into the full power of the universal life force, creating healing that transcends the limitations of time and space.

Section Summary
Multidimensionality and Parallel Universes

This section explored advanced Reiki practices, focusing on multidimensional healing, healing across parallel realities, and the quantum field's role in bridging science and spirituality. Reiki practitioners can facilitate healing beyond the physical realm by working across different dimensions, influencing the recipient's energy at multiple levels of existence, and how intention plays a crucial role in directing energy across time and space.

Multidimensional Healing: Connecting with Higher Realities

Reiki practitioners learn to work with the concept that individuals exist across multiple dimensions beyond the physical body. These dimensions, including emotional, mental, and spiritual bodies, hold vital energy that impacts the physical form. Reiki practitioners access these layers through symbols like Hon Sha Ze Sho Nen, facilitating healing that transcends physical symptoms and addresses deeper causes of imbalance. By healing across dimensions, practitioners bring balance to the entire being, affecting multiple layers of existence.

Healing Across Parallel Realities

The idea of parallel universes suggests that multiple realities exist simultaneously, each representing different outcomes or experiences. Reiki healing can extend across these realities, creating a ripple effect in which healing in one timeline affects others. Practitioners connect with alternate versions of the recipient's energy field in parallel realities, influencing outcomes across timelines and dissolving energetic patterns that may persist across different versions of the self. This multidimensional approach allows for holistic healing that impacts the present and alternate experiences.

Quantum Field: Bridging Science and Spirituality in Reiki Healing

Reiki finds its scientific foundation in the quantum field, a space where time and space dissolve, and all possibilities coexist. Non-locality and quantum entanglement illustrate how Reiki healing works in distance sessions, bypassing physical separation. Practitioners set clear intentions to direct healing energy within the quantum field, influencing not only the recipient's present timeline but also past and future dimensions. Visualization techniques help practitioners connect to this field and guide energy across multiple realities. This connection between quantum theory and Reiki bridges the gap between science and spirituality, highlighting the profound potential of energy healing.

Reiki healing has a profound reach when practitioners connect with multidimensional aspects of existence, affect parallel realities, and use the quantum field to transcend time and space for deep, holistic healing.

§

Collective Consciousness and Akashic Records

Accessing the Collective Consciousness for Healing Individuals and the Greater Whole

The concept of collective consciousness refers to the shared energy, thoughts, beliefs, and experiences of all beings within a society or even humanity. It is a vast, energetic field that connects everyone, and within it, all actions, emotions, and thoughts contribute to the overall state of human consciousness. In the context of Reiki and distance healing, practitioners can tap into this collective energy field to heal individuals and contribute to the healing of the collective whole.

In addition to individual healing, working with the collective consciousness allows practitioners to address larger societal imbalances. Issues such as collective fear, anxiety, or trauma are not confined to individuals but are shared across communities, nations, or even globally. Through Reiki, practitioners can direct healing energy to the collective consciousness, helping to bring balance and harmony to the greater field of human experience.

What is the Collective Consciousness?

The collective consciousness is the idea that all living beings are interconnected through an unseen, energetic network. As individuals have their own energy fields, so does the collective. This field is shaped by the thoughts, emotions, and experiences of all beings within it, and its energy reflects the overall state of consciousness at any given time. For example, during times of global crisis or widespread fear, the collective consciousness may resonate with lower frequencies, such as anxiety, uncertainty, or despair.

However, the collective consciousness is not a static field. It constantly shifts and evolves, influenced by positive and negative forces. As individuals heal and raise their consciousness, they contribute positively to the collective, helping elevate the overall frequency. Likewise, when collective healing occurs—such as during global moments of compassion, solidarity, or peace—individuals can benefit from the rise in the energetic frequency, experiencing more ease and alignment in their personal lives.

In Reiki, working with the collective consciousness means recognizing that the energy field of society, the planet, or even the universe can influence individual well-being. By tapping into this vast, energetic field, practitioners can send healing to one person and entire groups, communities, or humanity. This form of healing can be especially powerful when addressing global challenges or widespread emotional patterns, as it helps uplift the collective's vibrational frequency.

How Reiki Practitioners Access the Collective Consciousness

Reiki practitioners can access the collective consciousness in the same way they connect with an individual's energy field during a distance healing session. By setting the intention to work with the collective field, practitioners tune into the vibrational frequency of the collective, sensing areas where healing is needed and sending Reiki energy to address imbalances. This process is often guided by intuition, as practitioners may feel drawn to specific global issues or societal challenges calling for healing.

For instance, during times of widespread anxiety, such as global events that create uncertainty or fear, practitioners can set the intention to send healing energy to the collective consciousness, focusing on dissolving the fear and restoring a sense of calm and peace. This healing energy is directed into the collective field, helping to ease the energetic tension that individuals may be experiencing on a global scale. In this way, Reiki is a powerful tool for contributing to the overall healing of humanity (McTaggart, 2008).

One technique for accessing the collective consciousness is to use visualization. Practitioners can imagine the collective energy field as a vast, interconnected web of light surrounding the Earth, with each strand representing the energy of an individual, community, or global event. As they channel Reiki energy, practitioners visualize this light growing brighter, dissolving areas of darkness or imbalance, and restoring harmony to the web. This visualization helps to strengthen the connection between the practitioner and the collective consciousness, ensuring that the healing energy is directed where it is needed most.

Healing the Collective Through Individual Healing

Every person's energy field is connected to the collective, meaning that when an individual heals, they raise their frequency and, in doing so, uplift the collective energy field as well.

This dynamic is especially powerful when addressing ancestral patterns, collective trauma, or karmic imbalances passed down through generations. For example, an individual may carry the energetic imprint of trauma experienced by their ancestors, whether through historical events, cultural experiences, or family dynamics. By healing these imprints within the individual, Reiki practitioners help to release the burden from the collective consciousness, allowing future generations to experience greater freedom and alignment.

In this sense, healing work at the individual level has ripple effects that extend far beyond the person receiving the healing. As individuals heal, they contribute positively to the collective, creating a more harmonious and balanced energetic field for everyone. Practitioners who recognize this connection can approach individual healing sessions with an even greater sense of purpose, knowing that their work contributes to the evolution of collective consciousness.

Group Healing Sessions for Collective Consciousness

Group Reiki healing sessions are an excellent way to address the collective consciousness, as they bring together multiple practitioners or recipients to focus on a shared healing intention. These sessions can be directed toward specific global issues—such as peace, environmental healing, or reducing fear—or toward general collective well-being. Group healing amplifies the energy being sent, as the combined intentions of multiple practitioners strengthen the flow of Reiki and create a more powerful impact.

During a group healing session, practitioners can focus on the collective consciousness by visualizing the Earth and its inhabitants surrounded by healing light. They may set specific intentions for the healing, such as bringing peace to regions in conflict, addressing collective environmental challenges, or supporting humanity in times of emotional or spiritual crisis. By working together, practitioners create a unified field of healing energy that contributes to the overall balance and well-being of the collective.

These group sessions can also be performed at a distance, with practitioners worldwide setting a shared intention to send healing energy at a specific time. Distance Reiki is not limited by location, and the combined efforts of practitioners around the globe can create powerful shifts in the collective consciousness, helping to restore harmony and balance across societies and the planet as a whole (Brennan, 1988).

Akashic Records: Understanding How Distance Healing Can Tap Into This Energetic Repository of All Experiences Across Lifetimes

The Akashic Records are often described as an energetic repository that contains the history of every soul's experiences across all lifetimes. This vast field of knowledge, sometimes called the Book of Life, is believed to store information about every action, thought, emotion, and event that has ever occurred, not only for individuals but also for the collective consciousness. In distance healing, practitioners can access these records to bring profound insights and healing to individuals and the collective.

Tapping into the Akashic Records allows Reiki practitioners to gain a deeper awareness of the energetic imprints carried by individuals or groups, particularly those related to past lives, karmic patterns, or ancestral wounds. By working with this information during a distance healing session, practitioners can help release energetic blockages that may have been carried across lifetimes, facilitating healing at a soul level. Additionally, accessing the Akashic Records can provide valuable insights that guide the healing process, allowing practitioners to address the root causes of imbalances that may have originated in previous lifetimes.

What Are the Akashic Records?

The Akashic Records are a universal library containing every thought, action, and experience that has ever occurred for all souls. This energetic field exists outside of time and space so that practitioners can access past, present, and future records. Each soul has its own set of records within this vast repository, and these records hold the key to understanding the soul's journey, lessons, and purpose throughout its many lifetimes.

Practitioners can use the Akashic Records to gain insight into the karmic patterns or energetic imprints influencing a recipient's current life. For example, a person may be experiencing recurring patterns of emotional pain or physical illness that seem resistant to healing through traditional methods. By accessing the Akashic Records, practitioners may discover that these patterns are rooted in past life experiences or unresolved karmic lessons. With this awareness, practitioners can focus the healing energy on clearing these old imprints, allowing the recipient to release the burdens they have carried from one lifetime to the next (Schutz, 1997).

Additionally, the Akashic Records hold humanity's collective history, meaning that practitioners can access records related to the shared experiences of groups, communities, or even the planet as a whole. This collective information can be particularly valuable when working to heal ancestral trauma, inherited karmic patterns, or global imbalances. By accessing the collective Akashic Records, practitioners can help facilitate healing not just for individuals but for the broader collective consciousness as well.

How Reiki Practitioners Access the Akashic Records

Reiki practitioners access the Akashic Records through intention, meditation, and intuition. Before a healing session, the practitioner sets the intention to connect with the recipient's records, seeking guidance and insight into the energetic patterns that are influencing their current experience. The practitioner's intuitive awareness often guides this process, as they may receive impressions, images, or feelings that reveal crucial information about the recipient's soul journey.

One technique for accessing the Akashic Records is to enter a meditative state, where the practitioner's mind is quiet, and their awareness is open to receiving information from the universal energy field. During this meditation, the practitioner may visualize a sacred library or book of knowledge and mentally request access to the recipient's records. This process is carried out with great respect and humility, as the Akashic Records are considered sacred, and practitioners approach them intending to serve the recipient's highest good.

The Hon Sha Ze Sho Nen symbol, used in Reiki to transcend time and space, is an excellent tool for accessing the Akashic Records during distance healing sessions. This symbol allows the practitioner to connect with the recipient's soul-level information, bringing awareness to any karmic patterns, past life experiences, or ancestral imprints that need to be healed. By sending Reiki energy to these areas, the practitioner helps to clear the energetic imprints stored in the recipient's Akashic Records, allowing them to move forward with greater freedom and alignment (Petter, 2000).

Healing Past Life and Karmic Patterns

One benefit of accessing the Akashic Records during distance healing is the ability to heal past-life traumas and karmic patterns affecting the recipient's current life. Past-life energy can manifest in various ways, such as recurring emotional patterns, unresolved fears, or physical ailments that seem to have no clear cause in the present lifetime. These imprints may result from unresolved lessons or traumas the soul has carried across multiple lifetimes.

By accessing the recipient's past life records, Reiki practitioners can identify the root causes of these energetic imprints and send healing energy to dissolve the blockages. For example, suppose a recipient is experiencing chronic fear or anxiety that seems disproportionate to their current circumstances. In that case, the practitioner may discover that this fear is rooted in a traumatic event from a past life. By sending Reiki energy to the moment of trauma, the practitioner helps to release the emotional imprint, allowing the recipient to heal at a deep, soul level.

Karmic patterns, which are energetic imprints created by past actions or choices, can also be addressed through distance healing. The Akashic Records hold information about the karmic lessons that each soul is meant to learn, and these lessons often manifest as recurring patterns in multiple lifetimes. By working with the Akashic Records, Reiki practitioners can help recipients clear old karmic debts, resolve unfinished business from past lifetimes, and align with their soul's highest purpose (Schutz, 1997).

Working with Ancestral Energy and Collective Karma

In addition to individual records, the Akashic Records contain information about the ancestral lineage and the collective karmic patterns passed down through generations. These patterns can manifest as inherited emotional wounds, familial trauma, or even cultural imbalances that affect entire communities. By accessing the ancestral Akashic Records, Reiki practitioners can help recipients release the energetic imprints of their ancestors, healing the unresolved trauma passed down through the family line.

For example, a recipient may carry the emotional burden of grief or loss that their ancestors experienced during war, famine, or hardship. These imprints may affect the recipient's ability to experience joy or emotional freedom in their current life fully. By accessing the ancestral Akashic Records, the practitioner can help the recipient release these inherited burdens, freeing them from the energetic weight of the past and allowing them to create a more empowered future.

This work can also extend to healing humanity's collective karma. The Akashic Records contain the collective experiences of the entire planet, including the unresolved traumas and karmic lessons that have shaped human history. By working with the global Akashic Records, Reiki practitioners can contribute to healing collective wounds, such as war, environmental destruction, or societal injustice. This form of healing benefits the collective consciousness and helps create a more harmonious and aligned future for the planet and its inhabitants (Laszlo, 2007).

The Role of Intuition and Trust in Accessing the Akashic Records

Accessing and working with the Akashic Records requires practitioners to rely on their intuition and develop a deep trust in the information they receive. Because the Akashic Records exist outside of time and space, the information that comes through may not always be linear or immediately apparent. Practitioners must remain open and receptive to the subtle impressions, feelings, or images during the session, trusting that the Reiki energy will guide them to the areas that need healing.

Practitioners should approach the Akashic Records with a sense of humility and respect, as these records hold the sacred experiences of the soul's journey across lifetimes. By maintaining a heart-centered intention to serve the recipient's highest good, practitioners can access the Akashic Records with clarity and compassion, bringing healing aligned with the soul's purpose and path.

As we move forward, we will explore how meditation and Reiki symbols can further enhance the practitioner's ability to work with the Akashic Records, providing deeper insights and more powerful healing experiences.

Healing Across Timelines: Clearing Energetic Imprints from the Past

Reiki distance healing's ability to clear energetic imprints from the past, both in terms of individual experiences and collective history is transformative in its nature. These energetic imprints are the subtle influences that shape a person's emotional, physical, and spiritual well-being. They often arise from unresolved experiences, trauma, or karmic patterns that continue to impact the present moment, even though the original events may have occurred in a different lifetime or timeline.

By tapping into the Akashic Records and working with the collective consciousness, Reiki practitioners can access these past influences and release the energy that no longer serves the recipient. This healing across timelines allows practitioners to work on past lives, ancestral trauma, and even unresolved experiences from early childhood, ensuring that the recipient's energy field is clear and free of the burdens carried from the past.

Understanding Energetic Imprints and How They Shape the Present

Energetic imprints are the subtle residues left behind by past experiences, particularly those that were emotionally or physically intense. These imprints may include unresolved trauma, unhealed emotional wounds, or patterns of thought and behavior that were established in response to specific events. Over time, these imprints become embedded in the energy field, influencing the recipient's health, emotions, and relationships.

For example, a person who experienced a traumatic event in a past life may carry the energetic residue of that experience into their current life. This could manifest as recurring fear, emotional instability, or even physical symptoms, even though the person may not consciously remember the original event. Similarly, collective experiences—such as wars, natural disasters, or widespread societal upheaval—can leave collective energetic imprints that influence entire communities or generations.

These imprints are stored in the individual's energy field and in the Akashic Records, where they form part of the soul's history. By accessing these records, Reiki practitioners can identify the root cause of the energetic imprints and send healing energy to the original experience, helping to dissolve the old patterns and release the energy that has been carried forward (Schutz, 1997).

Healing Past Life Traumas

Many people carry unresolved trauma from previous lifetimes that continues to influence their present life. These traumas may manifest as recurring emotional patterns, irrational fears, or physical symptoms that seem unrelated to the person's current experiences.

Through the Akashic Records, practitioners can access the recipient's past lives and identify the specific moments where trauma occurred. By sending Reiki energy to those moments, practitioners help to release the emotional, physical, and spiritual wounds carried forward from one lifetime to the next. This process not only heals the recipient in the present but also creates a ripple effect that brings healing across multiple lifetimes and dimensions.

For example, a recipient who struggles with feelings of abandonment may discover that this pattern originates from a past life in which they experienced significant loss or rejection. By healing the energetic imprint of that experience, the practitioner helps the recipient release the old emotional pain, allowing them to move forward without the burden of the past (Petter, 2000).

Clearing Ancestral and Familial Energies

In addition to working with past lives, Reiki practitioners can help recipients clear ancestral and familial energies passed down through generations. These inherited imprints often take the form of ancestral trauma, such as patterns of emotional suppression, fear, or grief, that have been carried through the family line. These energies can block the recipient's energy field, preventing them from fully embracing their potential or experiencing emotional freedom.

By accessing the ancestral records within the Akashic field, Reiki practitioners can identify the patterns of trauma or imbalance that have been passed down through the lineage. For example, a recipient who experiences chronic anxiety may be carrying the energetic residue of fear that was passed down from ancestors who lived through war or famine. By sending Reiki energy to these ancestral imprints, practitioners can help to release the inherited trauma, freeing the recipient from the cycle of emotional pain that has affected their family for generations.

This healing can also positively affect the recipient's descendants, as clearing the energetic imprints of the past helps to create a more balanced and harmonious energy field for future generations. In this way, Reiki practitioners help heal the individual and contribute to the healing of entire family lines.

Healing Collective Trauma and Karma

In addition to individual and ancestral healing, Reiki practitioners can also work with the collective consciousness to address more extensive, shared experiences of trauma and karma. Collective trauma often arises from events that affect entire groups or populations, such as wars, natural disasters, or political upheaval. These events leave behind collective energetic imprints that can influence societies for generations, manifesting as ongoing conflict, fear, or societal imbalance.

By accessing the Akashic Records of the collective consciousness, practitioners can identify areas where healing is needed and direct Reiki energy to dissolve the energetic imprints of collective trauma. For example, practitioners may send healing energy to the energetic residues left behind by global events such as wars, which have created deep emotional and spiritual wounds in the collective psyche. Healing these imprints helps to release the collective energy that keeps societies stuck in patterns of fear, violence, or division.

Working with collective karma is particularly important when addressing social justice, inequality, or environmental harm. The karmic imprints of past actions—whether at the individual or societal level—can continue to influence the present and future. By sending Reiki energy to these areas, practitioners can help to clear the karmic debts that have been accumulated over time, creating space for healing, reconciliation, and positive change on a global scale (Laszlo, 2007).

Integrating Healing Across Timelines

The process of healing across timelines is not just about clearing old energy—it's also about integrating the lessons, wisdom, and growth from past experiences. As recipients release the energetic imprints of the past, they can reclaim the strength, resilience, and spiritual insights their souls have gained over many lifetimes. This integration process allows recipients to move forward with a more profound sense of purpose, alignment, and empowerment.

In distance healing, practitioners can facilitate this integration by helping recipients connect with their higher self and the universal life force. This process often involves sending Reiki energy to the recipient's soul-level awareness, helping them recognize and embrace the wisdom they have gained from past challenges and experiences. As recipients integrate these lessons, they can become a more authentic and aligned version of themselves, free from the energetic imprints of the past.

Section Summary
Collective Consciousness and Akashic Records

This section discussed the profound healing potential of Reiki by tapping into the collective consciousness, accessing the Akashic Records, and healing across timelines. Reiki practitioners can address imbalances not only at the individual level but also within the collective and karmic patterns that influence communities, ancestral lines, and the recipient's soul journey across lifetimes. By working in these expansive energetic fields, practitioners can clear blockages, release inherited trauma, and promote healing that transcends time and space.

Accessing the Collective Consciousness for Healing Individuals and the Greater Whole

Reiki practitioners can connect with the collective consciousness—the shared energy and experiences of humanity—to bring healing to individuals and the collective. This vast energetic field reflects societal imbalances, such as collective fear, anxiety, or trauma. By tapping into this field, practitioners can help dissolve collective challenges and uplift the overall vibrational frequency of humanity. Individual healing also positively impacts the collective, as every personal transformation contributes to the greater whole.

Akashic Records: How Distance Healing Can Tap Into This Energetic Repository of All Experiences Across Lifetimes

The Akashic Records hold the complete history of every soul's experiences across all lifetimes. Reiki practitioners can access these records to gain insights into past-life traumas, karmic patterns, and ancestral imprints that influence the recipient's present life. By sending healing energy to these imprints, practitioners can clear deep-seated energetic blockages, helping recipients resolve issues carried across lifetimes and ancestral lines. This healing process addresses the root cause of emotional, physical, or spiritual challenges and promotes freedom and growth at the soul level.

Healing Across Timelines: Clearing Energetic Imprints from the Past

Reiki distance healing allows practitioners to work across timelines, clearing energetic imprints from past experiences that continue to influence the present. These imprints, stored in the recipient's energy field and the Akashic Records, may stem from past-life trauma, ancestral patterns, or collective experiences. By healing these imprints, practitioners help recipients release the burdens of the past, including unresolved trauma or karmic patterns, and facilitate integration of the lessons learned across lifetimes. This process ensures that the recipient's energy field is clear and aligned with their highest potential.

In the next chapter, we will explore advanced techniques for enhancing Reiki distance healing, such as working with symbols, setting clear intentions, and using meditation to deepen the practitioner's connection to the recipient and the universal life force.

§

Soul Contracts and Life Purpose

Healing as a Means of Aligning with Soul Contracts and Life Purpose

Soul contracts are agreements each soul makes before incarnating into a physical body. These contracts are designed to provide growth, learning, and evolution opportunities by presenting individuals with specific challenges, relationships, and experiences that align with their soul's journey. While these contracts are often created to guide the soul toward its highest potential, they can also present energetic challenges that manifest as physical, emotional, or spiritual blockages.

One of the most powerful applications of energy work in Reiki distance healing is helping individuals align with their soul contracts and rediscover their life purpose. Reiki can help people reconnect with their soul's deeper calling, facilitating personal growth and spiritual evolution by releasing the energetic blockages that prevent individuals from fully embracing their path.

What Are Soul Contracts?

A soul contract is an agreement the soul makes before incarnation. It outlines the essential experiences, relationships, and challenges that the individual will encounter in their lifetime, all intended to support their spiritual growth and development. These contracts are not random; they are carefully crafted based on the soul's past experiences, karmic patterns, and the lessons that need to be learned to evolve.

Soul contracts may include relationships with specific individuals—such as family members, romantic partners, or friends—who will play important roles in the individual's life. They may also include life events or challenges designed to push the individual out of their comfort zone and help them grow on a spiritual level. While these contracts are made with the highest intentions, they can sometimes result in difficult or painful experiences that create energetic blockages in the individual's field.

Sometimes, individuals may feel disconnected from their life purpose, experiencing a sense of confusion, frustration, or stagnation. These feelings can arise when the person's energy field becomes blocked by unresolved experiences related to their soul contract. Reiki distance healing can help release these blockages, allowing the individual to reconnect with their soul's path and move forward with greater clarity and purpose (Judith, 2004).

Aligning with Life Purpose Through Healing

Aligning with one's life purpose involves clearing away the energetic imprints accumulated over time, allowing the individual to reconnect with the more profound truth of their soul's journey. These blockages often result from past life experiences, unresolved karma, or emotional wounds carried over into the present life. These blockages can create confusion, indecision, or fear, preventing the individual from fully stepping into their life purpose.

Reiki distance healing offers a powerful way to address these energetic blockages. By sending healing energy to the areas of the recipient's energy field holding onto old patterns, trauma, or fear, practitioners can help clear the pathways for the individual to rediscover their true purpose. This process often involves working with the third eye chakra (Ajna), which governs intuition and insight, and the solar plexus chakra (Manipura), which is associated with personal power and confidence.

During a distance healing session, practitioners can use Reiki symbols, such as Hon Sha Ze Sho Nen (the distance symbol) and Cho Ku Rei (the power symbol), to focus the healing energy on the recipient's higher self and their connection to their soul contract. These symbols help to clear the energetic pathways, allowing the individual to release the patterns and blockages preventing them from aligning with their true purpose.

Releasing Energetic Blockages to Follow the True Path

Many experience energetic blockages that prevent them from fully embracing their life purpose. These blockages may manifest as recurring emotional patterns, limiting beliefs, or physical symptoms that seem unrelated to any specific cause. In many cases, these blockages are directly connected to the soul's journey and the lessons embedded in the individual's soul contract.

For example, a person who struggles with self-doubt or fear of failure may have made a soul contract to overcome these challenges to step into their full potential. However, the unresolved energy of these experiences may create blockages in the solar plexus chakra, preventing the person from moving forward confidently in life. By working with Reiki energy, practitioners can help clear these blockages, allowing the recipient to release old patterns of fear and step into their personal power.

Similarly, individuals who feel disconnected from their intuition or spiritual path may be experiencing blockages in the third eye chakra, which governs insight and higher guidance. These blockages can make it difficult for the person to trust their inner wisdom or follow the path that aligns with their soul's purpose. Reiki distance healing can help clear these blockages, restoring energy flow to the third eye chakra and allowing the individual to reconnect with their inner guidance.

In many cases, clearing these blockages also involves addressing past life experiences or karmic patterns that have carried over into the present. By accessing the Akashic Records during a distance healing session, practitioners can gain insight into the specific experiences that have contributed to these blockages and send healing energy to dissolve them at their roots. This process allows the recipient to release the energetic burdens of the past and move forward with a renewed sense of clarity and purpose (Schutz, 1997).

Distance Healing's Role in Helping Individuals Embrace Their Life Purpose

Distance healing is a powerful tool for helping individuals embrace their life purpose and align with their soul's true path. Because Reiki energy transcends time and space, practitioners can connect with the recipient's higher self and soul contract during a distance healing session, providing deep, transformative healing that reaches beyond the physical realm.

By working with the higher chakras, such as the third eye and crown chakras, Reiki practitioners help recipients access their higher guidance and reconnect with their life purpose. The healing energy clears the confusion, fear, and limiting beliefs, preventing the recipient from fully embracing their soul's journey and allowing them to move forward confidently and clearly.

In addition to clearing blockages, Reiki distance healing can provide recipients with spiritual insights and intuitive guidance that help them better understand their life purpose. Through healing, many recipients experience spiritual awakenings or moments of profound clarity, in which they gain a greater understanding of their soul's path and the lessons they are meant to learn in this lifetime. These moments of awakening can be life-changing, providing recipients the motivation and inspiration to follow their true calling.

As we move forward to the next chapter, we will explore how distance healing can address generational trauma and ancestral karma, helping to heal family lines and create positive ripple effects for future generations.

Distance Healing's Role in Releasing Energetic Blockages to Help Individuals Follow Their True Path

The journey to discovering and living in alignment with one's life purpose often requires clearing energetic blockages accumulated over time. These blockages can stem from a wide range of experiences, including past trauma, limiting beliefs, societal conditioning, and unresolved karmic lessons. Many of these blockages operate on a subconscious level, making them difficult to address through traditional means. This is where Reiki distance healing can be a powerful tool, helping individuals release the energies preventing them from fully stepping into their life's true path.

Distance healing works by accessing the recipient's energy field and identifying areas where the energy flow has been disrupted or blocked. These disruptions often manifest as stagnation, confusion, or a sense of being "stuck" in life. By using Reiki to clear these blockages, practitioners can help the recipient realign with their soul contract and move forward on their journey with greater clarity, purpose, and freedom.

The Nature of Energetic Blockages

Energetic blockages occur when the natural flow of life force energy, or ki, becomes disrupted. These disruptions can be caused by unresolved emotions, past trauma, limiting beliefs, or karmic patterns. When energy becomes stagnant or blocked, it can create physical, emotional, or mental symptoms that make it difficult for the individual to move forward. These blockages can affect the chakras, the energy centers that regulate the flow of ki throughout the body, and the auric field, which serves as a protective and energetic boundary for the individual.

Energetic blockages are often tied to soul contracts, agreements made before birth to experience specific lessons or challenges for spiritual growth. However, when these lessons go unprocessed or unresolved, they can create an energetic residue that remains in the individual's energy field, causing blockages that prevent them from moving forward in alignment with their life purpose.

For example, a person who has made a soul contract to learn the lesson of self-worth may encounter challenges in life that test their confidence and sense of value. Suppose these challenges go unaddressed or are met with resistance. In that case, the individual may develop an energetic blockage in the solar plexus chakra associated with personal power and self-esteem. This blockage can manifest as feelings of inadequacy, self-doubt, or fear of taking action, ultimately preventing the individual from fully embracing their life purpose (Judith, 2004).

How Distance Healing Clears Energetic Blockages

Reiki distance healing works by channeling universal life force energy to areas of the recipient's energy field that are blocked or stagnant. The practitioner uses intention, Reiki symbols, and visualization techniques to direct healing energy to the specific areas that need attention. This process helps to dissolve the energetic blockages, allowing ki to flow freely once again.

One of the most powerful tools for clearing blockages during distance healing is the Cho Ku Rei symbol, also known as the power symbol. This symbol amplifies the flow of energy, making it particularly effective for breaking through areas of stagnation. By visualizing the Cho Ku Rei symbol over the blocked chakra or area of the auric field, the practitioner helps to release the dense or stuck energy that has been preventing the recipient from moving forward.

The Hon Sha Ze Sho Nen symbol is especially useful for blockages related to karmic patterns or past life trauma. This symbol transcends time and space, allowing the practitioner to access the root cause of the blockage, whether it originates in this lifetime or a previous one. By sending healing energy to the point of origin, the practitioner helps to resolve the unresolved karma or trauma that has been carried forward, freeing the recipient from its energetic grip (Petter, 2000).

Addressing Limiting Beliefs and Emotional Blockages

Many energetic blockages that prevent individuals from aligning with their life purpose are rooted in limiting beliefs or emotional wounds. These beliefs and emotions can create powerful, energetic patterns that shape the individual's reality, often without them realizing it. For example, people may subconsciously believe they are not worthy of success, love, or happiness. This belief creates a self-imposed limitation that manifests as fear, procrastination, or self-sabotage, preventing individuals from pursuing their true calling.

Reiki distance healing can help to clear these limiting beliefs by addressing the emotional energy that underlies them. The practitioner works to release the emotional wounds or traumas that gave rise to the limiting belief, allowing the recipient to let go of the patterns holding them back. As these emotional blockages are cleared, the recipient can reframe their beliefs and move forward with greater confidence and clarity.

In addition to emotional blockages, Reiki can also help to clear mental blockages, such as overthinking, doubt, or fear of failure. These blockages often affect the third eye chakra, which governs intuition and higher vision. By sending healing energy to this chakra, the practitioner helps to clear the mental fog that has been clouding the recipient's ability to see their life purpose. As the third eye chakra is cleared, the recipient gains greater access to their intuition and inner guidance, allowing them to make decisions aligned with their soul's true path (Judith, 2004).

Helping Individuals Rediscover Their Life Path

For many people, rediscovering their life purpose begins with inner discontent or restlessness. They may feel "off track" or that their current life circumstances do not reflect their deeper desires and aspirations. This feeling of being out of alignment with one's life purpose is often accompanied by energetic blockages that prevent the individual from making the necessary changes to get back on track.

Distance healing can play a vital role in helping individuals realign with their life path by clearing the energetic obstacles preventing them from moving forward. By addressing the emotional, mental, and spiritual blockages accumulated over time, practitioners help the recipient reconnect with their inner truth and higher guidance.

During the healing process, many recipients experience moments of clarity and insight in which they gain a deeper understanding of their life purpose. These moments of awakening often occur as the higher chakras (such as the third eye and crown chakras) are cleared, allowing the recipient to access the higher wisdom that has been guiding them all along. As these blockages are released, the recipient can see their life path more clearly and often feel renewed purpose and direction.

Releasing Fear and Resistance to Change

One of the most common blockages preventing individuals from following their true path is fear of the unknown, failure, or stepping into their own power. This fear can create a powerful, energetic barrier that keeps individuals stuck in familiar but unfulfilling patterns. Distance healing can help to release the energetic imprints of fear stored in the recipient's energy field, allowing them to move forward with greater courage and confidence.

By sending Reiki energy to the areas of the body and energy field where fear is held—often the root chakra (Muladhara) and the solar plexus chakra (Manipura)—practitioners help dissolve the energetic barriers that have been holding the recipient back. This process releases the fear and restores a sense of groundedness and personal empowerment, allowing the recipient to take the necessary steps to align with their life purpose.

As we move into the next chapter, we will explore how distance healing can address generational trauma and ancestral karma and the ripple effects that healing family lines can have on future generations.

Section Summary
Soul Contracts and Life Purpose

This section covered how Reiki distance healing serves as a profound tool for aligning individuals with their soul contracts and life purpose by releasing energetic blockages that hinder their path. And, that the principles behind soul contracts, the nature of energetic blockages, and how Reiki helps individuals clear these blockages, ultimately empowering them to pursue their true path with clarity, purpose, and alignment.

Healing and Aligning with Soul Contracts

Soul contracts are pre-incarnational agreements that outline key life experiences, relationships, and challenges designed for spiritual growth and evolution. However, these contracts can also lead to energetic challenges and blockages that hinder an individual's progress. Reiki distance healing allows practitioners to help individuals realign with their soul contracts by clearing the energetic blockages that arise from unresolved experiences or karmic lessons. By addressing these energetic patterns, Reiki facilitates personal growth, enabling recipients to reconnect with their life purpose and move forward with greater clarity and focus.

Releasing Energetic Blockages to Follow the True Path

Energetic blockages, caused by past trauma, limiting beliefs, or unresolved emotional and karmic patterns, often prevent individuals from fully stepping into their life purpose. These blockages can manifest as stagnation, confusion, or feelings of being "stuck." Reiki distance healing works by accessing the recipient's energy field, identifying the areas of disruption, and channeling healing energy to dissolve these blockages. By using Reiki symbols like Cho Ku Rei and Hon Sha Ze Sho Nen, practitioners help release dense or stagnant energy, allowing individuals to clear emotional, mental, and spiritual blockages that have been holding them back from living their true purpose.

Rediscovering Life Purpose and Moving Forward

Once the energetic blockages are cleared, individuals often experience a profound shift in their ability to follow their true path. Reiki helps individuals reconnect with their higher self, realign with their life purpose, and embrace their soul's journey with renewed confidence. The healing process also strengthens their connection to their inner guidance, empowering them to trust the flow of life and make decisions aligned with their higher calling. As individuals step into this alignment, they are better equipped to follow the signs and synchronicities that guide them toward fulfilling their soul contracts.

In essence, this section highlights the transformative power of Reiki in releasing the energetic imprints that obstruct an individual's alignment with their life purpose. By addressing and clearing these blockages, recipients can move forward on their soul's path with a renewed sense of purpose, clarity, and empowerment.

§

Knowledge Review
Chapter Five

Advanced Concepts in Distance Healing

1. Why is attuning to higher frequencies important for Reiki practitioners in distance healing?

2. Describe a simple meditation technique that can help raise a practitioner's vibrational frequency before a distance healing session.

3. How can gratitude be used as an attunement technique before a distance healing session?

4. Why is mindfulness important in a Reiki distance healing session?

5. Describe a basic mindfulness meditation technique to help practitioners stay present during a distance healing session.

6. How does visualization enhance the practitioner's intention during a Reiki distance healing session?

7. How can a practitioner maintain mindfulness throughout a distance healing session?

8. What is the quantum field, and how does it relate to the process of Reiki distance healing?

9. How does the principle of non-locality in quantum physics support the idea of distance healing in Reiki?

10. What role does intention play in the healing process within the quantum field, and how does it affect the outcome of a Reiki session?

11. How can visualization techniques enhance a Reiki practitioner's ability to work within the quantum field during distance healing?

12. How does integrating quantum theory with Reiki healing bridge the gap between science and spirituality?

13. What is the collective consciousness, and how does it influence individual and collective well-being?

14. How can Reiki practitioners contribute to healing the collective consciousness?

15. What techniques can be used to access the collective consciousness for healing purposes?

16. How does individual healing impact the collective consciousness?

17. What are the Akashic Records, and how do they inform Reiki healing?

18. How do Reiki practitioners access the Akashic Records during a distance healing session?

19. How can the Akashic Records help in healing past-life traumas and karmic patterns?

20. What role does intuition play in accessing and working with the Akashic Records?

21. What are energetic imprints, and how do they affect an individual's present life?

22. Which two chakras are most commonly associated with aligning with life purpose, and why?

23. How do Reiki practitioners heal past life traumas during distance healing sessions?

24. What is the significance of ancestral and familial energy healing in Reiki?

25. How can Reiki practitioners work with collective trauma and karma?

26. What is the process of integrating healing across timelines, and why is it important?

27. What is a soul contract, and how does it shape an individual's life experiences?

28. How can Reiki distance healing help individuals align with their soul contracts and life purpose?

29. What role do past life experiences and karmic patterns play in creating blockages, and how can Reiki help release them?

30. How does distance healing provide spiritual insights that help individuals understand and embrace their life purpose?

31. What causes energetic blockages, and how do they prevent individuals from following their life path?

32. How does Reiki distance healing clear energetic blockages, and which symbols are most effective

33. How can limiting beliefs and emotional blockages be cleared through Reiki distance healing?

34. Which chakras are often affected by mental and emotional blockages, and how does Reiki help restore balance?

35. How does Reiki help individuals release fear and resistance to change, and what are the key chakras involved?

Real-World Applications of Distance Healing

Healing Across Generations and Ancestral Lines

Addressing Generational Trauma and Ancestral Karma

The concept of generational trauma and ancestral karma suggests that the energy of unresolved trauma, pain, and life experiences can be passed down from generation to generation. This energy is often carried subconsciously and manifests through emotional, psychological, and even physical patterns in descendants' lives. These patterns are not always consciously recognized by individuals, yet they significantly impact how people experience the world, relate to themselves and others, and navigate life's challenges.

Reiki distance healing offers a powerful way to address and heal generational trauma and ancestral karma, providing individuals with the opportunity to break free from inherited patterns that no longer serve them. By working at the energetic level, practitioners can tap into the recipient's family lineage, accessing the deep-rooted energies that have been passed down through the generations and clearing the blockages that keep these patterns in place. This process not only heals the recipient but also creates positive ripple effects throughout the family line, healing past and future generations.

What Is Generational Trauma?

Generational trauma, also known as intergenerational trauma, refers to the transfer of traumatic experiences, unresolved emotional wounds, and psychological patterns from one generation to the next. This transfer happens through various means, including family dynamics, learned behavior, and energetic imprints. It is important to recognize that generational trauma is not just passed down through stories or learned behaviors—it is also carried at the energetic level, meaning that even those who are not consciously aware of their family's traumatic past may still carry the energetic residue of these experiences in their own energy field.

Examples of generational trauma can include the impact of war, famine, poverty, or systemic oppression on an entire family line. Suppose an ancestor lived through a period of extreme hardship or trauma. In that case, the unresolved emotional and energetic imprints of that experience may be passed down through the family line, affecting subsequent generations. This trauma can manifest as chronic emotional distress, a sense of fear or insecurity, or recurring patterns of behavior that seem resistant to change.

Reiki distance healing allows practitioners to tap into the energetic roots of this generational trauma, working to release the blockages that have been inherited from the family line. By accessing the ancestral energy field, practitioners can send healing energy to the moments when the trauma occurred, helping to dissolve the energetic imprints that have been carried forward. This process of healing allows recipients to break free from the patterns of the past, creating space for new growth, healing, and transformation (Schutz, 1997).

Healing Ancestral Karma

In addition to generational trauma, many people carry the energetic burden of ancestral karma. Ancestral karma refers to the unresolved karmic lessons, patterns, and debts passed down through the family line. These karmic imprints can result from actions, behaviors, or choices made by ancestors that were left unresolved or unbalanced. Just as individuals are responsible for resolving their karma, entire family lines can carry ancestral karma that needs to be addressed and healed.

For example, an ancestor may have harmed others by engaging in unjust practices, oppressing others, or acting out of greed or fear. The energetic consequences of these actions may have been passed down through the family line, manifesting as patterns of struggle, financial instability, or relationship difficulties in later generations. Reiki distance healing offers a way to address these karmic imprints by working with the Akashic Records and the ancestral energy field, helping to release the energetic debt and healing the entire family line (Laszlo, 2007).

When working with ancestral karma, Reiki practitioners often use symbols like Hon Sha Ze Sho Nen, allowing them to transcend time and space and connect with the karmic patterns created in the past. By sending Reiki energy to the root of the karmic imbalance, the practitioner helps to resolve the unresolved lessons or debts, freeing the recipient from the energetic burden that has been passed down. This process not only heals the recipient but also has a ripple effect on future generations, preventing the continuation of these karmic patterns in the family line.

The Role of the Root Chakra in Ancestral Healing

The root chakra (Muladhara) is critical in generational and ancestral healing. As the energy center responsible for grounding, safety, security, and connection to one's roots, the root chakra is where much of the ancestral energy is stored. When there are blockages or imbalances in the root chakra, individuals may experience a sense of disconnection from their family, insecurity, or an inability to feel grounded in life. These imbalances are often the result of unresolved trauma or karma that has been passed down through the family line.

During a Reiki distance healing session focused on ancestral healing, practitioners may direct energy specifically to the root chakra to clear the blockages preventing the flow of grounding energy. By using symbols such as Cho Ku Rei (the power symbol), practitioners help amplify the healing energy in the root chakra, releasing the energetic patterns inherited from the family line. As the root chakra is cleared, individuals often feel a more profound sense of connection to their roots and a renewed sense of safety and stability.

Healing Across Time and Generations

One of the most powerful aspects of Reiki distance healing is its ability to transcend time and bring healing to both the past and future. When working with generational trauma and ancestral karma, practitioners are not just healing the recipient—they are also sending healing energy to the ancestors who first experienced the trauma and future generations who would otherwise inherit these patterns.

By accessing the recipient's family lineage through the Akashic Records, practitioners can identify the key moments where trauma or karmic imbalances occurred and send healing energy directly to those moments. This process helps to clear the energetic residue that has been carried forward, allowing the recipient to break free from the patterns of the past and create a new path for themselves and their descendants.

This multidimensional healing process creates a ripple effect that transforms the recipient's life and brings healing to the entire family line. As the old patterns are cleared, future generations are no longer burdened by the same karmic or traumatic imprints, allowing them to live with greater freedom, clarity, and alignment.

The Ripple Effect on Future Generations

When healing is done at the ancestral level, it profoundly impacts future generations. The trauma, fear, or struggle patterns that would have been passed down are no longer present in the family's energetic field, creating space for new, positive patterns to emerge. This healing work transforms the individual and ensures that future generations can live without the energetic burden of their ancestors.

In Reiki distance healing, the power of intention plays a crucial role in directing the healing energy toward both the past and future. Practitioners set the intention to bring healing not only to the recipient but also to their ancestors and descendants, allowing the healing energy to flow through the entire family line. This intention helps create lasting change that benefits the entire lineage, energetically and spiritually.

Healing Family Lines and Its Ripple Effect on Future Generations

The healing of ancestral trauma and generational karma through Reiki distance healing is not confined to the individual alone; it can create a ripple effect that extends to both past ancestors and future descendants. As family lines are energetically intertwined, any shifts in one person's energy can influence the entire lineage, helping to break the chains of inherited trauma and karmic patterns that may have persisted across generations.

By addressing the root causes of these inherited patterns, practitioners can facilitate multidimensional healing that brings balance, peace, and renewal to the entire family. Future generations benefit immensely from this process, as they are no longer burdened by the same energetic imprints, allowing them to experience life with greater freedom, clarity, and alignment.

The Ripple Effect on Future Generations

When Reiki distance healing is directed toward healing ancestral lines, it brings about significant changes for the individual receiving the healing and their descendants. By clearing the energetic imprints of past trauma, karmic lessons, and unresolved emotions, the healing energy creates space for new patterns to emerge, free from the limitations of the past. This allows future generations to experience life without being weighed down by their ancestors' emotional and energetic baggage.

For instance, an individual whose ancestors experienced war, famine, or oppression may carry within them the energetic imprint of fear, insecurity, or a constant sense of survival mode. This imprint could manifest in the present as anxiety, self-sabotage, or a deep-seated belief in scarcity or lack. By addressing these inherited patterns during a Reiki session, practitioners can help to release the energy of fear and restore a sense of safety and security to the family line. As a result, future generations are no longer predisposed to these patterns, allowing them to experience a greater sense of ease, abundance, and emotional well-being.

Moreover, the ripple effect extends beyond the immediate family. As family members undergo healing, their energetic shifts can influence the collective consciousness of their wider community, helping to create an environment of healing, transformation, and growth. When ancestral trauma is healed, positive behavior, mindset, and emotional health changes can contribute to a more peaceful, harmonious world for future generations.

How Reiki Dissolves Inherited Emotional Patterns

Reiki distance healing effectively dissolves inherited emotional patterns because it works at the energetic level, bypassing the conscious mind and directly accessing the emotional imprints stored within the family line. These emotional imprints can be the result of traumatic events, unresolved grief, or even habitual patterns of behavior that have been passed down from one generation to the next. Often, these patterns persist because they have never been adequately addressed or processed by the family members who initially experienced them.

During a Reiki distance healing session, practitioners connect with the recipient's ancestral energy field, identifying the specific emotions or patterns that must be addressed. These may include feelings of guilt, shame, abandonment, or anger—emotions that have been passed down through the family line, creating recurring patterns of emotional imbalance. By sending Reiki energy to these emotional imprints, practitioners help dissolve the energetic residue that has been carried forward, allowing the recipient and their descendants to break free from these inherited emotions.

For example, suppose an ancestor experienced profound loss or grief that was never fully processed. In that case, this energy may have been passed down through the family line, manifesting as an inability to experience joy, difficulty forming meaningful relationships, or ongoing sadness or isolation. Reiki healing releases this emotional energy, helping the recipient process and heal the inherited grief. As this emotional energy is released, future generations are freed from carrying this unprocessed grief, allowing them to experience life with a greater sense of connection, joy, and emotional freedom.

Restoring the Flow of Energy in Family Lines

One key outcome of Reiki healing in ancestral lines is the restoration of energy flow throughout the family line. When trauma, karma, or emotional imprints are passed down, they can create energetic blockages that prevent the free flow of ki, or life force energy, within the family. These blockages can manifest as recurring patterns of struggle, dysfunction, or stagnation experienced by multiple generations. In some cases, these blockages may even create physical health problems as the unresolved energy manifests in the body.

Reiki distance healing works to clear these energetic blockages, restoring the natural flow of ki throughout the family line. Practitioners may focus on specific energy centers, such as the root chakra, which governs the family's connection to their lineage, or the heart chakra, which is responsible for emotional healing and compassion. By restoring balance to these energy centers, the practitioner helps to re-establish the free flow of energy throughout the entire family line, allowing for greater healing, harmony, and well-being.

As the flow of energy is restored, family members often experience a shift in consciousness, becoming more aware of the patterns that have influenced their lives and the lives of their ancestors. This heightened awareness allows them to make conscious choices that are free from the limitations of the past, empowering them to create new patterns of health, happiness, and success. This restoration of energy not only benefits the individual receiving the healing but creates a ripple effect that spreads throughout the entire family line, offering healing to both ancestors and descendants alike.

Creating Positive Patterns for Future Generations

One of the most rewarding aspects of ancestral healing through Reiki is creating positive patterns that will be passed down to future generations. As old trauma, fear, and limitation patterns are cleared, new opportunities for growth, empowerment, and joy emerge. The clearing of ancestral energy allows future generations to experience life with a clean slate, free from the energetic imprints of the past.

This process of creating positive patterns is not limited to the energetic realm—it also manifests in the physical, emotional, and behavioral choices individuals make in their daily lives. As family members heal, they model healthier behaviors and emotional responses for future generations. This may include fostering healthier communication, creating more supportive relationships, or embracing new opportunities for personal growth and spiritual development. As these new patterns take root, they become the foundation for future generations to build upon, ensuring that the family line continues to grow in alignment with love, compassion, and wholeness.

In Reiki distance healing, practitioners can set the intention to anchor positive energy and new patterns into the family line, helping to create a lasting legacy of healing and transformation. This may involve visualizing the family's energy field being filled with light, love, and abundance or using Reiki symbols like Cho Ku Rei to amplify the flow of positive energy throughout the family line. By doing so, practitioners help to ensure that the healing work they do today will benefit future generations for years to come.

As we move forward to the next chapter, we will explore the role of empathy, intuition, and psychic abilities in facilitating distance healing and how practitioners can strengthen these connections for more precise and effective healing.

Integrating Ancestral Healing Into Daily Life: Lasting Change for Future Generations

As Reiki distance healing facilitates the release of ancestral trauma and generational karma, the healing process doesn't end with the energetic session. For the transformation to truly take root and create lasting change, individuals and families must integrate healing into their daily lives. This integration process ensures that the energetic shifts initiated during the Reiki session are embodied in practical ways, fostering healthier patterns and behaviors that can be passed down to future generations.

Healing across ancestral lines is not just about removing blockages and traumas;

it's also about creating new legacies for families based on love, support, and balance. As individuals work to integrate energy healing, they must consciously reinforce the new patterns and create an environment that nurtures this continued growth. Reiki healing provides the initial energetic clearing, but true transformation requires commitment and mindful action in everyday life.

Anchoring the Healing Into the Physical and Emotional Body

Anchoring the energetic shifts into the physical and emotional body is an important part of integrating ancestral healing. After a Reiki session, recipients may feel lighter, more grounded, or emotionally free from old patterns. However, to make these shifts permanent, it's important to ensure that the new energy flow is integrated on all levels. The healing must move beyond the energetic and become embedded in the individual's body and consciousness.

Practitioners can guide recipients to practice techniques such as grounding meditations, body awareness exercises, or chakra balancing to help anchor healing energy into their physical and emotional systems. For instance, spending time in nature, practicing deep breathing, or using visualizations to strengthen the root chakra can all be beneficial in keeping the energy flow steady and clear. These practices help reinforce the healing by connecting the subtle energy shifts to the material body, ensuring the person remains balanced and aligned with the new energetic patterns (Judith, 2004).

Emotionally, recipients should be encouraged to acknowledge and process any feelings that arise as the old patterns clear. Often, as ancestral trauma is released, long-held emotions like grief, anger, or fear may come to the surface. By consciously working through these emotions, whether through journaling, meditation, or speaking with a therapist, individuals can ensure that they are not just bypassing the healing but actively engaging with it. This emotional processing allows them to make space for new, healthier emotional responses.

Creating New Patterns of Behavior and Thought

After Reiki distance healing has helped clear ancestral patterns, the next step in integration is to create new patterns of behavior and thought that align with the family's new energetic template. While the energetic clearing removes the blockages that were holding old patterns in place, it's up to the individual and their family to cultivate new habits, ways of thinking, and relationship dynamics that reflect the healing that has taken place.

For example, if a family has experienced a pattern of emotional distance or lack of communication passed down from previous generations, the healing process may open the door for deeper emotional connections and more supportive relationships. However, it's essential for family members to consciously foster these new dynamics by engaging in open communication, expressing their feelings, and nurturing emotional intimacy. The energy work clears the path, but the new behaviors must be practiced for the healing to take root.

On an individual level, recipients may find that after an ancestral healing session, they feel drawn to take different actions or adopt new mindsets more aligned with their true selves. For example, someone carrying the weight of ancestral trauma related to scarcity or lack may feel inspired to embrace a more abundant mindset and take steps to create financial security. To fully integrate this change, the recipient may need to shift their daily thoughts and actions to reflect this new sense of abundance, whether through positive affirmations, financial planning, or changing limiting beliefs around money (McTaggart, 2008).

The key to creating lasting change is mindfulness. By staying aware of their thoughts, behaviors, and choices, individuals can continuously reinforce the new energy patterns in their lives, ensuring that ancestral healing continues to impact them positively.

The Power of Ritual and Symbolism in Ancestral Healing

Rituals and symbolic acts are powerful tools for anchoring the energetic changes initiated through Reiki distance healing. These practices help solidify the connection to the healed ancestors and reinforce the new patterns established within the family line. By incorporating rituals into daily or seasonal practices, individuals and families can honor the healing that has taken place and invite continued growth and transformation.

One simple yet effective ritual is the creation of an ancestral altar. This altar can be where family members place pictures, mementos, or symbols representing their ancestors and objects that symbolize the healing and new patterns they wish to cultivate. Lighting candles, offering prayers, or expressing gratitude at the altar can help keep the connection to the healed ancestors alive while honoring the positive energy flowing through the family line. This practice deepens the family's connection to their roots and strengthens their commitment to living in alignment with the healing that has occurred.

Other rituals, such as seasonal ceremonies, family gatherings, or even personal meditative practices, can be incorporated to keep the family's energy aligned with the new patterns. For instance, during significant family transitions, such as births, marriages, or even holidays, families may come together to perform simple rituals of gratitude and connection, reinforcing the new energy cultivated through ancestral healing.

Symbols can also play a powerful role in anchoring the healing. Family members can visualize Reiki symbols, such as Hon Sha Ze Sho Nen or Cho Ku Rei, during healing sessions, meditation, or prayer to continue inviting healing energy into the family's energetic field. These symbols can also clear any lingering emotional residue or strengthen the bonds between family members, further integrating the healing into daily life (Petter, 2000).

Passing Down the Gift of Healing to Future Generations

As healing becomes integrated into the family line, the positive patterns that emerge have the potential to be passed down to future generations. Just as trauma and unresolved karma can be inherited, so can the gifts of healing, resilience, and love. By consciously creating an environment of emotional support, spiritual alignment, and energetic harmony, families ensure that the next generation will inherit a legacy of empowerment, strength, and connection.

Children and future generations benefit immensely from growing up in an environment that prioritizes emotional openness, healing, and spiritual growth. The energy shifts facilitated through Reiki distance healing create a foundation upon which future generations can thrive, free from the limiting patterns of the past. The healing that is done today impacts the current family and paves the way for the continued evolution of the family's spiritual lineage.

In teaching children about the importance of energy, healing, and connection to their ancestors, families can ensure that the next generation is equipped with the tools and understanding needed to continue this healing journey. This knowledge empowers them not only to break free from old patterns but also to carry forward the wisdom and strength that their ancestors have gained through the healing process.

Section Summary
Healing Across Generations and Ancestral Lines

By utilizing Reiki distance healing, practitioners can address deeply rooted patterns and blockages passed down through generations, facilitating healing for individuals and their entire family lineage. This chapter highlights the principles and practices essential for understanding and facilitating ancestral healing and how to ensure that this healing becomes a lasting legacy for future generations.

Addressing Generational Trauma and Ancestral Karma Through Distance Healing

Generational trauma and ancestral karma represent the unresolved pain, trauma, and karmic patterns passed down through families. These imprints can manifest as emotional, psychological, or physical challenges affecting descendants' lives. Reiki distance healing provides a means to access and clear these inherited energies by connecting with the recipient's family lineage and the Akashic Records. Practitioners send healing energy to moments of ancestral trauma and karmic imbalance, releasing the blockages that have been carried forward. This process frees the recipient from inherited burdens and creates healing that reverberates across the entire family line, benefiting both past and future generations.

Healing Family Lines and Its Ripple Effect on Future Generations

Reiki healing across ancestral lines creates a ripple effect that positively impacts future generations. By clearing inherited emotional patterns, trauma, and karmic lessons, Reiki distance healing helps dissolve blockages that have kept family members stuck in cycles of fear, insecurity, or struggle. This energy work restores the flow of ki throughout the family line, allowing new, positive patterns to emerge. As ancestral healing takes place, future generations can experience greater freedom, clarity, and alignment, free from the energetic burdens of the past. This healing extends beyond the individual and family, contributing to a more harmonious collective consciousness.

Integrating Ancestral Healing Into Daily Life: Lasting Change for Future Generations

For Reiki's transformative effects to create lasting change, it is crucial to integrate ancestral healing into daily life. This integration process involves anchoring the energetic shifts into the physical and emotional body through grounding techniques, meditation, and chakra balancing. By consciously creating new behavior and thought patterns, individuals and families can reinforce the positive energy cultivated during the Reiki session. Rituals, symbols, and practices such as building ancestral altars help to solidify the healing, ensuring that it becomes a lived experience. As this healing is passed down, future generations inherit a legacy of empowerment, strength, and spiritual alignment, allowing them to thrive with greater freedom and purpose.

§

Empathy, Intuition, and Psychic Abilities

The Role of Heightened Empathy and Psychic Abilities in Facilitating Distance Healing

One of the essential qualities a Reiki practitioner brings to a distance healing session is their capacity for empathy and their ability to tune into the recipient's energy field. Empathy, in this context, goes beyond the ability to feel for another person—it involves the deep sensitivity to sense and understand another person's emotions, energy patterns, and even physical sensations. Alongside empathy, developing intuitive and psychic abilities greatly enhances a practitioner's ability to facilitate effective distance healing by providing insights into the recipient's energetic condition, emotional state, and spiritual needs.

While the mechanics of Reiki healing—such as Reiki symbols, intention, and visualization—are essential, the practitioner's ability to sense energy and respond intuitively to the recipient's needs elevates the healing experience. This heightened sensitivity allows practitioners to guide the healing process with greater precision, ensuring that the recipient receives the energy where it is most needed. For those developing their practice in Reiki, distance healing, nurturing empathy, and refining intuitive and psychic abilities are integral to providing more effective, insightful, and transformative healing.

What Is Empathy in the Context of Energy Healing?

Empathy in Reiki healing is more than just the emotional resonance one feels for another. An energetic sensitivity allows the practitioner to perceive the recipient's energy field and understand its subtle shifts and patterns. Empathy will enable practitioners to tune into the frequency of the person they are working with, creating a profound connection that bridges the distance between them. In distance healing, this empathetic connection is essential because the practitioner cannot rely on physical touch or direct observation; instead, they must rely on their ability to feel the recipient's energy remotely.

Empathy also plays an important in helping practitioners to identify areas of energetic imbalance. Practitioners may sense emotional blockages, physical discomfort, or energetic stagnation as they connect with the recipient's energy. These sensations can manifest as emotional impressions, such as feeling the recipient's sadness, anxiety, or grief, or as physical sensations, such as tightness, heaviness, or warmth in certain areas of the body. By tuning into these empathetic cues, practitioners can direct Reiki energy to the areas that require healing, ensuring that the energy flows where it is most needed (Judith, 2004).

For practitioners, developing energetic empathy involves learning to differentiate between their emotions and the recipient's. This ability to discern ensures that the practitioner remains a clear conduit for the healing energy without becoming overwhelmed or burdened by the recipient's emotional or energetic state. Grounding practices, such as meditation or visualization, are essential for maintaining emotional clarity and protecting the practitioner's energy field while facilitating healing.

Intuition as a Guide in Distance Healing

Alongside empathy, intuition is one of the practitioner's most valuable tools in distance healing. Intuition is the inner knowing or gut feeling that guides practitioners in their decision-making process, helping them understand what the recipient needs during the session. In Reiki healing, intuition can offer insights not accessible through the logical mind, allowing practitioners to tap into the deeper layers of the recipient's energy field and uncover the root causes of imbalances.

During a Reiki distance healing session, intuitive insights may come from mental images, words, or symbols representing the recipient's energetic condition. For example, a practitioner may see a dark cloud around the recipient's heart chakra, indicating an emotional blockage related to grief or loss. Alternatively, they may sense a word or phrase, such as "trust" or "letting go," pointing to the emotional or spiritual lesson the recipient is working through. These intuitive messages help the practitioner tailor the healing session to the recipient's specific needs, ensuring that the energy is directed to the areas of the greatest significance (McTaggart, 2008).

Intuition also plays a critical role in helping practitioners choose the right tools during the healing session. For instance, a practitioner may feel intuitively guided to use a specific Reiki symbol, such as Hon Sha Ze Sho Nen (the distance healing symbol) or Sei He Ki (the emotional healing symbol), depending on what they sense the recipient requires. This intuitive guidance ensures that the session flows smoothly and that the recipient receives the energy to support their healing on all levels—physical, emotional, mental, and spiritual.

For Reiki practitioners, developing intuition involves learning to trust their inner voice and recognize the subtle cues that arise during a session. This process can be enhanced through meditation, visualization, and journaling, which help practitioners strengthen their connection to their intuitive faculties and better understand the information they receive during healing.

Developing Psychic Abilities for Deeper Insight

In addition to empathy and intuition, some Reiki practitioners possess or develop psychic abilities, which can further enhance the depth of their healing work. In the context of Reiki, psychic abilities refer to the practitioner's ability to perceive energy and information beyond the ordinary physical senses. These abilities may include clairvoyance(clear seeing), clairaudience (clear hearing), clairsentience (clear feeling), or claircognizance (clear knowing). While not every Reiki practitioner develops psychic abilities to the same degree, those who do find these skills can provide profound insights into the recipient's energetic and spiritual state.

For example, a practitioner with clairvoyant abilities may be able to see images of the recipient's energy field, including areas of blockage or imbalance. They may perceive colors, shapes, or symbols that offer insights into the recipient's emotional state or spiritual journey. Practitioners with clairsentient abilities may feel sensations in their own body corresponding to the recipient's physical or emotional condition, allowing them to direct healing energy more precisely.

Psychic abilities can also connect with the recipient's higher self, spirit guides, or ancestors, providing guidance that supports the healing process. These spiritual connections can offer profound insights into the recipient's life purpose, karmic patterns, or past experiences influencing their current state. By tapping into these higher levels of awareness, practitioners can provide healing beyond the physical and emotional levels, addressing the deeper spiritual dimensions of the recipient's journey (Brennan, 1988).

Creating a safe and supportive environment for psychic development is important for Reiki practitioners looking to develop their abilities. Practices such as meditation, psychic development exercises, and working with mentors who have experience in this area can help practitioners cultivate their abilities in a grounded and responsible way. Psychic development is an ongoing journey, and practitioners should approach it with patience, humility, and a commitment to using their abilities for the highest good.

Strengthening Intuitive Connections for More Precise Healing

Developing and honing intuitive abilities is essential for Reiki practitioners, especially those engaged in distance healing, where the lack of physical proximity makes it critical to rely on energetic perceptions. While intuition is an inherent ability within every person, it can be strengthened and refined through intentional practices and a conscious commitment to deepening the connection with one's inner guidance. As practitioners learn to trust their intuitive insights, they are better equipped to offer healing aligned with the recipient's highest good, addressing not only their physical and emotional needs but also the spiritual and energetic dimensions of their being.

Connecting intuitively allows practitioners to sense subtle energies, uncover hidden patterns, and gain insight into the root causes of the recipient's imbalances. This makes the healing process more precise and effective, as the practitioner is guided by an internal knowing that transcends rational thought or observation. By cultivating this intuitive awareness, practitioners become more attuned to the flow of energy within the recipient's field, making them capable of facilitating deep and transformative healing experiences.

Techniques to Strengthen Intuition for Distance Healing

Meditation and Quieting the Mind

Meditation is a powerful tool for developing intuition. Regular meditation helps to quiet the mind, allowing the practitioner to listen to their inner voice without interference from mental chatter or distractions. A calm and focused mind is essential for intuitive work, as it enables practitioners to be fully present during the healing session and more receptive to the subtle energetic signals coming from the recipient.

Meditation practices focusing on breath awareness, visualization, or mantras can help Reiki practitioners cultivate a deep inner stillness. During distance healing sessions, a meditative state allows practitioners to enter a space of expanded awareness to receive intuitive insights about the recipient's energy field. By consistently practicing meditation, practitioners build a strong foundation for intuitive work, making it easier to access intuitive information when needed most (McTaggart, 2008).

Journaling and Dream Work

Another technique for strengthening intuition is journaling and engaging with dream work. Writing down intuitive impressions, feelings, or images that arise during or after a healing session can help practitioners make sense of the information they receive. Journaling provides a space to reflect on intuitive insights and patterns, assisting practitioners to become more attuned to their inner guidance.

Dreamwork is another powerful way to develop intuition. Dreams often carry symbolic messages from the subconscious mind and can provide practitioners with insights into their healing work or the needs of their clients. By keeping a dream journal and paying attention to the themes or symbols in dreams, practitioners can develop a deeper connection to their intuitive faculties and receive valuable guidance for their healing practice (Judith, 2004).

Working with Reiki Symbols and Visualization

Reiki symbols are powerful tools for amplifying intuitive abilities, especially with visualization techniques. Symbols such as Cho Ku Rei (the power symbol) and Sei He Ki (the emotional healing symbol) can help practitioners focus their energy and enhance their ability to perceive the recipient's energy field. Visualization exercises, in which practitioners imagine the symbols being drawn or activated over the recipient's energy centers, can open intuitive channels and help guide the flow of healing energy.

When working with these symbols, practitioners can focus on opening their third eye chakra, the energy center responsible for intuition and inner vision. By visualizing the third eye chakra becoming clear and radiant, practitioners enhance their ability to receive intuitive messages and visual impressions during healing sessions. This practice strengthens the connection between the practitioner's intuition and the recipient's energy, allowing for more precise and effective healing (Petter, 2000).

Practicing with Feedback and Validation

One of the most effective ways to refine intuitive skills is by practicing with client feedback. During distance healing sessions, practitioners may receive intuitive impressions about the recipient's energy field, emotional state, or physical condition. Sharing these insights with the recipient and receiving feedback can help practitioners validate their intuitive experiences and build confidence in their abilities.

For example, A practitioner might sense an energetic blockage around the recipient's heart chakra and share this information with the client after the session. The recipient may confirm that they have been experiencing emotional pain or grief, validating the practitioner's intuitive perception. This process of receiving feedback and validation helps practitioners develop greater trust in their intuitive abilities, reinforcing their confidence in the accuracy of the information they receive during healing.

Trusting the Intuitive Process

Learning to trust the intuitive process can be a significant challenge for many Reiki practitioners. Intuition often presents itself in subtle ways—through fleeting images, sensations, or feelings—and practitioners may doubt the validity of these impressions, especially if they cannot immediately explain or understand them. However, intuition operates beyond the realm of the logical mind and often conveys information that becomes clearer over time.

Trusting intuition means letting go of the need for immediate answers or validation and allowing the intuitive process to unfold naturally. Practitioners must learn to honor the insights they receive, even if they initially seem vague or abstract. Over time, as practitioners deepen their connection to their intuitive faculties, they become more adept at interpreting the messages and sensations that arise during healing sessions, enabling them to offer healing tailored to the recipient's unique energetic needs (McTaggart, 2008).

Additionally, practitioners should be mindful of the ego's role in intuitive work. The ego may try to interfere by doubting or dismissing intuitive impressions, particularly if those impressions don't align with preconceived ideas or expectations. By cultivating humility and non-attachment to the outcomes of the healing session, practitioners can create space for their intuition to guide the healing process with greater clarity and authenticity.

Nurturing Empathy Through Self-Care and Boundaries

While a valuable asset in Reiki distance healing, empathy can also be emotionally taxing if not appropriately managed. Highly empathetic practitioners may find themselves absorbing the emotions or energy of their clients, leading to emotional fatigue or energetic overwhelm. To maintain balance and offer effective healing, practitioners must practice self-care and establish energetic boundaries that protect their energy field.

Engaging in regular grounding practices is critical in nurturing empathy. These practices help practitioners stay connected to their own energy and prevent them from becoming overly enmeshed in the energy of others. Grounding can be as simple as taking a few moments to focus on the breath, visualize roots extending into the earth, or engage in physical activities such as walking in nature. These practices help clear and stabilize the practitioner's energy, ensuring they remain centered and present during healing sessions.

Practitioners should create energetic boundaries before and after each healing session. This can be done by visualizing a protective shield of light around their energy field or setting a clear intention only to receive information that serves the recipient's highest good. After the session, it's important to release any energy or emotions that may have been picked up from the recipient by engaging in clearing practices, such as smudging with sage or taking a salt bath.

By nurturing their empathy and maintaining strong, energetic boundaries, Reiki practitioners can continue to offer healing with compassion, clarity, and emotional resilience.

Developing Psychic Abilities for Deeper Insight

For many Reiki practitioners, developing psychic abilities is a natural progression that enhances their capacity to offer profound distance healing. Psychic abilities allow practitioners to perceive energy and information beyond the ordinary senses, offering more profound insights into the recipient's physical, emotional, mental, and spiritual state. These abilities may include clairvoyance (clear seeing), clairaudience (clear hearing), clairsentience (clear feeling), or claircognizance (clear knowing). While psychic abilities vary from practitioner to practitioner, their cultivation can add a powerful dimension to the healing experience.

Developing psychic abilities in Reiki healing enables practitioners to tap into the subtle realms of energy, providing information often hidden or inaccessible through logic alone. These insights can help practitioners understand the root causes of a recipient's energetic imbalances, making the healing process more targeted and effective. Psychic abilities also allow practitioners to connect with higher spiritual realms, including the recipient's higher self, spirit guides, or ancestors, who can offer additional guidance and support during the healing session.

Types of Psychic Abilities in Reiki Healing

Clairvoyance (Clear Seeing)

Clairvoyance refers to the ability to see energy, images, symbols, or visions that provide information about the recipient's energy field. Practitioners with clairvoyant abilities may see the recipient's chakras or auric field in the form of colors, shapes, or energetic patterns. These visual cues can reveal blockages, areas of stagnation, or energetic imbalances that need to be addressed during the healing session.

For instance, a practitioner may see a dark or cloudy area around the recipient's heart chakra, indicating an emotional blockage related to grief or sadness. By recognizing this visual information, the practitioner can focus healing energy on the heart chakra, using Reiki symbols such as Sei He Ki (the emotional healing symbol) to clear and balance the energy. Clairvoyance can also reveal deeper spiritual insights, such as past life experiences or karmic patterns influencing the recipient's current state (Brennan, 1988).

Clairaudience (Clear Hearing)

Clairaudience is the ability to hear messages, words, sounds, or guidance from the subtle realms. Practitioners with clairaudient abilities may receive messages from the recipient's higher self, spirit guides, or other spiritual entities supporting the healing process. These messages can provide valuable insights into the recipient's spiritual journey and offer guidance on resolving energetic imbalances or emotional issues.

For example, during a distance healing session, a practitioner may hear the word "release" or "trust," indicating that the recipient needs to let go of something they've been holding onto or develop greater trust in the healing process. These auditory cues can help guide the practitioner's actions during the session, ensuring that the healing is aligned with the recipient's highest good. Clairaudience can also receive specific instructions about which Reiki symbols or techniques to use, making the healing process more focused and intentional (Petter, 2000).

Clairsentience (Clear Feeling)

Clairsentience involves feeling or sensing the recipient's energy or emotions within the practitioner's body. Practitioners with clairsentient abilities may experience physical sensations, such as warmth, pressure, or tingling, in areas of their body that correspond to the recipient's imbalances. They may also feel emotional sensations, such as sadness, joy, or anxiety, that provide insights into the recipient's emotional state.

Clairsentience allows practitioners to develop a deep, empathetic connection with the recipient, sensing the energy shifts in real time. For example, if the recipient holds unresolved grief in their solar plexus chakra, the practitioner may feel a tightness or heaviness in that area. This information helps the practitioner direct Reiki energy to the area that needs healing, ensuring that the session addresses the root cause of the imbalance.

Clairsentience is particularly useful in distance healing because it allows the practitioner to experience the recipient's energy field even when they are not physically present. This heightened sensitivity to energy enables the practitioner to offer more precise and intuitive healing, responding to the recipient's needs in a compassionate and attuned way (McTaggart, 2008).

Claircognizance (Clear Knowing)

Claircognizance is receiving knowledge or insights without external cues or explanations. Practitioners with claircognizant abilities often experience sudden flashes of insight or a deep inner knowing about the recipient's energy field, spiritual journey, or emotional state. This knowing may come in the form of a thought, idea, or inner conviction that guides the practitioner's actions during the healing session.

For example, a practitioner may suddenly know that the recipient's energetic imbalance is related to a past life trauma or a karmic pattern, even if they haven't received any visual or auditory confirmation. This clear knowing helps the practitioner focus the healing energy on the areas that need the most attention, allowing them to work efficiently and effectively. Claircognizance is often described as an instinctual or intuitive sense that transcends logic, guiding the practitioner toward the most appropriate course of action (Judith, 2004).

Cultivating Psychic Abilities for Distance Healing

While some Reiki practitioners naturally possess psychic abilities, others may need to cultivate these gifts through practice and intention over time. Developing psychic abilities requires patience, self-awareness, and a commitment to deepening one's connection with the subtle energy realms. Here are a few techniques to help practitioners cultivate and strengthen their psychic abilities for distance healing:

Meditation and Chakra Work

Meditation is a powerful tool for opening and activating the third eye chakra

(Ajna), which is responsible for intuition, psychic vision, and spiritual insight. By meditating on the third eye chakra and visualizing it as a radiant, clear energy center, practitioners can enhance their ability to perceive subtle energies and receive psychic impressions. Working with the crown chakra (Sahasrara) can also help practitioners connect with higher spiritual realms, allowing them to receive guidance from spirit guides, ancestors, or the recipient's higher self (Judith, 2004).

Psychic Development Exercises

Psychic development exercises can help practitioners strengthen their clairvoyant, clairaudient, clairsentient, or claircognizant abilities. These exercises may include visualization techniques, such as imagining energy fields or symbols and listening practices that help practitioners tune into subtle sounds or messages from the spiritual realm. Practicing these exercises helps practitioners become more attuned to the information they receive during distance healing sessions.

Working with Mentors or Guides

Many practitioners benefit from working with experienced mentors or guides who can help them develop their psychic abilities in a safe and supportive environment. Mentors can offer guidance, feedback, and techniques for refining psychic abilities, assisting practitioners to build confidence in their intuitive and psychic gifts. Spiritual guides, such as spirit guides or ancestors, can also provide support during healing sessions, offering insights that assist the practitioner in their work.

Trusting the Process

The development of psychic abilities requires practitioners to trust their inner guidance and allow the information they receive to flow naturally. Practitioners must release doubt and surrender control during the healing session, allowing psychic impressions to come through without judgment or over-analysis. By trusting the process, practitioners create a space for psychic information to emerge clearly and authentically, making the healing experience more powerful and effective (McTaggart, 2008).

Combining Psychic Abilities with Empathy and Intuition

When empathy, intuition, and psychic abilities are combined, they create a powerful foundation for Reiki distance healing. Practitioners who can tune into the recipient's energy field with empathy, trust their intuitive guidance, and receive psychic impressions from the subtle realms can offer healing that is deeply aligned with the recipient's needs. These abilities create a holistic and multidimensional healing experience, addressing the recipient's physical, emotional, mental, and spiritual well-being.

As practitioners continue to develop these gifts, they become more effective conduits for Reiki energy, offering transformative and insightful healing sessions. The combination of empathy, intuition, and psychic abilities allows practitioners to access the deeper layers of the recipient's energy field, providing healing beyond the surface and touching the core of the recipient's soul.

Section Summary
Empathy, Intuition, and Psychic Abilities

Practitioners can develop heightened sensitivity to energy, refine their intuitive faculties, and cultivate psychic skills like clairvoyance, clairsentience, and clairaudience to deepen their connection with the recipient's energy field. By integrating these abilities into their practice, Reiki healers can offer more precise and transformative healing that addresses the recipient's physical, emotional, and spiritual needs.

Heightened Empathy and Intuitive Abilities in Reiki Healing

Empathy and intuition are central to a Reiki practitioner's ability to connect with the recipient's energy during distance healing. Empathy allows practitioners to sense and understand emotional or physical imbalances, while intuition guides them in determining the most effective areas to focus the healing energy. Reiki practitioners develop these abilities by quieting the mind, trusting their inner guidance, and practicing mindfulness. By honing their empathetic and intuitive capacities, practitioners can sense the subtle shifts in energy, allowing for more precise and effective healing.

Strengthening Intuitive Connections for More Precise Healing

This section outlines specific techniques for developing and strengthening intuition, which is crucial for offering effective distance healing. Techniques such as meditation, journaling, and working with Reiki symbols help practitioners enhance their connection to their intuitive faculties. Meditation quiets the mind, making it easier for practitioners to access subtle energy, while journaling and dream work offer insights that deepen the practitioner's understanding of their intuitive impressions. Strengthening intuition helps practitioners tailor healing sessions to the recipient's unique needs, offering more personalized and impactful healing.

Developing Psychic Abilities for Deeper Insight

Psychic abilities, such as clairvoyance (clear seeing), clairaudience (clear hearing), and clairsentience (clear feeling), provide practitioners with the ability to perceive energy and information beyond the physical senses. Developing these abilities allows Reiki healers to offer profound insights into the recipient's energetic imbalances, uncover the root causes of issues, and connect with higher spiritual realms for guidance. Techniques like meditation, chakra work, and psychic development exercises help practitioners cultivate these gifts, deepening their capacity for distance healing and allowing them to access deeper layers of the recipient's energy field.

Reiki practitioners can offer a multidimensional healing experience beyond surface-level symptoms and address the recipient's physical, emotional, and spiritual well-being by integrating heightened empathy, intuition, and psychic abilities.

§

Using Sound and Vibrational Healing in Distance Reiki

Introduction to Using Sound (Solfeggio Frequencies, Mantras) to Amplify Healing Intentions at a Distance

As we explore how Reiki can be enhanced, sound emerges as a powerful, often under appreciated tool for amplifying healing energy. Sound is more than a sensation we hear—it is a vibration that moves through the universe, resonating with every aspect of our existence. Whether it is the soothing hum of a mantra or the ancient tones of Solfeggio frequencies, sound can affect our physical, emotional, and spiritual bodies. This influence becomes incredibly profound when combined with Reiki distance healing, where sound vibrations can act as carriers of intention, deepening the connection between practitioner and recipient, even across vast distances.

To better understand how sound and vibrational healing work, imagine a pebble dropped into a still pond. The ripple effect created on the water's surface is a visual metaphor for how sound waves travel, interacting with everything in their path. These sound waves create similar ripples in our energetic field when we chant a mantra or play a Solfeggio frequency. These ripples can help to clear stagnant energy, harmonize imbalances, and attune the body to its natural frequency. And just like water ripples, sound can travel beyond immediate physical space, reaching and influencing the recipient's energy field, no matter the distance.

In this section, we will explore how Reiki distance healing can be amplified using the vibrational power of sound. Whether you are new to Reiki or have practiced for years, integrating sound into your healing sessions can unlock deeper layers of transformation. We'll look at the history of Solfeggio frequencies—an ancient system of sound healing—and the use of mantras as tools for focusing and amplifying your healing intentions. As you will discover, sound has a unique relationship with the energetic body. When used with purpose and mindfulness, it becomes a bridge between the seen and unseen realms, enhancing the potency of distance Reiki.

The Power of Sound in Healing: More Than Just a Vibration

From ancient cultures to modern science, sound has long been recognized for its healing properties. Ancient civilizations used chanting, drumming, and singing bowls to restore balance in the body, believing that certain tones could harmonize the soul with the cosmos. Today, we understand that sound is a form of energy that can be measured in frequencies—specific vibrations that resonate with particular parts of the body.

For example, each tone corresponds to different healing qualities in Solfeggio frequencies. The frequency of 396 Hz, for instance, is known to help release guilt and fear, while 528 Hz is often referred to as the "miracle tone," believed to promote DNA repair and transformation. These frequencies work by resonating with the body's natural energy centers or chakras, helping to realign them and restore balance. When used in distance Reiki healing, these frequencies extend the practitioner's intention, providing another layer of vibrational energy that supports the healing process (Horowitz, 2012).

Imagine this process as tuning a musical instrument. When an instrument is out of tune, it creates dissonance. But with the right note or vibration, you can retune the instrument to its harmonious state. Similarly, the human body, too, responds to vibrations. Specific frequencies can "retune" our energy centers when physically or emotionally out of balance, aligning us with our natural, healthy state.

Sound in Reiki healing doesn't stop at frequencies but extends to mantras. These sacred sounds or phrases, often repeated, hold immense spiritual power. The repetition of a mantra creates a vibrational resonance that shifts the energy field of both the practitioner and recipient. When combined with Reiki, mantras act as vehicles for healing energy, helping to sharpen focus and direct intention and enhance the flow of ki (life force energy).

Sound as a Bridge Between Energy Fields

Reiki distance healing connects the recipient's energy field across space and time. Sound's intrinsic ability to travel through air and beyond physical barriers can help bridge this gap. Sound's vibrational nature resonates at the quantum level, meaning it interacts with the energetic field in ways that transcend the physical distance between the practitioner and recipient. Think of sound as a radio wave, capable of traveling vast distances and delivering information instantly and precisely.

You create a vibrational resonance that amplifies energy flow by incorporating sound into your distance healing sessions—whether through chanting, playing Solfeggio frequencies, or even silently repeating a mantra. Just as quantum entanglement allows particles to remain connected across space, sound is a vibrational connection that enhances the healing process, no matter how far apart the practitioner and recipient are.

A practical example can be seen in using the 528 Hz frequency, often called the "miracle tone." In one case, a Reiki practitioner used this frequency during a distance healing session for a recipient struggling with emotional trauma. The practitioner played the tone softly in the background while sending Reiki energy. Over time, the recipient reported a deep sense of peace and emotional release, which they attributed to the calming and transformative effects of the healing session. The combination of sound and Reiki amplified the healing process, allowing the recipient to move through their emotional blockages with greater ease and grace.

Integrating Sound Into Your Distance Reiki Practice

Adding sound to your Reiki practice doesn't require complex equipment or specialized training. Simple tools like a singing bowl, tuning fork, or recorded frequencies can easily be incorporated into your healing space. As you begin a distance healing session, set the tone—literally—by playing a Solfeggio frequency that aligns with the recipient's needs or chanting a mantra that amplifies your intention.

For example, if your recipient is dealing with feelings of anxiety or fear, you might use 396 Hz, known for its grounding and fear-releasing qualities. If you focus on heart-centered healing, the 528 Hz frequency or the mantra Om Mani Padme Hum (which resonates with the heart chakra) can help direct your energy more precisely. You create a symphony of healing energy by attuning yourself to these vibrations, harmonizing your intentions with the recipient's needs.

Whether through Solfeggio frequencies, mantras, or other forms of sound, these vibrational tools become a bridge of connection between you and the recipient, amplifying the flow of Reiki energy across distance and deepening the healing experience.

The Relationship Between Sound Frequencies and the Energetic Body

When we think about healing, focusing on the physical body is easy. But in energy healing practices like Reiki, we know that the energetic body—which includes the chakras, auras, and subtle energy fields—plays an equally important role in maintaining health and well-being. Our energetic body is constantly in motion, vibrating at frequencies that reflect our mental, emotional, and spiritual state. Sound, with its ability to generate vibrations that penetrate deeply into the human system, directly and profoundly affects these energetic fields.

Just as a musical note can create harmony or discord, so can the vibrations within our energy field be in tune or out of balance. This is where sound healing becomes a valuable tool for Reiki practitioners. By introducing specific sound frequencies, we can restore the natural vibrational state of the energetic body, much like tuning an instrument. Combined with Reiki, sound enhances the practitioner's ability to retune the recipient's energy, bringing harmony to areas that may be blocked or imbalanced.

We must first explore how different frequencies interact with the chakras to understand the relationship between sound frequencies and the energetic body. These seven primary energy centers govern various aspects of our physical, emotional, and spiritual health. Each chakra has its vibrational frequency, and sound healing aligns these frequencies, helping to clear blockages and restore balance to the system.

Chakras and Their Corresponding Sound Frequencies

The body's seven main chakras are often depicted as spinning wheels of energy, each vibrating at its frequency. When these chakras are aligned and functioning correctly, they support overall well-being. However, when a chakra becomes blocked or out of balance, it can lead to physical, emotional, or spiritual distress. Sound frequencies are one of the most effective ways to restore balance to the chakras, as they resonate with the body's natural energy systems.

Let's explore how specific sound frequencies correlate with each of the chakras:

Root Chakra (Muladhara)

The Root Chakra is located at the base of the spine and is associated with grounding, security, and survival instincts. When this chakra is balanced, we feel safe, secure, and connected to the earth. The 396 Hz frequency is particularly effective for the Root Chakra, as it helps to release fear and anxiety, bringing the recipient into a state of groundedness and calm.

Sacral Chakra (Svadhisthana)

Located just below the navel, the Sacral Chakra governs creativity, passion, and emotional expression. When blocked, it can lead to issues with emotional imbalance or creative blocks. The 417 Hz frequency clears stagnant energy from this chakra, helping to spark creativity and restore emotional flow.

Solar Plexus Chakra (Manipura)

The Solar Plexus Chakra is associated with personal power, confidence, and willpower. An imbalance in this chakra can manifest as self-doubt or a lack of direction. The 528 Hz frequency, often called the "miracle tone," is ideal for the Solar Plexus Chakra, promoting self-confidence, inner strength, and transformation.

Heart Chakra (Anahata)

The Heart Chakra is at the center of our emotional body, representing love, compassion, and forgiveness. When this chakra is blocked, it can lead to feelings of isolation, grief, or emotional pain. The 639 Hz frequency helps to heal relationships, open the heart, and invite love and harmony into the recipient's life.

Throat Chakra (Vishuddha)

The Throat Chakra is the center of communication and self-expression. Blockages in this chakra can result in difficulty expressing thoughts or emotions. The 741 Hz frequency effectively clears this energy center, helping to enhance clarity in communication and the ability to speak one's truth.

Third Eye Chakra (Ajna)

The Third Eye Chakra governs intuition, inner vision, and spiritual insight. When blocked, it can lead to confusion, lack of clarity, or difficulty trusting one's intuition. The 852 Hz frequency helps to activate and clear this chakra, strengthening intuitive abilities and enhancing spiritual awareness.

Crown Chakra (Sahasrara)

Located at the top of the head, the Crown Chakra represents our connection to the divine, the universe, and higher consciousness. A balanced Crown Chakra allows for a sense of spiritual connection and enlightenment. The 963 Hz frequency activates the Crown Chakra, opening pathways to deeper spiritual insights and divine connection (Judith, 2004).

How Sound Frequencies Influence the Energy Body in Distance Healing

In distance healing, sound frequencies become a bridge between the practitioner and recipient, facilitating healing at the energetic level even when they are physically apart. Since sound waves move through energy, not just matter, they can penetrate the subtle energy bodies surrounding the physical form, such as the etheric, emotional, and mental layers.

For example, when a practitioner plays the 639 Hz frequency to heal the Heart Chakra, the sound waves create a vibrational resonance that travels through the energy body, helping to dissolve emotional blockages related to grief or heartache. As the sound frequency interacts with the recipient's auric field, it assists in clearing away stagnant emotional energy, allowing the flow of life force energy, or ki, to return to its natural state of balance.

Sound can also harmonize the auric field, which acts as a protective energetic layer around the body. Over time, stress, emotional trauma, and negative thought patterns can create disruptions in the auric field, leading to imbalances that affect the physical and emotional body. Practitioners can smooth out these disruptions by introducing specific sound frequencies during a distance healing session, restoring harmony to the auric field and enhancing the recipient's overall well-being.

Sound frequencies are particularly effective when used with Reiki symbols, such as Hon Sha Ze Sho Nen(the distance symbol) or Sei He Ki (the emotional healing symbol). The Reiki symbols act as energy keys, opening pathways for the healing energy to flow, while the sound frequencies create a vibrational foundation that supports and amplifies the healing process. Together, they create a powerful synergy that enhances the effectiveness of the distance healing session (Petter, 2000).

Practical Applications: Using Sound in Distance Reiki Sessions

Incorporating sound into distance Reiki healing is both simple and transformative. You can start by selecting a Solfeggio frequency or mantra that resonates with the recipient's current needs. Before beginning the session, spend a few moments setting your intention for the healing. As you play the frequency or chant the mantra, visualize the sound waves extending from your space to the recipient's energy field, carrying healing energy across the distance.

For example, if the recipient is dealing with self-doubt, you may play the 528 Hz frequency while focusing on sending Reiki energy to their Solar Plexus Chakra. As the session progresses, allow the sound frequency to guide the flow of Reiki energy, trusting that it enhances the healing at both the energetic and emotional levels.

Another approach is to use a singing bowl or tuning fork during the session. As you generate the sound, imagine the vibrations traveling through space and time, aligning with the recipient's energy centers and helping to clear any blockages. You can also use sound to bring yourself into a deeper state of focus and meditation, ensuring you remain fully present throughout the healing session.

By integrating sound frequencies into your distance Reiki practice, you create a multi sensory healing experience that addresses the recipient's needs on multiple levels—physical, emotional, mental, and spiritual. Sound amplifies the flow of Reiki energy, making the healing process more holistic, powerful, and transformative.

In the next chapter, we will explore the final steps toward mastering distance healing, offering practical techniques to develop and grow your Reiki practice and real-world examples of how sound and Reiki can create profound shifts in recipients' lives.

Section Summary
Using Sound and Vibrational Healing in Distance Reiki

Sound, as a vibrational tool, can amplify healing intentions, deepen connections between the practitioner and recipient, and restore harmony within the energetic body. Incorporating specific frequencies and mantras can significantly elevate the distance healing process, making it more effective, precise, and transformative.

Introduction to Using Sound (Solfeggio Frequencies, Mantras) to Amplify Healing Intentions at a Distance

Sound is an effective tool for amplifying Reiki energy during distance healing sessions. Solfeggio frequencies—specific sound vibrations with healing properties—and mantras act as carriers of intention, resonating with the recipient's energy field to clear blockages and restore balance. The section explains how these frequencies work similarly to instrument tuning, aligning the body's natural energy centers. It emphasizes that integrating sound, whether through playing specific frequencies or chanting mantras, can significantly enhance the flow of Reiki energy across distances, providing a more profound healing experience.

The Relationship Between Sound Frequencies and the Energetic Body

This section explores how sound frequencies directly interact with the energetic body, including the chakras and auras. Each chakra corresponds to a specific Solfeggio frequency that resonates with it, helping to clear blockages and restore harmony. For example, the 396 Hz frequency targets the Root Chakra, while the 528 Hz frequency, known as the "miracle tone," aligns with the Solar Plexus Chakra. Sound frequencies penetrate the recipient's energy body during Reiki distance healing, facilitating a deeper connection and enhancing the flow of healing energy. Sound is a powerful ally in achieving holistic balance and transformation by working in tandem with Reiki symbols.

§

Knowledge Review
Chapter Six

Real-World Applications of Distance Healing

1. What is generational trauma, and how can it manifest in a person's life?

2. How does Reiki distance healing address ancestral karma?

3. Which chakra plays a key role in ancestral healing, and why?

4. What is the significance of healing across time and generations in the context of Reiki distance healing?

5. How does Reiki distance healing create a ripple effect across generations?

6. What types of inherited emotional patterns can be dissolved through Reiki?

7. How does Reiki help restore energy flow in family lines, and why is this important?

8. What is the benefit of anchoring positive energy for future generations through Reiki?

9. Why is integrating ancestral healing into daily life after a Reiki session important?

10. How can individuals anchor the energetic shifts from Reiki healing into their physical and emotional bodies?

11. What role do rituals and symbols play in ancestral healing?

12. How can families create new behavior and thought patterns to align with ancestral healing?

13. How can the gifts of healing be passed down to future generations?

14. What is the difference between emotional empathy and energetic empathy in the context of Reiki distance healing?

15. How can intuition guide a Reiki practitioner in a distance healing session?

16. What are psychic abilities, and how do they contribute to Reiki distance healing?

17. Why is it important for Reiki practitioners to develop grounding practices alongside their empathy and psychic abilities?

18. Why is intuition important in Reiki distance healing, and how does it benefit the healing process?

19. How does meditation help strengthen a practitioner's intuitive abilities during distance healing sessions?

20. What role does feedback play in developing a Reiki practitioner's intuition?

21. What self-care practices can help Reiki practitioners maintain balance and avoid emotional fatigue?

22. How does clairvoyance benefit Reiki distance healing sessions, and what type of information can a practitioner receive through clairvoyant abilities?

23. What is clairsentience, and how can it enhance a practitioner's ability to connect with the recipient during a distance healing session?

24. What are some effective techniques for cultivating psychic abilities for Reiki distance healing?

25. Why is trusting the process important when developing psychic abilities, and how can practitioners overcome doubt during healing sessions?

26. How does sound enhance Reiki distance healing, and what role does it play in bridging the energy between the practitioner and the recipient?

27. What is the significance of Solfeggio frequencies in sound healing, and how do they correspond to different healing qualities?

28. How can mantras be used in conjunction with Reiki distance healing, and how do they affect the healing process?

29. Describe a practical way to incorporate sound tools into a Reiki distance healing session.

30. What role does sound play in influencing the energetic body during a Reiki healing session?

31. How do sound frequencies work with Reiki symbols in distance healing?

32. What is the benefit of using the 528 Hz frequency in a Reiki distance healing session?

CHAPTER SEVEN

Mastering Distance Healing: A Practitioner's Guide

Developing Your Distance Healing Practice

Techniques for Mastering Distance Healing

Much like in-person Reiki, distance healing requires practice, dedication, and trust in the universal flow of energy. As you embark on the journey to master distance Reiki, you may find that the key to deepening your practice lies in refining your skills, strengthening your connection with the recipient, and developing a profound confidence in your ability to work with energy across space and time. Whether you are just beginning to offer distance healing or looking to elevate your practice to new heights, this chapter will guide you through the essential techniques for mastering distance Reiki.

While Reiki distance healing can feel abstract to those new to the practice, it operates on the same principles that govern all energy work: intention, focus, and the flow of universal life force energy. The only difference is that distance healing transcends the limitations of physical proximity, allowing practitioners to send Reiki energy to recipients regardless of where they are in the world. Think of it as tuning into a radio frequency: when the practitioner's intention and focus are clear, the energy is sent and received, much like a song played across airwaves that can be heard miles away.

In this section, we'll explore specific techniques that will help you hone your ability to send Reiki energy at a distance, build a stronger connection with the recipient, and overcome any challenges that may arise as you refine your practice.

Setting the Stage: Preparing for a Distance Healing Session

Just like an in-person Reiki session, the success of distance healing relies heavily on the practitioner's ability to create a sacred, focused environment. Before beginning any distance healing, it is essential to take a few moments to prepare yourself and your space. This preparation helps center your energy and ensures that you are fully present and grounded for the work ahead.

Grounding Yourself

Grounding is an essential first step in any Reiki practice, particularly in distance healing, where the absence of physical touch can sometimes make it more challenging to stay connected. Before you begin, take a few minutes to ground yourself by engaging in a simple meditation or breathing exercise. Imagine roots growing from the base of your spine deep into the earth, anchoring you in place and providing stability. This grounding process helps to ensure that your energy is balanced and that you can maintain a strong, clear channel for the Reiki energy to flow through.

Setting Intentions

Intentions are the cornerstone of all distance healing work. They act as the energetic compass, guiding the flow of Reiki energy to where it is needed most. Before beginning a session, setting clear, focused intentions for the healing is essential. This can be done through a simple prayer, affirmation, or visualization. For example, you might set the intention to "bring balance and harmony to the recipient's energy field" or "release any blockages that are preventing the flow of love and light."

In addition to setting your own intentions, connecting with the recipient beforehand is helpful to understand their specific needs or concerns. This can be done via email, phone, or video call, allowing you to tailor your healing session to their unique circumstances. Once you've gathered this information, use it to refine your intention, focusing on the areas where the recipient needs the most support (McTaggart, 2008).

Creating a Sacred Space

Even though the recipient is not physically present, the space in which you conduct the healing is just as important. Set up a sacred, peaceful environment where you won't be disturbed. Light a candle, burn some sage or incense, and play soft music if it helps you focus. Arrange any tools you need, such as crystals, Reiki symbols, or sound instruments, and ensure you are comfortable. By creating a sacred space, you help elevate the vibration of the session, making it easier to connect with the recipient's energy and maintain your focus throughout the healing.

Connecting with the Recipient's Energy Field

The most magical aspect of distance Reiki is its ability to bridge the gap between the practitioner and the recipient, no matter how far apart they may be. But how exactly does one connect with another's energy field when they're not physically present? The answer lies in the combination of intention, visualization, and trust.

Visualizing the Recipient

Once you've grounded yourself and set your intentions, it's time to connect with the recipient's energy. Visualization is a powerful tool that helps you create a clear, energetic link with the recipient. Begin by closing your eyes and imagining the recipient in your mind's eye. You don't need a perfect mental image; hold a clear intention of their presence. Imagine them sitting or lying down, relaxed and open to receiving the healing energy.

As you visualize the recipient, you can imagine them surrounded by light, perhaps in a protective bubble or a circle of healing energy. This visualization creates a robust, energetic link, allowing you to access their energy field from a distance. Trust that this connection has been established and that the recipient is ready to receive the healing energy you will send.

Using Reiki Symbols to Strengthen the Connection

One of the most effective ways to strengthen the connection between you and the recipient is by using Reiki symbols, particularly the Hon Sha Ze Sho Nen symbol. This powerful symbol, often referred to as the "distance healing symbol," is a key that unlocks the door to the recipient's energy field, regardless of the physical distance between you.

To use this symbol, begin by visualizing or drawing Hon Sha Ze Sho Nen in the air or the palm of your hand. As you focus on the symbol, silently repeat its name three times, feeling the connection between you and the recipient grow stronger with each repetition. Imagine the symbol creating a light bridge between you and the recipient, allowing Reiki energy to flow freely across the distance. This simple practice can help you establish a powerful, energetic link, ensuring that the healing energy reaches the recipient with precision and clarity (Petter, 2000).

Trusting the Process

An essential skill a Reiki practitioner can develop is the ability to trust the process. Distance healing may feel less tangible than in-person sessions, but the principles guiding energy flow remain the same. Once you've set your intention and connected with the recipient's energy field, trust that the energy will flow precisely where needed, even if you can't physically witness the effects. The energy will be received per the recipient's highest good, whether immediately or over time.

It's natural to wonder whether the recipient is truly feeling the effects of the healing, especially when working across great distances. However, the key to mastering distance Reiki lies in surrendering control and trusting in the universal energy flow. Know that the energy you send is guided by the recipient's needs and the wisdom of the universe, and trust that the healing will unfold in perfect harmony.

Building Focus and Maintaining Presence During Distance Healing

Maintaining focus is crucial during distance healing sessions, as the lack of physical proximity can make it easier for distractions or doubt to creep in. Here are some tips for maintaining focus and presence throughout the session:

Stay Grounded: Periodically check in with yourself throughout the session to ensure that you remain grounded. If you feel your mind wandering, take a few deep breaths and visualize yourself reconnecting with the earth.

Use Anchors: Keep an anchor, such as a crystal or Reiki symbol, in your hand as you work. This physical object can remind you to stay focused on the healing process and maintain your connection with the recipient.

Set a Timer: To prevent distractions, set a timer for the duration of the session. This allows you to immerse yourself fully in the healing without the need to check the clock.

By practicing these techniques, you can strengthen your ability to send Reiki energy at a distance, deepen your connection with the recipient, and ensure that the healing flows smoothly and effectively.

Building Rapport and Energetic Connections with Distant Clients

When conducting distance Reiki, one of the most critical factors in creating a successful session is building rapport and connection with your client. Even though the practitioner and recipient may not be in the same physical space, a meaningful and energetic bond is essential to the effectiveness of the healing. Establishing trust, open communication, and emotional connection ensures that the practitioner and recipient feel attuned to each other, making it easier for the healing energy to flow smoothly and effectively across distance.

While in-person sessions allow for immediate verbal and nonverbal feedback, distance healing requires additional attention to how you connect with your client before, during, and after the session. This section will explore specific techniques for building rapport, maintaining an energetic connection, and fostering an ongoing relationship with distant clients to ensure your sessions are healing and transformative.

The Importance of Communication Before and After the Session

Effective communication is the foundation for building rapport with your distant clients. Before the session, it's essential to establish clear and open lines of communication so that both you and the recipient feel aligned and connected. While this may seem straightforward, connecting with the client before the healing session begins sets the stage for deeper trust and allows you to tailor the healing process to their unique needs.

Pre-Session Communication

Before starting a distance Reiki session, take a moment to check in with the recipient. Whether through email, phone, or video call, invite the recipient to share their current state of mind, body, and spirit. Ask them about any specific issues they would like addressed, such as physical pain, emotional stress, or spiritual concerns. This open dialogue helps to clarify the recipient's needs and allows you to set clear intentions for the session. Additionally, it will enable the recipient to feel seen, heard, and cared for, strengthening the energetic bond between you.

During this conversation, explain how the distance healing process works, especially if the recipient is new to Reiki. Describe the steps you'll be taking, including any symbols, mantras, or sound frequencies you might use, and emphasize that their comfort and openness are vital in receiving the full benefits of the session. Reassure the client that there is no right or wrong way to feel during the session and that their experience may be unique to their own energy needs (McTaggart, 2008).

Post-Session Follow-Up

After the session, it's equally important to follow up with the client to discuss how they felt and what insights may have emerged during the healing. This post-session communication helps to reinforce the connection and ensures that the recipient feels supported, even after the energy has been sent. Ask open-ended questions like, "How did you feel during the session?" or "Did anything come up for you that we should explore further?"

During this follow-up, you can also share any intuitive insights you received while conducting the healing. For example, if you sensed blockages in specific chakras or received visual images during the session, discussing these impressions with the client can deepen their understanding of their energy field and clarify areas that need continued healing.

Providing practical suggestions for post-session care, such as staying hydrated, journaling about the experience, or doing a grounding exercise, can help the recipient integrate the healing on a deeper level. This ongoing support fosters trust and strengthens the relationship, making future sessions more effective.

Creating a Personal Connection: Beyond the Physical

Building rapport in distance healing extends beyond verbal communication. It also involves creating an energetic connection that transcends physical limitations. Establishing a deep personal connection with the recipient enhances energy flow and allows for a more meaningful healing experience. Here are some ways to cultivate this connection:

Tuning into the Client's Energy Field

Even though your client isn't physically present, you can still tune into their energy field by setting a clear intention and focusing your mind on their presence. Once you've established communication and set the stage for the session, take a few moments to close your eyes and visualize the recipient's energy field. As you do this, imagine that you are connecting with their higher self—the pure, spiritual essence of the individual that exists beyond the physical body.

Feel into the client's energy as if they are right in front of you. Sense their emotional state, physical body, and energetic patterns. Trust that this intuitive connection will guide the flow of Reiki energy. The more deeply you attune to the recipient's energy, the stronger the healing session. Use your breath to stay connected and focused, allowing the Reiki energy to flow naturally between you and the client.

Using Reiki Symbols to Strengthen the Connection

As discussed in the previous section, Reiki symbols are vital in strengthening the energetic link between you and your distant client. The Hon Sha Ze Sho Nen symbol, in particular, acts as a bridge between the practitioner and recipient, connecting you across space and time. By visualizing or drawing this symbol, you create a direct line of energy between yourself and the client, ensuring that the Reiki energy is transmitted clearly and effectively.

In addition to using the distance symbol, you might incorporate Sei He Ki (the emotional healing symbol) or Cho Ku Rei (the power symbol) to help clear emotional blockages or amplify the energy flow. As you send Reiki energy, visualize the symbols lighting up and expanding, creating a bright, healing connection that envelops you and the recipient in protective light.

Setting Sacred Space for Distance Healing

While the recipient may be far away, creating a sacred space on your end can help foster a more profound sense of connection and presence. Set up your healing space with intention, lighting candles, burning incense, or using crystals that resonate with the client's needs. As you prepare for the session, infuse the space with loving energy and set the intention that it will be a conduit for healing.

By treating the session with the same level of care and reverence as an in-person session, you energetically communicate to the recipient that their well-being is a priority. This sacred container you create on your end of the healing session helps to ensure that the Reiki energy flows smoothly and that the recipient feels nurtured, even from afar.

Nurturing Long-Term Relationships with Clients

Distance healing offers the opportunity to build long-term, supportive relationships with clients. These ongoing relationships allow for more profound healing as the practitioner and recipient become more attuned to each other's energy fields. Here are some tips for nurturing long-term connections with distant clients:

Regular Check-Ins

One of the simplest ways to build rapport is through regular check-ins. Even if your client isn't scheduled for a session, sending a quick message to see how they are doing helps to maintain the connection. These brief moments of communication show that you care about their well-being and are invested in their healing journey.

Offering Guidance Between Sessions

Clients often benefit from ongoing support between sessions. You can offer simple tips for maintaining their energy, such as daily grounding exercises, meditation practices, or chakra balancing techniques. Providing this guidance reinforces your role as a trusted healer and encourages the recipient to stay engaged in their healing process.

Sharing Insights and Reflections

You'll notice patterns in their energy field as you work with distant clients. Sharing your insights and reflections with them can help them better understand their spiritual and energetic journey. These insights might include recurring themes, emotional patterns, or energetic blockages that arise during the sessions. Discussing these with your clients empowers them to take a more active role in their healing and personal growth (Brennan, 1988).

Building strong rapport and an energetic connection with your distant clients are essential to developing a successful distance Reiki practice. Focusing on clear communication, creating a personal connection, and offering ongoing support ensures your clients feel seen, heard, and healed, even across great distances.

Practical Steps for Growing Your Distance Healing Business

As your confidence and skill in distance Reiki deepen, you may feel drawn to expand your practice, reaching more clients and creating a sustainable, thriving business. While the essence of Reiki healing lies in the energy work itself, building a successful distance Reiki business requires attention to practical aspects such as attracting new clients, managing your schedule, and maintaining a solid professional presence. This section will explore practical strategies to grow your business, including marketing, client retention, and ethical considerations, all while staying true to the heart-centered approach that defines Reiki healing.

Distance Reiki offers the unique opportunity to connect with clients worldwide, transcending the geographical limitations of an in-person practice. Whether transitioning from in-person sessions to distance healing or establishing a new distance-based business, the following steps will help you create a strong foundation for growth while maintaining the integrity of your healing work.

Attracting New Clients: Creating a Professional Online Presence

In today's digital age, establishing a professional online presence is an effective way to attract new clients for your distance healing practice. Your website, social media profiles, and other online platforms are the primary ways potential clients will find and engage with you. When creating your online presence, focus on authenticity and clarity, showcasing your unique approach to Reiki and making it easy for clients to understand your offer.

Build a Website

Your website is the cornerstone of your business and acts as a virtual storefront where potential clients can learn about your services. Keep the design simple, professional, and inviting when building a website. Clearly outline your Reiki distance healing services, including session details, pricing, and how clients can book with you. It's also helpful to include an FAQ section to address common questions about distance healing, especially for new clients to Reiki.

Include a biography highlighting your journey as a Reiki practitioner, your training, and what inspired you to offer distance healing. Share your philosophy and approach to Reiki in a way that feels authentic to you, as this helps to establish trust with potential clients. Testimonials from current or past clients can also be added to lend credibility and offer social proof of your effectiveness.

Use Social Media

Social media platforms such as Instagram, Facebook, and LinkedIn provide excellent opportunities to reach a wider audience. Use these platforms to share insights about Reiki, the benefits of distance healing, and practical tips for maintaining energetic health. Regularly posting educational content—such as articles, videos, or infographics—positions you as an expert in your field and attracts clients who resonate with your approach.

Social media also allows for a more personal connection with your audience. Share stories about your experiences as a practitioner, offer guidance on spiritual or energetic well-being, and engage with your followers by responding to their comments and questions. The more authentic you appear, the more likely you are to attract clients who align with your energy and values.

Search Engine Optimization (SEO)

Once your website is live, ensure it is optimized for search engines. Search engine optimization (SEO) is the practice of enhancing your website content so that it appears in search engine results when potential clients search for services like "distance Reiki" or "Reiki healing for anxiety." Using relevant keywords throughout your website, such as in-service descriptions, blog posts, and page titles, will help improve your visibility and attract more organic traffic.

Additionally, consider writing blog posts on Reiki and energy healing topics. Blog posts help with SEO and provide valuable information to potential clients, establishing you as a knowledgeable and trustworthy practitioner.

Retaining Clients and Building Long-Term Relationships

While attracting new clients is important, cultivating long-term relationships with your existing clients is vital to maintaining a sustainable business. The clients who experience positive results from your distance healing sessions are more likely to return for ongoing support and refer you to others. Here are some strategies for building and retaining your client base:

Offer Follow-Up Sessions

Distance healing can often open up new layers of emotional, mental, or spiritual healing that may need continued support. After an initial session, suggest follow-up appointments to monitor the recipient's progress and work through any additional imbalances. Many clients appreciate the opportunity to receive regular healing as part of their personal growth or spiritual development.

Consider offering session packages at a discounted rate, encouraging clients to book multiple sessions in advance. For example, you might offer a package of four distance Reiki sessions at a reduced price. This provides ongoing support to the client and creates a consistent flow of appointments for your practice.

Create Personalized Healing Plans

As you become more familiar with each client's energy field and unique needs, you can create personalized healing plans catering to their concerns. For example, suppose a client is struggling with emotional trauma. In that case, you might develop a plan that includes a series of distance Reiki sessions focused on the heart chakra, complemented by suggestions for self-care practices between sessions.

By tailoring your approach to each client, you offer a highly personalized service that makes clients feel cared for and supported on their healing journey. This level of personalization builds trust and loyalty, increasing the likelihood of long-term client relationships.

Maintain Regular Communication

Regularly checking in with clients, even between sessions, helps to reinforce your connection with them. A simple email or message asking how they are feeling or whether they've noticed any shifts since their last session can go a long way in building rapport. These check-ins show that you are genuinely invested in their well-being, fostering a sense of care and support.

You can also create a monthly newsletter offering insights, tips for energetic health, and information about upcoming events or offerings. This keeps you in touch with your clients and provides them with ongoing value, even when they aren't actively booking sessions.

Ethical Considerations and Maintaining Integrity

Upholding the ethical principles central to Reiki healing is crucial. Practicing with integrity, compassion, and professionalism ensures your clients' well-being and strengthens your practice's reputation. Here are some key ethical considerations to keep in mind:

Client Confidentiality

Confidentiality is a cornerstone of trust in the healer-client relationship. Always maintain your clients' privacy by keeping their personal information, session details, and any insights gained during the session strictly confidential. If you plan to use case studies or testimonials in your marketing materials, be sure to get written consent from the client and respect their preferences for anonymity if desired.

Respecting Client Boundaries

While distance Reiki offers a profound healing experience, respecting the client's personal boundaries is essential. Always obtain consent before initiating a healing session, and never assume that a client is ready for deeper emotional or spiritual work unless they express interest. The recipient should feel empowered to guide their healing journey, and your role as a practitioner is to support them with compassion and non-judgment.

Staying Grounded and Balanced as a Practitioner

It's important to prioritize your energetic well-being. Working with multiple clients, especially on sensitive emotional or spiritual issues, can sometimes lead to energetic fatigue or overwhelm. Schedule regular self-care practices, such as meditation, grounding exercises, and personal Reiki sessions, to maintain your energetic balance.

Additionally, establish clear boundaries between work and personal life. It's easy to feel the need to be constantly available for clients, especially as your practice grows. However, taking time to rest and recharge is essential for maintaining your effectiveness as a healer.

By maintaining professionalism, integrity, and self-care, you create a sustainable practice that honors your clients' and your own well-being.

§

Conclusion

Summarizing the Journey

As we come to the end of this exploration into the transformative power of distance healing, we are reminded of the profound interconnectedness of the universe, where scientific principles, metaphysical truths, and spiritual wisdom converge. Throughout this journey, we have seen how the boundaries between science and spirituality blur, revealing a more profound reality where energy flows, unseen yet undeniable, connecting all living beings across time and space.

The practice of distance healing, grounded in ancient traditions like Reiki, is a living testament to the idea that energy is not limited by physical proximity. Whether through the lens of quantum physics, which offers insights into non-locality and quantum entanglement, or the rich spiritual traditions that have long understood the flow of life force energy, we see how these diverse systems of thought are inherently linked. Both recognize that the energy connecting us all is a constant force capable of transcending space and time, allowing healing to occur even at great distances.

This interconnectedness is not simply an abstract concept but the foundation upon which distance healing is built. Quantum mechanics gives us the scientific framework to understand how energy transmission works, while spiritual principles provide the context for using this knowledge with intention, compassion, and purpose. This fusion of scientific theory and spiritual practice opens a gateway to understanding our reality's deeper, more subtle layers.

Through the practice of distance healing, we facilitate personal transformation and well-being and contribute to the raising of collective consciousness. Every time a practitioner sends healing energy with intention, they tap into the universal energy field, helping to balance, heal, and restore the energy flow within individuals. As more people engage in these practices, the ripple effect expands, influencing families, communities, and the world.

Distance healing fosters greater balance and harmony by helping individuals release energetic blockages, alleviate physical pain, or clear emotional and mental burdens. When individuals are energetically balanced, their actions and thoughts align with higher vibrational frequencies, contributing to humanity's upliftment. Over time, this creates a shift in personal consciousness and the collective energy field that surrounds and connects us all.

In this journey, we've explored how scientific discoveries, like the law of vibration, the zero-point field, and quantum healing, mirror long-held spiritual truths about the interconnected nature of life. Distance healing bridges these worlds, offering a scientifically sound and deeply spiritual practice. It teaches us that healing is not confined to the body but includes the mind, spirit, and soul—all parts of a greater whole that are influenced by the subtle flow of energy.

Ultimately, distance healing is a powerful tool for transformation. Whether addressing physical ailments or promoting emotional, mental, and spiritual growth, it offers a pathway to personal well-being while helping to raise humanity's consciousness. As more people embrace the power of energy healing, the ripple effects will continue to expand, contributing to a more balanced, compassionate, and interconnected world.

This journey, then, is not just about healing individuals but about tapping into the vast network of energy that unites us all. It is a call to recognize the oneness of existence and the potential we hold to create lasting change—both for ourselves and for the world—through the intentional use of energy and consciousness.

The Future of Distance Healing

As we move into an era where science, technology, and spirituality increasingly converge, the future of distance healing holds extraordinary promise. Imagine a world where ancient wisdom meets cutting-edge advancements, creating new possibilities for health and well-being on a personal and planetary scale. In the future, distance healing will be a complementary practice and an integral part of mainstream health systems, valued for its holistic benefits and profound impact on the collective consciousness.

One of the most exciting aspects of this future lies in the advancements of quantum physics and energy medicine. As scientific research into the quantum field deepens, the principles that underlie distance healing—such as quantum entanglement, non-locality, and the infinite potential of the zero-point field—will be further validated. With each discovery, the gap between science and spirituality narrows, offering a clearer understanding of how Reiki and other forms of energy healing transcend time and space. Imagine a future where quantum sensors and biofeedback devices can map subtle energy fields in real-time, providing insights into how energy flows between a practitioner and recipient during a distance healing session. This could lead to more precise, personalized healing protocols, allowing energy healers to target imbalances accurately.

On a technological front, we see innovations that amplify and enhance the effects of distance healing. Virtual reality (VR) and augmented reality (AR) platforms, combined with biometric data, offer immersive environments where recipients can more tangibly experience the healing process. A Reiki practitioner could guide someone through a virtual healing landscape, making the energy exchange feel more immediate and accessible despite physical distance. Technologies like bio-resonance devices, which detect and correct energetic imbalances, may evolve to integrate seamlessly with spiritual practices, bridging the gap between the physical and energetic realms.

Moreover, spiritual evolution will significantly influence how distance healing shapes the future. As more people awaken to their inherent energetic potential, distance healing may become more widely embraced by healers and individuals seeking to maintain their well-being. We will likely witness a deeper societal understanding of how thoughts, intentions, and emotions influence health. Practices like Reiki, meditation, and mindful intention-setting will increasingly be seen as essential components of a balanced life, helping individuals take greater responsibility for their healing journey.

On a larger scale, the ripple effect of distance healing could profoundly impact humanity's collective consciousness. Imagine the possibility of global healing sessions addressing widespread emotional, spiritual, or environmental imbalances. Reiki circles, where thousands of practitioners and recipients unite with a shared intention to heal the planet, could become regular events, contributing to restoring Earth's energetic equilibrium. In this way, distance healing might evolve from an individual practice into a powerful tool for planetary transformation.

Ultimately, the future of distance healing will likely mirror the expansion of human consciousness itself. As we collectively grow more aware of our interconnectedness—both with each other and with the Earth—the practice of healing from a distance will continue to evolve, offering new possibilities for health, harmony, and spiritual growth. Whether through scientific innovation or spiritual awakening, distance healing is poised to become a cornerstone in humanity's quest for balance and well-being, shaping not only our future but the future of the planet.

In the coming years, combining science, technology, and spirituality will drive the evolution of distance healing, offering an expanded view of what's possible when we tap into the universal energy field. This future promises to redefine how we think about health—not just as the absence of illness but as the harmonious flow of energy within and between all beings.

§

Conducting a Distance Reiki Healing Session

A Step-by-Step Guide

This guide outlines the detailed steps for Reiki practitioners to conduct a successful distance healing session, incorporating grounding, intention-setting, energy connection, and follow-up support for the recipient.

Pre-Session

Before beginning a distance Reiki session, a clear and open line of communication with the recipient is crucial. It allows the practitioner to tailor the session to the recipient's unique needs and provides reassurance about the process. Use this pre-session checklist to guide the conversation and ensure both you and the recipient are aligned before the healing begins.

Establishing Communication

1. Contact the recipient via phone, email, or video chat.
2. Ensure a comfortable and relaxed tone.
3. Clarify the purpose of the conversation (pre-session check-in).

Reach out to the recipient to begin the conversation. A simple introduction, such as: "Hi [Recipient's Name], I wanted to take a few minutes to check in with you before our distance Reiki session. This will help me understand where to focus the healing energy and make sure we are on the same page about your needs." This brief conversation will set a relaxed tone and establish trust.

Discussing the Recipient's Current Emotional, Mental, and Physical State

1. Ask open-ended questions about the recipient's current emotional, mental, and physical state.
2. Take note of any areas they would like the session to focus on.
3. Ask how they are feeling on an energetic or spiritual level, if relevant.

Questions to Ask:

"How are you feeling emotionally today? Are there any emotions you're dealing with that you'd like me to focus on?"

"Mentally, are you feeling clear, or are you experiencing any stress or mental fog?"

"Is there any physical discomfort or tension in your body that you'd like addressed during the session?"

"Would you like me to focus on any specific areas of your energy field or chakras?"

"How are you feeling energetically or spiritually right now? Do you feel connected or in need of balance?"

During this part of the conversation, encourage the recipient to share how they've been feeling. This will give you a clearer idea of where to direct the Reiki energy. For example, if they mention feeling emotionally overwhelmed, you can focus more on the heart chakra. If they express physical discomfort, you may focus on areas where energy blockages might exist.

Addressing Specific Areas of Focus

1. Clarify any specific areas or concerns the recipient wants to be addressed.
2. Make notes of key points (physical pain, emotional distress, mental clarity, etc.).
3. Confirm with the recipient that these will be the areas of focus during the session.

Questions to Ask:

"Is there a specific physical area where you're feeling discomfort, such as your back, neck, or shoulders?"

"Are there any emotional issues, such as stress, anxiety, or sadness, that you'd like me to concentrate on?"

"Would you like me to pay attention to your mental clarity or help with focus during the session?"

"Are there any other specific issues or concerns you'd like the healing session to address?"

Clarifying specific areas of focus helps you direct the healing more effectively. For example, if the recipient mentions experiencing anxiety, you might focus more on the solar plexus or heart chakra to help release emotional blockages. Use their feedback to guide your intention-setting and energy work.

Explaining the Process and Setting Expectations

1. Briefly explain how the distance healing session will work.
2. Reassure the recipient that they don't need to do anything special during the session.
3. Confirm they are comfortable with the process and have no additional questions.

Questions to Ask:

"Would you like me to explain how the distance Reiki session works?"

"Do you have any concerns or questions about the session?"

"Is there anything you'd like to know about what to expect during or after the session?"

Provide a brief overview of how the session will unfold, such as: "I will be connecting with your energy field remotely, using Reiki symbols to help guide the energy where it's needed. You don't need to do anything except relax and allow the energy to flow." Reassure them that they can follow up with questions or observations after the session.

Preparing the Recipient for the Session

1. Ensure the recipient knows how to prepare themselves (e.g., find a comfortable space, quiet environment, etc.).
2. Remind them to relax, release expectations, and be open to receiving healing energy.
3. Confirm the time of the session and how they should feel afterward.

Questions to Ask:

"Do you have a quiet, comfortable space where you can relax during the session?"

"Would you like any tips on how to prepare for the session? For example, relaxing music or meditation."

"How do you usually feel after receiving energy healing? Are there any post-session tips you'd like?"

Help the recipient prepare by suggesting that they create a peaceful environment for the session. Remind them that distance healing is just as effective as in-person Reiki, and they should relax and be open to the process. You can say: "I recommend you lie down in a comfortable space where you won't be disturbed, perhaps with some soft music playing. Just relax and focus on your breath."

Post-Session Check-In and Follow-Up

1. Schedule a post-session check-in to discuss how the recipient feels afterward.

2. Offer any post-session tips for grounding and integrating the healing (such as drinking water, resting, or journaling).

3. Make a note to follow up in the next day or two to check on any further feedback or shifts.

Questions to Ask:

"How would you like to follow up after the session? Would you prefer a phone call, email, or video chat?"

"Are there any specific post-session self-care practices you'd like me to suggest?"

"Would you like to schedule a brief follow-up in the next day or two to see how you're feeling after the healing session?"

A post-session check-in allows you to ensure that the recipient is integrating the healing effectively. Mention: "I'll follow up with you after the session to hear how you're feeling. It's a good idea to drink some water and rest afterward."

This pre-session checklist helps you conduct an effective distance Reiki healing session by opening clear lines of communication and addressing the recipient's physical, emotional, and mental needs. By engaging in this conversation, you ensure that the healing is personalized and that the recipient feels reassured and supported throughout the process.

Setting the Stage: Preparing for a Distance Healing Session

Creating a focused, sacred space is crucial for a successful distance Reiki session. This checklist will guide you through the essential steps to ground yourself, set intentions, create an energetic space, and establish protection to ensure you remain fully present and clear during the session.

Grounding Yourself

Grounding is a vital step in maintaining stability, clarity, and balance during a Reiki session, especially for distance healing, where there is no physical contact with the recipient.

1. Close your eyes and take deep, cleansing breaths.
2. Visualize roots growing from the base of your spine deep into the Earth.
3. Focus on your connection with the Earth to anchor your energy.
4. Clear your energy by releasing any tension or negative thoughts into the ground.

Start your session by grounding yourself through visualization or meditation. Imagine roots growing from your spine and extending deep into the Earth, anchoring your energy and providing stability. This practice not only helps clear your own energy but also ensures you are a stable conduit for Reiki energy to flow through.

Affirmation: "I am grounded, centered, and connected to the Earth. I am a clear and stable channel for Reiki energy."

Setting Clear Intentions

Setting clear, focused intentions before the session ensures that Reiki energy flows to the areas where healing is most needed. Intentions act as a guide and amplify the healing process.

1. Reflect on the recipient's needs (either through prior communication or intuitive guidance).

2. Set a clear, specific intention for the session.
3. Silently affirm or state your intention aloud.
4. Align your intention with the recipient's highest good.

Setting intentions is a powerful way to direct Reiki energy. Based on the recipient's concerns or needs, set a focused intention such as, "My intention is to bring emotional balance and healing to [Recipient's Name]." This intention acts as a compass, guiding the flow of energy where it's needed most.

Affirmation: "I set the intention for this session to bring peace, balance, and healing to [Recipient's Name]. I trust that the energy will flow for their highest good."

Creating a Sacred Space

The space where you conduct your Reiki session has a significant impact on the energy flow. Even though the recipient is not physically present, creating a peaceful and sacred environment helps elevate the session's vibration.
1. Light a candle to signify the beginning of the session.
2. Burn sage, incense, or essential oils to cleanse the space.
3. Play soft, relaxing music to enhance focus (optional).
4. Arrange any Reiki tools, crystals, or sound instruments.
5. Ensure you are seated or lying comfortably in a quiet area, free from distractions.

A sacred space raises the vibration of your healing session, making it easier to connect energetically with the recipient. Prepare your space by lighting a candle, burning sage, or playing gentle music. Have your tools, such as crystals, nearby, and make sure your environment is free from distractions. This ritual helps shift your energy and signals the beginning of the healing process.

Affirmation: "I create this space as sacred, peaceful, and filled with light, allowing the energy to flow freely and harmoniously."

Protection and Energetic Boundaries

Protection is necessary for maintaining your energy field and preventing the absorption of the recipient's energy, especially if they are dealing with emotional trauma or dense energy.

1. Visualize a protective bubble of light surrounding your body.
2. Use the Cho Ku Rei Reiki symbol for additional energetic protection.
3. Intend that only healing energy flows to and from you during the session.
4. Check in with yourself throughout the session to maintain energetic boundaries.

Before beginning the healing, visualize yourself surrounded by a protective bubble of white light. This energetic shield ensures that you maintain boundaries and do not absorb any negative or dense energy from the recipient. You can also draw the Cho Ku Rei symbol over your body to strengthen this protection. By setting these boundaries, you protect your energy while remaining fully present for the healing process.

Affirmation: "I am surrounded by a protective shield of light. Only healing energy flows through me, and I remain grounded and protected throughout the session."

By following this pre-session checklist, you can ensure that you are fully grounded, protected, and aligned with your healing intentions. Preparing your space, setting clear boundaries, and connecting with the recipient all contribute to creating a deeply transformative and focused distance Reiki session.

Connecting with the Recipient's Energy Field

In distance Reiki, connecting to the recipient's energy field is key to the healing process. This connection is established through visualization, intention, and trust. By following these steps, you can create a strong energetic link that transcends physical distance.

Visualizing the Recipient

Visualization is a powerful tool that allows you to form an energetic link with the recipient, even when they are not physically present.

1. Sit quietly, close your eyes, and take a few deep breaths.
2. Hold the recipient in your mind's eye; it doesn't have to be a perfect image.
3. Visualize the recipient in a calm, relaxed state, as if they are ready to receive healing.

4. Surround the recipient with white or golden light, symbolizing their openness to healing energy.

5. Imagine the recipient's energy field glowing, signaling their readiness for the Reiki energy.

Visualization helps create a focused, energetic link between you and the recipient. Close your eyes, take a few breaths, and picture the recipient sitting or lying down in a relaxed state. You don't need a perfect mental image—just hold the intention of their presence. See them bathed in light, open to receiving healing energy, as this visualization strengthens the connection between your energy fields.

Affirmation: "I am now connected to [Recipient's Name], and their energy field is open to receiving healing light and love."

Using Reiki Symbols to Strengthen the Connection

Reiki symbols are essential tools for enhancing the flow of energy during a distance healing session. The Hon Sha Ze Sho Nen symbol, in particular, is used to bridge distances, allowing energy to flow freely to the recipient.

1. Visualize or draw the Hon Sha Ze Sho Nen symbol on your palm or in the air.

2. Repeat the name "Hon Sha Ze Sho Nen" three times to activate the symbol.

3. Imagine the symbol forming a glowing light bridge between you and the recipient.

4. Trust that this bridge will allow Reiki energy to flow smoothly across the distance.

The Hon Sha Ze Sho Nen symbol is the key to connecting with the recipient's energy from afar. Visualize or draw this symbol in your palm or in the air, and repeat its name three times to strengthen the connection. Imagine it creating a light bridge between you and the recipient, allowing Reiki energy to flow freely across the distance and ensuring that the healing energy reaches them regardless of how far apart you are.

Affirmation: "Hon Sha Ze Sho Nen, Hon Sha Ze Sho Nen, Hon Sha Ze Sho Nen. I am connected to [Recipient's Name] through this light bridge, and the healing energy flows freely between us."

Trusting the Process

Distance Reiki requires the practitioner to trust in the flow of universal energy, which transcends time and space. Doubt can block the flow of energy, so it's essential to release any uncertainties and trust that the energy will reach the recipient where and how it's needed.

1. After setting your intention and visualizing the recipient, release any doubts or concerns.

2. Trust that the Reiki energy is flowing to the recipient, even if you can't see immediate effects.

3. Remind yourself that distance Reiki operates beyond the limits of time and space.

4. Let go of the need to control or direct the healing outcome—trust the energy to do its work.

Trust is the foundation of successful distance Reiki. After connecting with the recipient and setting your intention, it's crucial to release any doubts or concerns about whether the energy is reaching them. Trust that the Reiki energy is flowing exactly where it's needed, even if you can't see immediate results. Distance Reiki works on a level that transcends physical time and space, so let go of the need to control the outcome and have faith in the universal energy.

Affirmation: "I trust that Reiki energy flows to [Recipient's Name] exactly where it is needed, for their highest good and healing."

By following this checklist, you can establish a strong, energetic connection with the recipient, ensuring the smooth flow of Reiki energy during the session. Visualization, Reiki symbols, and trust are the key components that allow you to bridge the physical distance and provide effective healing.

Building Focus and Maintaining Presence

Maintaining focus and presence is crucial during distance healing, as the lack of physical proximity can make it easier for distractions to arise. You can remain focused and present throughout the healing process by grounding yourself, using physical or symbolic anchors, and setting practical parameters for your session.

Stay Grounded

Grounding is essential to maintaining focus during a distance healing session, especially as distractions can pull you out of the moment. Periodically check in with your energy and reconnect with the earth to stabilize your attention.

Checklist:

1. Begin the session with a grounding meditation, visualizing roots extending from your spine deep into the earth.

2. Take a few deep breaths and reconnect with the earth whenever your mind wanders.

3. Feel the earth's energy anchoring and supporting you throughout the session, creating a stable foundation.

4. If you are sitting, keep your feet flat on the ground, or visualize being connected to the earth if you are lying down.

Staying grounded throughout the session helps maintain a solid connection to the earth, stabilizing your energy and focus. If you notice your mind drifting or feel disconnected, take a few deep breaths and visualize yourself re-rooting into the earth. Imagine energy flowing from the ground through your body, keeping you centered and clear as a channel for Reiki.

Affirmation: "I am grounded and connected to the earth. My energy flows in balance, and I remain fully present for this healing session."

Use Anchors

Using physical objects as anchors can help you stay connected to the healing energy and prevent your mind from wandering. These objects serve as tangible reminders of your focus and intention.

Checklist:

1. Choose a small object, such as a crystal, Reiki symbol, or another sacred tool, to hold during the session.

2. Keep the anchor in your hand, or place it nearby in your sacred space as a reminder of your intention.

3. Periodically touch or glance at the object during the session to re-focus your energy.

4. Choose an object that holds personal meaning or significance for you as a Reiki practitioner.

Anchors can be incredibly helpful during distance healing as physical reminders to keep you focused. Select a small object, like a crystal, or draw a Reiki symbol in your palm. Hold it in your hand or place it in your sacred space as a tangible reminder of your connection to the recipient. When your mind drifts, gently touch or look at the anchor to re-direct your energy to the healing process.

Affirmation: "This [anchor/crystal/Reiki symbol] grounds my focus and keeps my attention fully aligned with the recipient's healing energy."

Set a Timer

Setting a timer ensures you can immerse yourself in the healing session without being distracted by the need to check the time. This helps maintain your presence and prevents interruptions.

Checklist:

1. Decide on the length of your healing session (e.g., 15, 30, or 60 minutes) based on the recipient's needs and your intuition.

2. Set a timer for the session so you won't need to check the time while working.

3. Indicate when the session is complete with a gentle, nonintrusive sound, avoiding harsh or startling alarms.

4. Trust the timer to free you from any time concerns, allowing you to engage with the Reiki energy fully.

One of the simplest ways to stay focused during distance healing is by setting a timer for the session. Decide in advance how long the healing will last, and set a gentle timer to go off at the end of the session. This allows you to immerse yourself in the healing without the distraction of checking the time. Knowing you have a set timeframe helps you stay fully present and focused.

Affirmation: "I trust the flow of time during this session. My focus is unwavering, and the energy flows freely and without distraction."

Pre-Session Questions to Ask Yourself:

Before beginning the session, ask yourself the following questions to ensure you are prepared to maintain focus throughout the healing:

Am I Grounded?

"Have I taken the time to ground myself? Am I centered and connected to the earth, ready to channel Reiki energy?"
What Will Be My Anchor?
"Do I have a crystal, Reiki symbol, or other object to use as an anchor to help maintain focus? How does this object connect to my intention?"
What Is the Duration of the Session?
"Have I set a clear timeframe for this session, and is my timer set so I can remain fully immersed without distraction?"

Grounding yourself, using an anchor, and setting a timer can enhance your ability to stay focused and present throughout the distance healing session. These tools ensure that your energy remains directed toward the recipient and that you can maintain a strong connection with the healing process. The key is to create a structure that supports your focus, allowing you to offer the most effective and transformative healing possible.

Sending Healing Energy

Now that you've established the connection with the recipient and maintained focus, it's time to send Reiki energy to facilitate the healing process. This stage is about directing the energy where it is most needed, using symbols and intuitive techniques to ensure the recipient receives the healing they require.

Starting the Session

Once your intentions are set, symbols activated, and the recipient visualized, begin sending Reiki energy.

1. Clear your mind and focus on the recipient.
2. Visualize white or golden light flowing from your hands to the recipient's energy field.
3. Imagine the recipient enveloped in this light, and feel it flowing into their body and energy centers.
4. If applicable, visualize Reiki symbols (e.g., Sei He Ki for emotional healing or Cho Ku Rei for amplifying energy) flowing into the recipient's energy field.
5. Focus on sending love, peace, and healing energy where it is most needed based on the recipient's concerns and your intuition.

Begin the session by centering yourself and holding a clear vision of the recipient. Visualize pure, white light flowing through your body and into the recipient, enveloping them in healing energy. Imagine this light penetrating deeply into their energy field, working to heal, balance, and clear any blockages. If the recipient has shared specific areas of concern, direct the energy toward these areas, visualizing Reiki symbols guiding the energy to flow freely.

Affirmation: "I send love, peace, and healing to [Recipient's Name], trusting that the Reiki energy flows exactly where it is most needed for their highest good."

Scanning the Energy Field

As you send Reiki energy, scan the recipient's energy field to detect any imbalances or blockages.

1. Begin scanning by intuitively or energetically "hovering" your hands over the recipient's energy body.
2. Use the Byosen Scanning technique, visualizing your hands moving over the recipient's energy field to detect imbalances.
3. Pay attention to sensations such as heat, tingling, pressure, or resistance, as these may indicate blockages.
4. Focus additional energy on areas where you sense imbalances or blockages, using appropriate Reiki symbols if necessary.

While sending energy, use your hands or intuitive guidance to scan the recipient's energy field. The Byosen Scanning technique involves using your hands (in your mind's eye) to feel the recipient's energy for any areas of imbalance. If you sense heat, tingling, or pressure, it may indicate a blockage or area requiring more attention. Direct more energy to these areas, visualizing the healing light dissolving blockages and restoring balance.

Affirmation: "I trust my hands and intuition to guide the healing energy to the areas that need it most, clearing blockages and restoring harmony."

Balancing the Chakras (Western Reiki)

Reiki can help balance the recipient's chakras, restoring the flow of energy throughout their body.

1. Visualize the recipient's chakras, starting from the root and moving up to the crown.

2. Send Reiki energy to each chakra, visualizing them glowing in their natural, vibrant color.

3. Use Cho Ku Rei to amplify energy flow and Sei He Ki to heal emotional blockages as needed.

4. Spend additional time on any chakra that feels blocked or imbalanced.

5. Focus on specific chakras based on the recipient's concerns (e.g., heart chakra for emotional healing or solar plexus chakra for confidence).

Move through each of the recipient's chakras, visualizing them spinning freely and glowing in their corresponding colors. Start at the root chakra, sending energy and focusing on clearing blockages. Use the Cho Ku Rei symbol to enhance energy flow and the Sei He Ki symbol for emotional healing, particularly for chakras related to emotional pain. Spend additional time on any chakra that feels blocked, ensuring it is balanced and flowing harmoniously.

Affirmation: "I balance and clear the chakras, restoring the free flow of energy through [Recipient's Name], supporting their physical, emotional, and spiritual well-being."

Balancing the Hara Energy System (Traditional Japanese Reiki)

The Hara energy system focuses on grounding and centering the recipient's energy. Balancing the Hara ensures the recipient's energy flows in alignment with their physical, emotional, and spiritual well-being.

1. Visualize the recipient's Hara line, running vertically from the crown of the head through the center of the body and into the Earth.

2. Focus on the Tanden (lower abdomen), sending Reiki energy to stabilize and ground the recipient's vital life force energy.

3. Move to the Ubu (solar plexus), visualizing it glowing and radiating confidence and willpower. Use the Cho Ku Rei symbol to enhance energy flow.

4. Direct energy to the Heart (Shin), allowing emotional balance, compassion, and love to flow freely. Use Sei He Ki for emotional healing.

5. Spend additional time at any Hara center that feels blocked or imbalanced, using Reiki symbols to promote healing.

6. Focus on specific Hara centers based on the recipient's concerns (e.g., Tanden for grounding and stability, Ubu for confidence, Shin for emotional healing).

Begin by visualizing the recipient's Hara line, extending from their crown to the Earth. Focus first on the Tanden, the seat of their vital energy, visualizing it glowing with warmth and stability. Gradually move to the Ubu, ensuring it radiates power and confidence, using Cho Ku Rei to amplify energy flow. Shift your attention to the Heart (Shin), balancing emotional energy and promoting love and compassion with Sei He Ki for healing. Spend additional time at any center that feels energetically blocked or imbalanced, ensuring that energy flows harmoniously throughout the Hara line.

Affirmation: "I balance and clear the Hara energy system, grounding [Recipient's Name] and restoring the flow of energy through their Tanden, Ubu, and Shin, supporting their physical, emotional, and spiritual well-being."

This checklist will guide you using the Hara system for distance healing, ensuring the recipient experiences balance, grounding, and emotional harmony.

Sealing the Healing

As you near the end of the session, it's important to seal the energy to ensure the recipient's energy field remains balanced and protected.

1. Visualize the recipient's entire body glowing with radiant, balanced energy.
2. Draw or visualize the Dai Ko Myo symbol (if attuned) to seal the healing with spiritual energy.
3. Visualize a protective, golden light surrounding the recipient, sealing in the healing energy.
4. Express gratitude to the recipient and the universal energy for the healing that has taken place.

Toward the end of the session, visualize the recipient's body glowing with balanced, flowing energy. Draw or visualize the Dai Ko Myo symbol (if you are attuned) to bring in spiritual energy and seal the healing. Imagine a golden light surrounding the recipient, protecting and integrating the healing energy. This helps ensure the recipient's energy remains balanced long after the session has ended.

Affirmation: "I seal this healing session, surrounding [Recipient's Name] with light and balance. The energy is protected and integrated for their highest good."

Post-Session Care and Follow-Up

The process of distance Reiki does not end once you stop sending energy. Proper aftercare and follow-up are crucial for integrating the healing and ensuring ongoing support for the recipient. Below is a detailed guide to help you close the session, provide support, and reflect on your practice.

Give Thanks and Release

Once the energy has been sent and the session concludes, closing the session with gratitude and releasing the connection with the recipient is essential.

1. Silently thank the recipient's energy for allowing the healing to take place.
2. Express gratitude to the universal energy, Reiki symbols, and any spiritual guides or energies that assisted during the session.
3. Visualize the light bridge or energy cord between you and the recipient dissolving gently, releasing any remaining connection to the recipient's energy.
4. Close your eyes, take a deep breath, and feel a sense of completion.

After you have sent Reiki energy, take a few moments to silently express gratitude for the opportunity to work with the recipient's energy. Give thanks to any spiritual guides or energies that helped facilitate the healing. Visualize the connection between you and the recipient dissolving, ensuring you are not holding onto their energy after the session. This step helps release any residual energetic ties, allowing you and the recipient to integrate the healing properly.

Affirmation: "I thank [Recipient's Name] for allowing this healing. I release the connection and trust that the healing will continue to unfold in perfect harmony."

Ground and Cleanse

After sending Reiki energy, it's essential to ground yourself and cleanse any residual energy from the session.

1. Ground yourself by taking deep breaths, visualizing roots growing from your feet into the Earth.
2. Walk outside or stand barefoot on the ground to reconnect with the Earth's energy.
3. Wash your hands to clear any lingering energy from the session.
4. Use sage, incense, or visualizations of white light to cleanse your energy field.

Grounding and cleansing after a Reiki session ensures that you return to your own energetic state and release any energy picked up during the session. Deep breathing exercises or walking outside barefoot can help reconnect you to the Earth's stabilizing energy. Washing your hands or using sage to smudge can cleanse your energy field, clearing any energetic residue from the session. Visualize a bright white light surrounding your body, clearing away any remaining energy.

Affirmation: "I am grounded, cleansed, and fully present in my own energy field. I release all that is not mine."

Offering Follow-Up Support

After the session, checking in with the recipient helps them process their experience and provides valuable feedback on the healing. This also lets you reflect on the session and plan for further support.

1. Reach out to the recipient through phone, email, or message.
2. Ask the recipient how they felt during and after the session.
3. Encourage them to share any sensations, emotions, or experiences they had.
4. Offer guidance on post-session care, such as staying hydrated, resting, or engaging in grounding exercises.

After the session, following up with the recipient to discuss their experience and offer support is essential. Ask them if they felt any shifts or sensations during the healing process and encourage them to reflect on their physical, emotional, or spiritual state. Offer guidance on integrating the healing by recommending post-session care, such as drinking water, resting, journaling, or practicing grounding exercises. Remind them that the healing process may continue for hours or days after the session, and offer reassurance if they experience any intensified symptoms or emotions.

Questions to Ask:

"How are you feeling after the session?"
"Did you notice any sensations or emotions during the healing?"
"Do you feel any physical, emotional, or mental shifts?"

Affirmation: "The healing energy will continue to work for [Recipient's Name] in the coming days. I remain available for further support as needed."

Journaling Your Observations

Keeping a journal of your Reiki sessions can help track the recipient's progress, reflect on patterns, and improve your techniques for future sessions.

1. Set aside time after the session to write down your observations.
2. Note any significant impressions, sensations, or intuitive messages received during the session.
3. Record areas where blockages were detected and the symbols or techniques you used.
4. Reflect on the session, noting any areas for improvement or continued focus in future sessions.

Journaling after a distance Reiki session allows you to reflect on the session's flow, noting any important insights or patterns that arose. Write down your impressions about the recipient's energy field, areas where blockages were detected, and the Reiki symbols or techniques used. This practice is beneficial when multiple sessions are required, as it helps you monitor progress and adjust future healing plans. Journaling also strengthens your intuitive practice and deepens your understanding of the healing process.

Affirmation: "I reflect on the session with gratitude, learning from the insights I've received. I trust that my practice grows with each session."

Following this detailed after-session guide ensures that you and the recipient are fully supported, grounded, and prepared to integrate the healing energy. This approach fosters ongoing growth and transformation, allowing the recipient to continue benefiting from the session long after it has ended.

Additional Considerations: Healing Crisis

It's important to inform the recipient that they might experience a "healing crisis" after the session. This is a temporary intensification of symptoms before an improvement in their condition.

1. Explain what a healing crisis is and provide reassurance that it is part of the healing process.
2. Offer tips for self-care during this time, such as rest, hydration, and gentle self-compassion.

3. Suggest journaling or mindfulness practices to help the recipient process any emotions or symptoms that arise.

A healing crisis can sometimes occur after a Reiki session, where symptoms intensify before improving. This is a natural part of healing as the body releases blockages. If the recipient experiences this, encourage them to rest, stay hydrated, and practice mindfulness or journaling to work through emotions or physical sensations. Reassure them that this phase is temporary and leads to deeper healing.

§

Recommended Reading

This list of books (in no particular order of importance) is intended to complement the teachings in *Beyond Space and Time: The Science and Spirit of Distance Healing in Reiki* and your journey in distance energy healing.

1. *The Tao of Physics* by Fritjof Capra. This classic book bridges the gap between Eastern spirituality and modern physics, offering a foundational understanding of the quantum world, which is crucial for grasping the science behind distance healing.

2. *The Holographic Universe* by Michael Talbot. Talbot explores the idea of the universe as a hologram, which aligns with the concept of interconnectedness and non-locality in Reiki healing.

3. *Hands of Light: A Guide to Healing Through the Human Energy Field* by Barbara Brennan. This essential guide delves deeply into the human energy field, chakras, and energy healing techniques, offering valuable insights into how energy can be transmitted over distance.

4. *Energy Medicine: The Science and Mystery of Healing* by Jill Blakeway. This is an excellent resource for understanding the broader field of energy healing, this book examines scientific and anecdotal evidence of how energy medicine works, particularly in long-distance contexts.

5. *The Power of Intention* by Dr. Wayne Dyer. Dyer's book focuses on the profound influence of intention on healing and manifesting desired outcomes. This is key to understanding how Reiki practitioners harness intention for effective distance healing.

6. *The Field: The Quest for the Secret Force of the Universe* by Lynne McTaggart. McTaggart introduces the idea of the zero-point field, which aligns with the scientific foundation for distance healing. The book provides evidence for the interconnectedness of all things at a quantum level.

7. *Your Hands Can Heal You* by Master Stephen Co & Eric B. Robins, M.D. A practical guide on how energy and intention can be used for healing, with techniques applicable to hands-on and distance healing practices.

8. *Quantum Healing: Exploring the Frontiers of Mind/Body Medicine* by Deepak Chopra. This exploration of how the mind and body are interconnected through quantum phenomena is essential for understanding the deeper layers of energy healing across time and space.

9. *Reiki and the Healing Buddha* by Maureen J. Kelly. This book provides an overview of Reiki's spiritual foundations and offers insights into how its principles connect to Buddhist teachings. It emphasizes interconnectedness and karma, key elements in distance healing.

10. *The Divine Matrix: Bridging Time, Space, Miracles, and Belief* by Gregg Braden. Braden explores how all things are connected through an energetic matrix and how this can be used for healing. His work resonates with the concept of Reiki healing transcending time and space.

11. *The Akashic Records: Unlock the Infinite Power, Wisdom, and Energy of the Universe* by Sandra Anne Taylor. For readers interested in delving deeper into the metaphysical concept of the Akashic Records and how they relate to distance healing, this book offers practical insights.

12. *The Biology of Belief: Unleashing the Power of Consciousness, Matter, & Miracles* by Bruce H. Lipton, Ph.D. Lipton explains how our beliefs and consciousness influence our biology. This connects well to intention and energy work in distance healing.

13. *Vibrational Medicine: The #1 Handbook of Subtle-Energy Therapies* by Richard Gerber, M.D. This comprehensive guide covers various energy healing modalities and provides scientific and metaphysical perspectives on how subtle energy can be used for healing across distances.

§

Knowledge Review Questions and Answers

Chapter One: The Foundations of Energy Healing

The Essence of Reiki

What do the words "Rei" and "Ki" mean, and how do they relate to the concept of Reiki?

Answer: "Rei" means universal, and "Ki" means life energy. Together, "Reiki" represents the universal life force that permeates all living things. This energy is comparable to "Chi" in Chinese and "Prana" in Sanskrit.

What happens when the flow of life energy becomes blocked, and what are some causes of these blockages?

Answer: Blockages in life energy can lead to physical discomfort, emotional imbalance, or disease. Common causes of blockages include stress, trauma, negative thoughts, or illness. Free-flowing energy is associated with health and vitality.

How does a Reiki practitioner channel healing energy, and what is their role in the process?

Answer: A Reiki practitioner channels universal life energy to the recipient by acting as a conduit. They do not create the energy but direct and amplify it using their intention. The energy flows through the practitioner's hands to where it is needed for healing.

Why is intention important in Reiki, and how does it influence the healing process?

Answer: Intention acts as a guiding force in Reiki, aligning the practitioner's focus with the recipient's needs. It is like planting a seed of healing, which grows as the practitioner nurtures it with focused energy. Intention bridges the physical and energetic worlds, facilitating healing on all levels.

How does the practitioner's trust in the intelligence of energy affect the outcome of a Reiki session?

Answer: In Reiki, the practitioner trusts the universal life energy to flow intuitively to where it is needed most. They do not control the outcome but hold space, allowing the energy to facilitate healing in alignment with the recipient's current state. This trust and non-attachment are essential to the Reiki process.

How does a Reiki practitioner channel energy into a recipient's energy field during a session?

Answer: A Reiki practitioner channels universal life energy through their body and hands into the recipient's energy field and physical body. The practitioner acts as a conduit, not generating the energy themselves but allowing it to flow from an abundant, universal source.

How does the energy know where to go during a healing session in Reiki?

Answer: In Reiki, energy is drawn by the recipient's body and energy system. It goes where it is most needed to restore balance. The practitioner does not need to direct or force the energy—it naturally flows to physical, emotional, mental, or spiritual imbalance areas.

How does Reiki work on a holistic level to promote healing?

Answer: Reiki addresses the immediate physical symptoms and the root causes of imbalances across the emotional, mental, and spiritual layers of the recipient's being. By clearing energy blockages, Reiki supports the body's natural healing mechanisms and promotes harmony across all levels.

Why are hand positions important in Reiki, and how do they relate to energy centers (chakras)?

Answer: Hand positions in Reiki correspond to the recipient's energy centers, or chakras, which regulate energy flow in the body. By placing their hands over these centers, the practitioner helps clear blockages and restore the free flow of energy, promoting balance and healing in the recipient's entire energy system.

What is non-locality, and how does it explain the ability of Reiki energy to be transmitted across distance?

Answer: Non-locality is a concept in quantum physics that suggests particles can influence each other instantaneously, regardless of distance. In Reiki, this principle explains how energy can be transmitted between a practitioner and a recipient across great distances without physical connection, reflecting the universal interconnectedness of energy.

How does distance healing in Reiki operate under the same energetic principles as hands-on healing?

Answer: Distance healing operates on the same energetic principles as hands-on healing because it channels the same universal life energy. The practitioner sets an intention to send energy, which flows naturally to the recipient, regardless of physical proximity. The recipient draws in the energy they need, just as in an in-person session.

What is the purpose of the Hon Sha Ze Sho Nen symbol in distance Reiki healing?

Answer: The Hon Sha Ze Sho Nen symbol is used in Reiki to bridge the physical gap between the practitioner and recipient. It facilitates energy flow across time and space, allowing healing without physical proximity. The symbol represents the timeless and spaceless nature of Reiki energy.

How can Reiki energy be sent across time, and what benefits does this offer in healing past or future events?

Answer: In Reiki, energy is not bound by linear time, allowing practitioners to send healing to past events or future situations. This helps heal unresolved traumas or set positive intentions for the future. The energetic web connecting all things allows the practitioner to direct healing across the timeline of a person's life.

Beyond Time and Space

What is non-locality in quantum mechanics, and how does it apply to Reiki energy healing?

Answer: Non-locality in quantum mechanics refers to the phenomenon where two entangled particles can affect each other instantly, regardless of distance. In Reiki, this principle explains how energy can be transmitted across time and space, allowing a practitioner to send healing energy to a recipient who is not physically present.

How does non-locality enable a Reiki practitioner to send healing energy over distance?

Answer: In distance Reiki healing, non-locality allows the practitioner to connect energetically with the recipient, creating a link similar to quantum entanglement. Through this energetic connection, healing energy is drawn by the recipient's energy field and flows to the areas where it is most needed, regardless of physical separation.

What role does the Hon Sha Ze Sho Nen symbol play in distance Reiki healing?

Answer: The Hon Sha Ze Sho Nen symbol helps create an energetic bridge between the practitioner and the recipient, transmitting healing energy across time and space. It transcends physical limitations and facilitates the flow of energy, reflecting the timeless and spaceless nature of Reiki healing.

What is the unified field, and how does it relate to Reiki's ability to heal across distances?

Answer: The unified field is a concept from quantum physics and metaphysics that suggests all things in the universe are interconnected within a vast web of energy. Reiki practitioners tap into this field, drawing on universal life energy to send healing across distances. This interconnectedness supports the idea that energy is not bound by space and can reach recipients wherever they are.

How does Reiki view time differently from the typical linear perception, and how does this allow healing to transcend time?

Answer: In Reiki, time is seen as fluid, like a spiral or web, where all moments are interconnected. This non-linear view allows Reiki energy to move freely along the past, present, and future continuum, making it possible to heal past traumas and influence future events.

How can Reiki heal past traumas, and how does this affect the present?

Answer: Reiki can be sent to past events or traumas by setting the intention to heal unresolved emotional blockages that disrupt the flow of energy in the present. By releasing the energetic charge associated with these events, the recipient experiences healing that positively impacts their current well-being, often freeing them from limiting patterns.

How does sending Reiki energy to future events influence outcomes, and what is the intention behind this practice?

Answer: Sending Reiki to future events helps create an energetic environment that supports the recipient's well-being. This practice is not about controlling the outcome but aligning the recipient with positive, supportive conditions for the highest good. It helps the individual approach future situations, such as job interviews or medical procedures, with greater confidence and ease.

What is the purpose of the Hon Sha Ze Sho Nen symbol in Reiki healing, and how does it function when healing across time?

Answer: The Hon Sha Ze Sho Nen symbol bridges the gap between the present and past or future events. It allows the practitioner to send Reiki energy across time and space, helping to heal past traumas or prepare for future events. The symbol represents the concept of "no past, no present, no future," facilitating energy flow beyond time constraints.

Why is the present moment so important in Reiki healing?

Answer: The present moment is crucial in Reiki because it is the only time we can directly engage with our energy, thoughts, and emotions. Reiki energy flows freely in the now, helping us align with our most authentic selves and allowing for healing and transformation to occur in real time.

How does Reiki help recipients become more grounded and reduce stress in the present moment?

Answer: Reiki quiets the mind and brings awareness to the present moment, reducing the distractions of past worries and future anxieties. This grounding effect allows the recipient's body's natural healing processes to function more effectively, promoting relaxation and reducing stress.

How does mindfulness play a role in Reiki, and how does Reiki support emotional awareness?

Answer: Mindfulness in Reiki involves becoming fully aware of one's thoughts, feelings, and surroundings without judgment. Reiki amplifies the energy of the present moment, supporting emotional awareness and release by helping the recipient observe and process their emotions without resistance.

What is the impact of Reiki on mental and emotional blockages, and how does it provide clarity?

Answer: Reiki clears energetic noise, such as mental distractions or emotional burdens, which block access to inner wisdom. As the recipient relaxes into the flow of Reiki energy, they gain clarity, insights, and a deeper understanding of their emotions or thoughts, which are vital to their healing process.

Chapter Two: Scientific Foundations

Quantum Mechanics and the Unified Field

What is quantum entanglement, and how does it help explain Reiki distance healing?

Answer: Quantum entanglement refers to the phenomenon where two particles, once connected, remain linked regardless of distance, and a change in one particle affects the other instantly. This concept provides a scientific explanation for how Reiki energy can flow between a practitioner and a recipient, even if great distances separate them.

How does a Reiki practitioner's and recipient's energetic connection mirror quantum entanglement?

Answer: In Reiki, the practitioner and recipient become energetically "entangled" during a session, meaning they are connected within the same energetic field. Just as in quantum entanglement, this link allows energy to flow between them instantly, transcending physical distance.

How do intention and Reiki symbols like Hon Sha Ze Sho Nen contribute to Reiki distance healing?

Answer: The practitioner uses focused intention and Reiki symbols, such as Hon Sha Ze Sho Nen, to create an energetic link with the recipient. This symbol bridges time and space, allowing the energy to flow from the practitioner to the recipient, guiding the healing process based on the recipient's needs.

How does quantum entanglement affirm the spiritual principle of universal interconnectedness in Reiki?

Answer: Quantum entanglement supports the spiritual idea that all things in the universe are interconnected. This concept echoes ancient wisdom in Reiki, where energy is believed to move freely between all beings, reinforcing that healing is possible across physical and energetic distances.

What is the unified field theory, and how does it relate to Reiki energy healing?

Answer: The unified field theory posits that everything in the universe is interconnected within one vast energy field. This theory helps explain how Reiki energy can flow between a practitioner and a recipient, transcending physical distance and time. In Reiki, the practitioner taps into this field to channel healing energy.

How does Reiki energy flow through the unified field, and why is physical proximity unnecessary?

Answer: Reiki energy flows through the unified field, a web of interconnected energy that permeates the entire universe. Since everything is connected in this field, Reiki does not require physical proximity to the recipient. The practitioner can channel healing energy through this network, allowing it to flow freely to the recipient, regardless of distance.

How does the unified field theory align with the spiritual concept of oneness in Reiki?

Answer: The unified field theory supports the spiritual principle of oneness, which teaches that all beings and things are interconnected. In Reiki, this idea is reflected in the understanding that the energy used to heal one person is part of the same universal life force that flows through everything, creating a ripple effect that can influence the greater collective energy.

How does Reiki practice contribute to the healing of the collective, beyond just the individual recipient?

Answer: Reiki energy does not stop at the individual recipient when channeled through the unified field. Because we are all interconnected, healing one person sends positive energy into the larger collective field. This ripple effect contributes to the overall balance and harmony of the world, helping to heal the collective consciousness.

What is non-locality in quantum mechanics, and how does it relate to Reiki healing?

Answer: Non-locality in quantum mechanics refers to the phenomenon where two particles, once connected, can influence each other's behavior regardless of the distance between them. In Reiki, this principle explains how a practitioner can send healing energy across space to a recipient, creating an energetic link that transcends physical separation.

How do Reiki practitioners use the non-local field to send healing energy across distances?

Answer: Reiki practitioners tap into the non-local field, creating an energetic connection with the recipient through the universal life force. This connection allows healing energy to flow instantly, guided by the practitioner's intention, regardless of the physical distance between them and the recipient.

How does the practitioner's intention influence Reiki healing, similar to the observer effect in quantum mechanics?

Answer: In Reiki, the practitioner's focused intention guides the flow of healing energy to the recipient. This mirrors the observer effect in quantum mechanics, where observation influences the behavior of particles. The practitioner's intention acts as a catalyst, directing the universal life energy to flow where it is most needed.

How does non-locality enable Reiki to heal events from the past and influence the future?

Answer: Non-locality allows Reiki to transcend the traditional boundaries of time, enabling the practitioner to send energy to heal past traumas or affect future events. In the non-local field, time is fluid, meaning the past, present, and future are interconnected, allowing energy to flow where it is most needed across the timeline.

The Observer Effect and Energy Healing

What is the observer effect, and how does it relate to quantum mechanics?

Answer: The observer effect refers to the phenomenon where the act of observation influences the behavior of particles. In quantum mechanics, particles like electrons behave differently when observed, either as particles or waves. This suggests that consciousness can directly impact physical reality.

How does the observer effect relate to the role of a Reiki practitioner during a healing session?

Answer: In Reiki, the practitioner's focused observation and intention guide the flow of healing energy, similar to how the observer effect influences particle behavior. By focusing on the recipient's energy field, the practitioner directs the energy flow toward areas that need healing, shaping the energy's movement during the session.

How does the practitioner's intention influence the energy flow in a Reiki session?

Answer: The practitioner's intention guides the energy flow, helping align the energy with the recipient's needs. While the practitioner doesn't control the outcome, their intention ensures that the energy flows in the most beneficial direction for the recipient's healing.

Why is the practitioner's presence and focus critical during a Reiki session?

Answer: The practitioner's focused presence enhances the connection with the recipient's energy field, amplifying the flow of healing energy. If the practitioner is distracted, the energy connection weakens, potentially reducing the session's effectiveness. Therefore, mindfulness and focus are crucial for successful healing.

How does the practitioner's intention guide the flow of Reiki energy during a session?
Answer: The practitioner's intention acts as a guiding force that directs the universal life energy toward the recipient's specific needs. By setting a clear intention, the practitioner creates the conditions for the energy to flow in the right direction, much like a gardener nurturing seeds to grow.

Why is the recipient's openness important in the Reiki healing process, and how does it complement the practitioner's intention?
Answer: The recipient's openness allows the healing energy to flow more freely, making the session more effective. When both the practitioner sets a focused intention, and the recipient is open to receiving energy, a powerful synergy is created, enhancing the healing process.

What is coherence in the context of Reiki, and how does intention help create it?
Answer: Coherence refers to aligning and synchronizing energy patterns, allowing for a more organized and effective energy flow. In Reiki, the practitioner's intention brings coherence to the session, aligning their energy with the recipient's needs and facilitating more profound healing.

What is the principle of non-attachment, and why is it essential in Reiki healing?
Answer: Non-attachment means that while the practitioner sets an intention for healing, they do not become attached to a specific outcome. This allows the universal life energy to flow freely, addressing the recipient's needs without interference. Trusting the process and releasing control is essential to creating a healing environment that serves the recipient's highest good.

How does the practitioner's intention create an energetic connection with the recipient during a distance Reiki session?
Answer: The practitioner's focused intention establishes a bridge between themselves and the recipient, allowing the universal life energy to flow. Through meditation, visualization, and Reiki symbols, the practitioner connects energetically to the recipient, regardless of physical distance.

Why is visualization and the Hon Sha Ze Sho Nen symbol important in distance Reiki healing?
Answer: Visualization helps the practitioner focus on the recipient's energy field, while the Hon Sha Ze Sho Nen symbol bridges the physical and energetic gap between practitioner and recipient. These tools enable the Reiki energy to flow freely, transcending time and space.

How can a Reiki practitioner use intention to send healing energy to past or future events?

> *Answer:* A Reiki practitioner can use intention to direct healing energy to past traumas or future events, helping to release emotional blockages or prepare for upcoming life transitions. By visualizing the event and setting the intention for healing, the practitioner can influence these moments across time.

Why is non-attachment important in distance healing, and how does it enhance the session's effectiveness?

> *Answer:* Non-attachment allows the practitioner to release control over the outcome, trusting that the universal life energy will flow in the most beneficial way for the recipient. This trust creates a space for healing, even without directly observing the recipient's physical cues.

Zero-Point Energy and Infinite Potential

What is zero-point energy, and how does it relate to the universal life force in Reiki?

> *Answer:* Zero-point energy is the lowest possible energy in the quantum vacuum, even in the absence of matter. It parallels the universal life force in Reiki, as both represent ever-present, infinite energy that can be accessed for healing and transformation.

How do zero-point energy and the universal life force energy share similar characteristics regarding availability and abundance?

> *Answer:* Both zero-point energy and the universal life force are always present and abundant. Reiki practitioners do not generate energy; instead, they tap into this infinite source, allowing the energy to flow through them to the recipient for healing purposes.

What is coherence in quantum mechanics, and how does it enhance the flow of Reiki energy during a session?

> *Answer:* Coherence in quantum mechanics refers to the alignment and synchronization of quantum states, allowing for smooth and efficient energy flow. In Reiki, coherence occurs when the practitioner aligns their energy with the universal life force, enabling a powerful and harmonious flow of healing energy.

How does the concept of zero-point energy help explain the limitless potential of Reiki healing?

> *Answer:* Zero-point energy, with its vast potential stored even in empty space, mirrors Reiki's limitless healing capacity. Just as zero-point energy contains immense power, Reiki energy can address various imbalances, including physical, emotional, mental, and spiritual, offering infinite possibilities for healing.

Why are grounding and centering important in Reiki, and how do they help practitioners channel energy?

> *Answer:* Grounding stabilizes the practitioner's energy by connecting them to the

Earth while centering focuses their attention on the present moment. These practices create a balanced, stable foundation, allowing the practitioner to be a clear conduit for universal life energy during a Reiki session.

How does meditation help a Reiki practitioner achieve coherence and deepen their connection to the universal life force?

Answer: Meditation quiets the mind and allows the practitioner to enter a state of relaxation and focus, facilitating coherence. This alignment with the universal life force energy enables a smoother and more effective flow of healing energy during the session.

How do Reiki symbols like Cho Ku Rei and Sei He Ki enhance the energy flow in a session?

Answer: Cho Ku Rei amplifies the energy flow, increasing its intensity, while Sei He Ki brings balance and harmony to the recipient's energy field. These symbols help practitioners direct the energy more effectively, aligning it with the recipient's needs.

Why are non-attachment and gratitude important in Reiki practice, and how do they influence energy flow?

Answer: Non-attachment allows the practitioner to release expectations about the healing outcome, trusting that the energy will flow where needed most. Gratitude reinforces the energetic connection between the practitioner, recipient, and universal life force, helping solidify the healing process and align the practitioner with the infinite potential of the energy field.

What is the quantum field, and how does it relate to Reiki healing?

Answer: The quantum field, or zero-point field, is an infinite web of energy that connects all things and holds the healing potential. In Reiki, practitioners tap into this field to access and channel universal life energy for healing, transcending time and space.

How do expanded visualization and quantum attunement allow Reiki practitioners to access the quantum field?

Answer: Expanded visualization helps practitioners mentally connect with the quantum field, visualizing the recipient surrounded by infinite energy. Quantum attunement involves aligning the practitioner's energy with the frequency of the quantum field, allowing them to draw from its limitless energy for healing.

How do resonance and sound-based practices like chanting or toning improve the practitioner's connection with the quantum field?

Answer: Resonance creates vibrational alignment between the practitioner's energy and the quantum field. Sound-based practices like chanting or toning help raise the practitioner's vibration, harmonizing their energy with the universal life force, thereby enhancing the flow of Reiki energy.

Why is energetic expansion through breath-work important in Reiki, especially for distance healing?

Answer: Energetic expansion allows practitioners to extend their energy field beyond their physical body, connecting with the recipient and the quantum field. This practice is particularly useful in distance healing, enabling a stronger, energetic connection and amplifying the flow of universal life energy for powerful healing results.

How can expanded visualization be used in hands-on Reiki to enhance healing?

Answer: Practitioners can visualize the recipient's energy field as an expansive, luminous light that extends beyond the physical body. This allows them to tap into the quantum field and address imbalances on a deeper, more subtle, energetic level, promoting more comprehensive healing.

What role does quantum attunement play in distance Reiki sessions, and how does it enhance the energy flow?

Answer: In distance healing, quantum attunement allows practitioners to align their energy with the quantum field. This connection enables them to access infinite healing energy and channel it to the recipient, regardless of physical distance, by focusing on the energetic field rather than the physical separation.

How can sound and resonance improve the vibrational frequency in Reiki sessions?

Answer: Practitioners can use chanting, toning, or music tuned to healing frequencies (432 Hz or 528 Hz) to raise their vibrational frequency and align more closely with the quantum field. This resonance enhances the energy flow, promoting deeper healing and transformation for the recipient.

Why is energetic expansion necessary in distance Reiki, and how does it strengthen the healing connection?

Answer: By consciously expanding their energy field, practitioners can bridge the physical distance between themselves and the recipient. This expanded field creates a stronger, energetic link. It allows for a more potent exchange of healing energy through the quantum field, making distance healing as effective as hands-on Reiki.

Chapter 3: Metaphysical and Spiritual Perspectives

The Laws of the Universe and Healing

What is the Law of Vibration, and how does it relate to Reiki healing?

Answer: The Law of Vibration states that everything in the universe vibrates at a specific frequency. In Reiki healing, this law explains how practitioners work with the universal life force, aligning their vibration with the recipient to facilitate energy flow and healing.

How do Reiki practitioners attune their vibration to the recipient during distance healing?
Answer: Practitioners use visualization, intention, and Reiki symbols to connect with the recipient's energy field. By aligning their vibration with the recipient's frequency, the practitioner allows the healing energy to flow seamlessly across distance, addressing any energetic imbalances.

How do different emotional states impact the vibrational frequency during a Reiki session?
Answer: Positive emotions like love, gratitude, and compassion vibrate at higher frequencies, while negative emotions like fear, anger, and sadness resonate at lower frequencies. During a Reiki session, the practitioner raises the recipient's vibrational frequency, promoting emotional balance and well-being.

How does raising the recipient's vibrational frequency during a Reiki session impact their physical, emotional, and spiritual well-being?
Answer: Raising the recipient's vibration helps to clear energetic blockages, not only addressing physical ailments but also balancing emotional, mental, and spiritual energy. This holistic approach promotes harmony and healing on all levels of the recipient's being.

What is the Law of Attraction, and how does it relate to Reiki healing?
Answer: The Law of Attraction states that like attracts like, meaning the energy and intentions we put into the universe attract similar energy back to us. In Reiki, this law governs the alignment between the practitioner's and recipient's vibrations, ensuring that the healing energy flows effectively when both are aligned with high-frequency outcomes.

Why is aligning the practitioner's intention with the desired healing outcome crucial for effective Reiki healing?
Answer: The practitioner's intention sets the vibrational tone for the healing session. When aligned with high-frequency emotions like love, compassion, and gratitude, the practitioner attracts similar healing energies, amplifying the session's effectiveness and helping direct the universal life force energy to the recipient's needs.

How does the recipient's openness impact the effectiveness of a Reiki session based on the Law of Attraction?
Answer: The recipient's openness and willingness to receive healing energy create vibrational alignment with the practitioner's intention. If the recipient is open, their energy field harmonizes with the universal life force, enhancing the resonance and allowing the healing energy to flow more smoothly.

Why is non-attachment important when applying the Law of Attraction in Reiki healing, and how does it support the process?

Answer: Non-attachment allows the practitioner to set a clear intention while trusting the universal life force to guide the healing in the best way possible. By releasing the need to control the outcome, the practitioner attracts high-frequency energy without interference, ensuring the healing flows naturally and aligns with the recipient's highest good.

What is the Law of Cause and Effect (Karma), and how does it influence a person's energy in Reiki healing?

Answer: The Law of Cause and Effect (Karma) teaches that every action, thought, and intention carries an energetic charge that shapes future outcomes. In Reiki, these energetic imprints from past actions can create blockages in the recipient's energy field, impacting their emotional, mental, and physical well-being.

How can Reiki practitioners help release karmic imprints and energetic blockages from past experiences?

Answer: Reiki practitioners can set an intention to send healing energy to past traumas or unresolved emotional experiences, helping the recipient release energetic blockages. By aligning with the universal life force, they dissolve negative energy imprints, restoring balance and allowing the recipient's energy to flow freely.

How does Reiki transcend time and space, and how can distance healing address karmic patterns or future events?

Answer: Reiki operates beyond the constraints of linear time, allowing practitioners to send healing energy to past or future events. Distance healing can target energetic imprints from past lives, traumas, or upcoming events, helping the recipient release karmic patterns or prepare for future outcomes with greater energetic alignment.

Why are self-care and energetic hygiene important for Reiki practitioners in the context of the law of cause and effect?

Answer: Reiki practitioners are also subject to the Law of Cause and Effect, meaning their past actions, thoughts, and experiences can influence their ability to channel healing energy. Maintaining self-care and resolving their karmic imprints ensures they remain a clear, balanced conduit for the universal life force, enabling effective healing sessions for their recipients.

Sacred Geometry and Healing

What role do sacred geometric patterns play in energy healing and Reiki?

Answer: Sacred geometric patterns represent the underlying order of the universe and illustrate how energy flows through harmonious and repetitive structures. These patterns provide Reiki practitioners with a visual framework to align themselves with the universal life force, deepening their understanding of how energy moves in the human energy field.

How do the Flower of Life and Metatron's Cube help in energy healing during a Reiki session?

Answer: The Flower of Life symbolizes interconnectedness and harmony in energy flow, helping practitioners visualize energy as a continuous, interconnected field during Reiki sessions. Metatron's Cube is used to clear and balance energy by connecting with the universal elements, promoting harmony, and removing blockages within the recipient's energy field.

How can sacred geometric patterns be applied in distance Reiki healing?

Answer: During distance healing sessions, practitioners can visualize sacred geometric patterns like the Flower of Life or Metatron's Cube surrounding the recipient's energy field. These patterns help bridge the physical distance by connecting the practitioner to the recipient through the universal life force, allowing healing energy to flow seamlessly across space.

How does the Sri Yantra symbol raise the recipient's vibrational frequency during Reiki healing?

Answer: The Sri Yantra represents the union of masculine and feminine energies and higher consciousness. By focusing on the geometric symmetry of the Sri Yantra, Reiki practitioners help the recipient clear lower vibrational energies, facilitating spiritual alignment and enhancing the connection to higher frequencies of love, wisdom, and light.

What does the Merkaba represent in sacred geometry, and how is it relevant to energy healing?

Answer: The Merkaba is a three-dimensional geometric star tetrahedron representing the union of light, spirit, and body. In energy healing, it is a tool for accessing higher consciousness and balancing energy. It is instrumental in distance healing, where it helps establish a deep connection with the recipient's energy field.

How can a Reiki practitioner activate the Merkaba field for distance healing?

Answer: The practitioner can visualize two interlocking tetrahedra around the recipient's body, one spinning clockwise (masculine energy) and the other counterclockwise (feminine energy). This spinning creates a protective and balanced Merkaba field, facilitating the flow of universal life energy from the practitioner to the recipient, transcending time and space.

How does the Merkaba help balance and align the recipient's energy field during a Reiki session?

Answer: By visualizing the Merkaba spinning around the recipient's body, the practitioner can clear stagnant or blocked energy and help align the recipient's chakras and energy channels. This symmetrical, harmonious structure ensures that the recipient's energy flows freely, restoring balance at all levels.

What is the purpose of Merkaba meditation for Reiki practitioners, and how is it performed?

Answer: Merkaba meditation helps practitioners align their energy with the universal life force, strengthening their ability to channel healing energy. It involves visualizing two interlocking tetrahedra spinning around the practitioner's body, creating a protective and expansive energy field that enhances their healing potential. This meditation also deepens the practitioner's connection to higher dimensions of consciousness.

How does sacred geometry provide a blueprint for understanding energy flow in the universe and its application in Reiki healing?

Answer: Sacred geometry represents the fundamental patterns and structures that govern the cosmos. In Reiki healing, these geometric patterns, such as the Flower of Life and Metatron's Cube, reflect the natural order and harmony of the universe. Practitioners use them to align the recipient's energy field with these universal patterns, promoting balance and healing.

What role do symmetry and proportion play in sacred geometry, and how does it apply to restoring balance in Reiki sessions?

Answer: Symmetry and proportion in sacred geometry, exemplified by the Golden Ratio, represent the ideal harmony of nature and the human body. In Reiki healing, using geometric patterns helps restore balance by aligning the recipient's energy field with these universal symmetry principles, promoting physical, emotional, and spiritual harmony.

How can a Reiki practitioner use geometric visualization, such as the Flower of Life or the Merkaba, to guide energy during a healing session?

Answer: The practitioner can visualize the recipient surrounded by sacred geometric patterns like the Flower of Life or the Merkaba. These patterns help guide energy flow harmoniously and balanced, clearing blockages and facilitating healing at deeper levels of the energy field.

How can sacred geometry be used to harmonize group energy and enhance the vibrational frequency of healing spaces?

Answer: In group healing sessions, visualizing sacred geometric patterns like the Flower of Life around participants helps unify and harmonize collective energy. Incorporating these geometric symbols into the physical space through images or visualizations raises the vibration of the healing environment, enhancing the flow of universal life force energy for all participants.

Fractal Universe and Holographic Reality

What are fractals, and how do they relate to energy healing in the context of Reiki?

Answer: Fractals are infinitely repeating patterns that exist at all scales of the universe, from the largest galaxies to the smallest cells. In Reiki, they represent the idea that every part of a system reflects the whole, allowing practitioners to influence the entire energy field by working on specific parts. This concept helps explain how healing energy can be transmitted effectively during distance healing.

How does the fractal nature of the human energy field facilitate healing at both local and distance levels?

Answer: Since every part of the human energy field reflects the whole, Reiki practitioners can direct energy to one part of the recipient's system (e.g., a chakra or meridian), knowing that the healing will resonate throughout the entire being. This fractal structure allows distance healing to work by influencing the interconnected energy field, even when the practitioner and recipient are not physically close.

How does the universe's fractal nature challenge traditional notions of hands-on healing?

Answer: The fractal nature of the universe suggests that healing is holographic, meaning that the energy transmitted during a Reiki session resonates through the recipient's entire system, even without direct physical contact. This challenges the traditional view that healing must occur through physical touch and supports the effectiveness of distance healing, where the practitioner works with the recipient's energy field across space and time.

How can practitioners use fractal visualization techniques to enhance Reiki healing?

Answer: Practitioners can visualize the recipient's energy field as a fractal structure, recognizing that each part reflects the whole. By focusing on a specific area of imbalance while understanding that the entire energy field will be affected, practitioners can amplify the healing effects and align with the infinite patterns of the universe, allowing energy to flow freely and create holistic healing.

What is the holographic principle, and how does it apply to Reiki healing?

Answer: The holographic principle asserts that every part of the universe contains the whole, just as each fragment of a hologram contains the entire image. In Reiki healing, this means that when a practitioner connects with any part of the recipient's energy field, they connect with the entirety of the recipient's being. This allows for healing to occur holistically, even at a distance.

How does the holographic nature of the universe make distance healing effective?

Answer: The holographic nature of reality means that every part of the universe, including the recipient's energy field, contains the whole. This allows a Reiki practitioner to send healing energy across time and space because they work with the recipient's entire energetic matrix, not just a single part. As a result, the healing energy can resonate throughout the recipient's being, regardless of physical distance.

What scientific theories support the holographic universe concept, and how do they relate to energy healing?

Answer: Theories such as David Bohm's implicate order and Gerard't Hooft's holographic universe model support the idea that the universe operates like a hologram, where each fragment contains information about the whole. In Reiki healing, this explains how practitioners can affect the recipient's entire energy system by focusing on any part, as all aspects of the recipient's being are interconnected.

How can Reiki practitioners use holographic visualization to enhance their healing sessions?

Answer: Practitioners can visualize the recipient's energy field as a holographic structure, understanding that each part reflects the whole. By focusing on healing one specific area, such as an emotional or physical block, practitioners can trust that the healing energy will flow through the entire being. This visualization enhances the practitioner's ability to channel holistic healing energy, aligning with the interconnected nature of the universe.

How does the concept of time as a fluid and interconnected web apply to Reiki healing?

Answer: Time is viewed as non-linear in Reiki, meaning that the past, present, and future are interconnected. Reiki can influence these different timelines by addressing energetic imprints, allowing healing to occur across time. By sending healing energy to past traumas or future events, practitioners help realign the recipient's energy field with balance and well-being in the present and future.

How can Reiki help heal past traumas that continue to affect the present?

Answer: Reiki can heal past traumas by sending healing energy to the time when the trauma occurred, addressing the energetic imprints left in the recipient's energy field. This process helps release stagnant or blocked energy, allowing the recipient to move forward without being held back by the trauma's lingering effects.

What role does Reiki play in preparing for future events, and why is it effective?

Answer: Reiki practitioners can send healing energy to future events, such as surgeries or important life transitions, to align the recipient with the highest possible outcome. This works because all moments are interconnected in the holographic and fractal time model. By influencing the energy surrounding a future event, Reiki helps ensure a balanced and harmonious experience for the recipient.

What is the significance of clearing ancestral energies in Reiki healing, and how is it done?

Answer: Clearing ancestral energies is important because individuals often inherit their lineage's emotional, behavioral, or spiritual patterns. Reiki practitioners can send healing energy to ancestral lines, helping to clear these inherited imprints and create space for healthier, more positive patterns to emerge. This is done by visualizing the recipient's connection to their family line and sending healing energy throughout the lineage.

How does reality's holographic and fractal nature explain Reiki's effectiveness across time and space?

Answer: In the holographic and fractal view of reality, every part of the universe contains the whole, and every moment is interconnected. This means that a Reiki practitioner can influence the recipient's entire being, across time and space, by focusing on a specific part of their energy field. Healing energy resonates through the recipient's timeline, creating effects in the past, present, and future.

The Role of Karma and Past Lives

What is karma, and how can unresolved karmic imbalances affect present-day health?

Answer: Karma is the universal principle of cause and effect, where every action, thought, and intention generates energy that influences future experiences. Unresolved karmic imbalances from past lives can manifest as physical, emotional, or mental issues in the present, such as chronic pain, recurring emotional patterns, or behavioral tendencies that seem resistant to change. These imbalances represent unresolved energies carried over across lifetimes, creating challenges in the current incarnation.

How can past life traumas manifest physically, emotionally, or mentally in the present?

Answer: Past life traumas can manifest in several ways, including unexplained physical symptoms, such as chronic pain or tension in areas of the body related to injuries or traumas from a past life. Emotionally, individuals may carry fears, anxieties, or emotional reactions tied to unresolved experiences from past lives. Mentally, recurring thought patterns or behaviors may reflect unresolved karmic imprints, such as a person repeatedly struggling with trust issues due to abandonment in a past life.

Why is it essential to address karmic imbalances as part of spiritual growth and healing?

Answer: Karmic imbalances often present opportunities for spiritual growth and healing, as they are linked to life lessons involving forgiveness, compassion, self-empowerment, or unconditional love. Addressing these imbalances allows individuals to release old patterns, heal emotional wounds, and align more fully with their higher self. Healing these imprints promotes both personal and spiritual development, contributing to the resolution of long-standing energetic blockages.

How can Reiki help in healing past life traumas and karmic imbalances?

Answer: Reiki helps heal past life traumas by facilitating the flow of universal life force energy to clear energetic imprints tied to past traumas or unresolved karma. Practitioners can use Reiki symbols like Hon Sha Ze Sho Nen to transcend time and space, directing healing energy toward past life events or karmic blockages. This process helps the recipient release energetic patterns from the past, leading to healing in the present.

What is the role of the Reiki practitioner in guiding recipients through karmic healing?

Answer: The Reiki practitioner is a facilitator and guide in karmic healing. Rather than "fixing" the recipient's karma, the practitioner creates a safe, healing space where the recipient can become aware of their karmic patterns and release them. The practitioner supports the recipient in accessing universal life force energy, guiding them through awareness, forgiveness, and release, helping to restore balance and harmony to their energy field.

How does distance Reiki healing address past life traumas and karmic imbalances?

Answer: Distance Reiki healing transcends time and space, allowing practitioners to send healing energy to past life events. By using the Reiki symbol Hon Sha Ze Sho Nen, practitioners can access the energetic imprints left by past traumas and dissolve the blockages or unresolved emotions that have persisted across lifetimes. This process helps the recipient release the energetic ties to past experiences, leading to healing and balance in the present.

What are ancestral wounds, and how can they affect present-day health?

Answer: Ancestral wounds are unresolved emotional, mental, or spiritual imprints passed down through generations. They often manifest as recurring family patterns, such as addiction, emotional dysfunction, or poverty. These inherited karmic patterns can influence the recipient's energy field, contributing to physical, emotional, or spiritual imbalances. By addressing these ancestral imprints through distance Reiki, practitioners can help release inherited energy and clear the way for healthier patterns to emerge.

How do Reiki practitioners use intention to guide the healing process across time and space?

Answer: Intention is vital in distance Reiki, particularly when working with past-life or ancestral healing. The practitioner sets a focused intention to send healing energy to a specific past event, ancestor, or karmic pattern. This clear intention helps direct the flow of the universal life force energy to the precise point of need, whether a past-life trauma or a generational wound, facilitating deep healing at the root cause of the issue.

What are the holistic benefits of healing past life traumas and ancestral wounds through distance Reiki?

Answer: Healing past life traumas and ancestral wounds through distance Reiki benefits the individual by releasing old karmic patterns and contributing to the collective consciousness. As individuals heal, they raise the vibrational frequency of their personal energy field and contribute to the collective healing of families, communities, and future generations. This process can potentially create transformation on both individual and collective levels, promoting growth, evolution, and spiritual alignment.

How does distance Reiki allow for healing across lifetimes and ancestral lines?

Answer: Distance Reiki allows for healing across lifetimes and ancestral lines by transcending the physical boundaries of time and space. Practitioners can connect with the recipient's energy field at different points in time, such as past lives or ancestral timelines, using symbols and intention to guide the universal life force energy to these distant events or patterns. This healing clears old imprints and helps restore balance, freeing the recipient from energetic blockages that have persisted across time.

How do energetic imprints from past traumas or experiences influence a person's present-day health and emotional state?

Answer: Energetic imprints from past traumas or experiences can reside in the individual's energy field, causing blockages or distortions in the flow of life force energy. These imprints can manifest as physical symptoms, emotional challenges, or mental patterns that persist in the present, even if the individual is not consciously aware of the original trauma. For example, unresolved grief from a past life or ancestral lineage may manifest as chronic sadness or physical tension in the chest, influencing overall well-being.

How does distance Reiki help in clearing energetic imprints from past lives?

Answer: Distance Reiki transcends the limitations of time and space, allowing practitioners to send healing energy to past life events or specific moments when trauma occurred. By using symbols like Hon Sha Ze Sho Nen, practitioners can connect with the recipient's energy at the time of the trauma and help dissolve the imprints embedded in the energy field. This process facilitates the release of emotional, mental, and spiritual blockages, freeing the recipient from the effects of the past.

What are karmic patterns, and how can Reiki help clear them?

Answer: Karmic patterns are repetitive cycles of behavior or emotional responses that arise from unresolved lessons from past lives. These patterns often manifest as recurring relationship issues, chronic health problems, or feelings of being "stuck" in life. Reiki can clear karmic patterns by addressing the energetic imprints that keep these cycles in place. Through distance healing, practitioners can help recipients release the old patterns and integrate the lessons they need to learn, allowing for greater spiritual growth and freedom from repetitive challenges.

What is ancestral healing, and how can distance Reiki address inherited patterns within a family?

Answer: Ancestral healing involves working with the energy of the recipient's family lineage to release unresolved trauma, pain, or karmic patterns passed down through generations. These inherited energies may manifest as recurring emotional or physical challenges within a family, such as addiction or mental illness. Distance Reiki allows practitioners to send healing energy to the recipient's ancestors or the entire lineage, helping to clear the energetic blockages and release the burden of inherited patterns, thus freeing the recipient from the effects of ancestral karma.

How does integrating lessons from past experiences contribute to healing across timelines?

Answer: The integration process allows the recipient to reclaim the strength, resilience, and spiritual wisdom gained from past experiences, even as they release the energetic imprints of trauma. Healing across timelines involves clearing old patterns and embracing the lessons and growth from past lives or ancestral experiences. This integration brings a sense of wholeness and alignment with the recipient's higher self, allowing them to move forward on their spiritual path with clarity and empowerment.

Chapter 4: Tools for Enhancing Distance Healing

Symbols, Intentions, and Amplifying Distance Healing

How does Hon Sha Ze Sho Nen enable Reiki practitioners to send healing energy across physical distances?

Answer: Hon Sha Ze Sho Nen is the Reiki symbol transcending time and space. It creates an energetic bridge between the practitioner and the recipient, allowing healing energy to flow freely despite physical distance. The symbol reinforces the interconnectedness of all energy and bypasses the limitations of linear time, enabling healing across the past, present, and future.

Describe the process of invoking Hon Sha Ze Sho Nen during a distance healing session.

Answer: To invoke Hon Sha Ze Sho Nen, the practitioner can visualize the symbol in their mind, draw it in the air, or trace it on paper. This is done at the beginning of a distance Reiki session to create an energetic connection with the recipient. The practitioner then sets a clear intention to send healing energy, trusting that it will reach the recipient regardless of physical location or time.

Why might a practitioner combine Hon Sha Ze Sho Nen with symbols such as Cho Ku Rei and Sei He Ki during a distance healing session?

Answer: Combining Hon Sha Ze Sho Nen with Cho Ku Rei or Sei He Ki amplifies the healing energy. Cho Ku Rei enhances the power and intensity of the energy flow, while Sei He Ki addresses emotional and mental imbalances. Using these symbols together creates a stronger, more focused healing environment that effectively targets physical and emotional issues.

What role does intention play when a practitioner uses Hon Sha Ze Sho Nen in distance healing, and how does it impact the session's outcome?

Answer: Intention is crucial in Reiki, as it directs the flow of healing energy. When using Hon Sha Ze Sho Nen, the practitioner's clear intention to heal and connect with the recipient guides the energy to its intended target. A focused mind and compassionate heart amplify the power of the symbol, ensuring that the healing is effective and reaches the recipient across time and space.

How does setting a focused intention enhance the effectiveness of a Reiki distance healing session?

Answer: Focused intention guides the energy flow in Reiki distance healing by aligning the practitioner's mental, emotional, and energetic focus with the healing goal. This clear focus ensures that the healing energy reaches the recipient's energy field and the specific area where it is most needed, enhancing the overall potency of the session.

What role do affirmations play in Reiki distance healing, and how can they amplify the healing process?

Answer: Affirmations are positive statements that reinforce the practitioner's intention during a distance healing session. They align the practitioner's energy with the desired outcome and raise the vibrational frequency of both the practitioner and the recipient. For example, affirmations like "The recipient is healed, whole, and at peace" create a supportive, high-vibrational environment for healing.

Give examples of effective affirmations for addressing physical, emotional, and spiritual issues during a Reiki session.

Answer: Physical Healing: "The recipient's body is strong, healthy, and full of vibrant energy." Emotional Healing: "The recipient releases all fear and embraces peace, love, and harmony." Spiritual Growth: "The recipient is aligned with their higher self and connected to the universe's infinite wisdom."

Why is meditation important for Reiki practitioners during distance healing, and how does it support intention and affirmations?

Answer: Meditation helps practitioners maintain mental clarity, emotional balance, and focus during a Reiki distance healing session. By calming the mind and centering their energy, practitioners can set strong intentions and align their thoughts with positive affirmations. This enhances the flow of healing energy, ensuring it remains clear and aligned with the recipient's needs.

What is the significance of maintaining a high vibrational frequency in Reiki, and how can practitioners ensure they stay aligned with positive emotions?

Answer: A high vibrational frequency enhances the potency of healing energy during a Reiki session. Practitioners can maintain this frequency by aligning with positive emotions such as love, compassion, gratitude, and peace. Focused intention, affirmations, and meditation help practitioners maintain this high vibrational state, ensuring the energy they channel is powerful and effective.

What is the role of meditation in Reiki healing, and how does it improve the practitioner's ability to channel healing energy effectively?

Answer: Meditation helps the practitioner enter a state of mental clarity and emotional balance, allowing them to focus on the recipient's energy field and the flow of universal life force. This clear, calm state enhances the practitioner's ability to sense subtle shifts in the recipient's energy and ensures a strong connection throughout the session.

Why is grounding meditation important before a Reiki distance healing session, and how do you perform it?

Answer: Grounding meditation ensures the practitioner is energetically stable, balanced, and fully present during the session. To perform grounding meditation, the practitioner focuses on their breath while visualizing energy rising from the Earth, filling their body with stability, and releasing tension into the ground. This practice creates a solid foundation for the healing session.

How does visualization help direct Reiki energy to specific areas of the recipient's body, and what are some examples of effective visualizations?

Answer: Visualization allows the practitioner to mentally guide the energy flow to specific areas that need healing. An example is the golden light visualization, where the practitioner imagines the recipient surrounded by a glowing light that dissolves blockages and restores balance. This technique intensifies the energy flow and creates a more focused healing effect.

How do Reiki symbols, such as Hon Sha Ze Sho Nen and Cho Ku Rei, enhance the healing process when combined with meditation and visualization?

Answer: Reiki symbols amplify the flow of healing energy by serving as visual and energetic guides. In meditation and visualization, practitioners can imagine these symbols over the recipient's body or energy field, helping to focus and strengthen the healing energy. For example, Hon Sha Ze Sho Nen connects the practitioner to the recipient, while Cho Ku Rei intensifies the energy in specific areas.

How does maintaining a state of presence and flow throughout a Reiki healing session improve the effectiveness of the healing?

Answer: Maintaining a state of presence and flow ensures that the practitioner remains fully attuned to the recipient's energy field and the flow of universal life force. By staying focused and connected, the practitioner can channel energy more effectively, sense subtle energy shifts, and adjust the energy flow as needed, resulting in a more transformative healing session.

Chakras and the Etheric Body

What is the etheric body, and how does it relate to physical health?

Answer: The etheric body is the energetic counterpart of the physical body, often referred to as its blueprint. It mirrors the physical form and maintains the body's vitality and health. Any imbalances in the etheric field can eventually manifest as physical symptoms, such as pain or illness. Distance healing works on the etheric field to restore balance and clear blockages, supporting overall physical health.

How can Reiki practitioners use distance healing to clear blockages in the etheric field?

Answer: Reiki practitioners use distance healing techniques to connect with and work on the recipient's etheric field, often invoking Reiki symbols and visualization. By sensing imbalances or blockages in the field, they send Reiki energy to dissolve these blockages, restoring the free flow of life force energy and promoting healing. This approach helps prevent energetic imbalances in the etheric field from manifesting as physical ailments.

What role do chakras play in distance healing, and how can clearing them support holistic well-being?

Answer: Chakras are energy centers within the etheric body that regulate the flow of life force energy throughout the body. Each chakra governs different aspects of physical, emotional, and spiritual well-being. During distance healing, Reiki practitioners focus on clearing and balancing these chakras to remove energetic blockages, allowing the recipient to experience improved health, emotional balance, mental clarity, and spiritual connection.

How does distance healing integrate across the etheric, emotional, mental, and spiritual bodies?

Answer: Distance healing works holistically across all layers of the energy field—etheric, emotional, mental, and spiritual. While the etheric body is closely tied to physical health, the emotional, mental, and spiritual bodies influence feelings, thoughts, beliefs, and spiritual connection. Reiki practitioners address imbalances in all these areas, helping to clear emotional pain, mental confusion, and spiritual disconnection, leading to comprehensive healing across the recipient's entire energy system.

What is the primary function of the chakra system, and why is it important to balance these energy centers during Reiki distance healing?

Answer: The chakra system regulates the flow of life force energy (ki or prana) throughout the physical and subtle energy bodies. Each of the seven main chakras governs different aspects of an individual's physical, emotional, mental, and spiritual well-being. Balancing these energy centers is vital because blockages can lead to physical illness, emotional distress, and spiritual disconnection. In distance healing, balancing the chakras ensures the free flow of energy, promoting holistic healing.

How can a practitioner use Reiki symbols and visualization to balance the recipient's root chakra during a distance healing session?

Answer: The practitioner can visualize a bright red light at the base of the recipient's spine, representing the root chakra (Muladhara). They may use the Cho Ku Rei symbol to increase energy flow, ensuring the recipient feels grounded, stable, and secure. The practitioner focuses on clearing blockages in this area, helping the recipient connect with the Earth and restore a sense of physical and emotional safety.

Which Reiki symbol is most commonly associated with emotional healing, and how can it be used to balance the sacral chakra during distance healing?

Answer: The Sei He Ki symbol is commonly associated with emotional healing. To balance the sacral chakra (Svadhisthana), the practitioner can visualize a warm, orange light swirling around the recipient's lower abdomen while using the Sei He Ki symbol to dissolve emotional blockages. This restores emotional balance and helps recipients reconnect with their creativity, joy, and sensuality.

What are the typical signs of an imbalanced third eye chakra, and how can distance healing address these symptoms?

Answer: An imbalanced third eye chakra (Ajna) can manifest as a lack of intuition, mental fog, difficulty making decisions, or feeling disconnected from inner guidance. In distance healing, the practitioner can visualize a deep indigo light on the recipient's forehead and use the Sei He Ki symbol to clear mental and emotional blockages clouding the recipient's intuition. This helps restore clarity, mental focus, and a deeper connection to inner wisdom.

What is the role of the crown chakra in spiritual connection, and how can distance healing strengthen this connection?

Answer: The crown chakra (Sahasrara) governs spiritual connection, higher consciousness, and a sense of purpose. When this chakra is blocked, the recipient may feel disconnected from their spiritual path or experience a lack of meaning. Distance healing can strengthen the recipient's spiritual connection by visualizing a bright violet or white light at the top of the recipient's head and using the Hon Sha Ze Sho Nen symbol to align them with their higher self and the divine. Balancing the crown chakra allows the recipient to feel more spiritually connected and aligned with their life's purpose

What is the primary function of the emotional body, and how can distance healing address emotional wounds?

Answer: The emotional body governs feelings, emotional experiences, and relationships and is closely linked to the heart chakra. Distance healing addresses emotional wounds by sending Reiki energy to release emotional blockages caused by unresolved trauma, suppressed emotions, or stress. Symbols like Sei He Ki promote emotional healing, allowing recipients to process their feelings and find inner peace.

How does the mental body influence thoughts and beliefs, and what techniques can a practitioner use to clear mental blockages during distance healing?

Answer: The mental body governs thoughts, beliefs, and mental clarity and is connected to the third eye and throat chakras. When the mental body is out of balance, it can manifest as limiting beliefs, confusion, or overthinking. Practitioners can use the Hon Sha Ze Sho Nen symbol to transcend time and space, addressing the root causes of mental patterns and helping dissolve negative thought loops. This allows the recipient to gain clarity and release limiting beliefs.

Describe how Reiki distance healing can strengthen the recipient's connection to their higher self through the spiritual body.

Answer: The spiritual body governs the recipient's connection to their higher self, divine energy, and spiritual path. In Reiki distance healing, the practitioner can send energy to the crown chakra, using the Hon Sha Ze Sho Nen symbol to align the recipient with their spiritual essence. This helps open pathways for spiritual growth and strengthens the connection to the divine, leading to a renewed sense of purpose and inner peace.

What are the benefits of integrating healing across the emotional, mental, and spiritual bodies during a distance healing session?

Answer: Integrating healing across the emotional, mental, and spiritual bodies creates a holistic healing experience that addresses all aspects of the recipient's well-being. By working on one layer, such as releasing emotional blockages, the practitioner indirectly influences the mental and spiritual bodies, creating a ripple effect of balance and healing throughout the recipient's entire energy field. This interconnected approach leads to more profound and transformative healing.

What Reiki symbol is associated with emotional healing, and how does it help in distance healing sessions?

Answer: The Sei He Ki symbol is associated with emotional healing and balance. In distance healing, practitioners use Sei He Ki to clear emotional blockages in the recipient's emotional body, helping to dissolve stored emotions such as grief, anger, or fear. This symbol facilitates emotional release and creates space for healing and inner peace.

Meditation, Mindfulness, and Energy Healing

Why is attuning to higher frequencies important for Reiki practitioners in distance healing?

Answer: Attuning to higher frequencies allows practitioners to connect more deeply with the universal life force, enabling them to channel more focused, potent energy during distance healing sessions. It strengthens the energetic connection between the practitioner and recipient, making the healing energy flow more effectively across time and space.

Describe a simple meditation technique that can help raise a practitioner's vibrational frequency before a distance healing session.

Answer: A simple meditation technique involves focused breathing. The practitioner sits comfortably and focuses on their breath. They imagine drawing in pure, healing energy with each inhale, filling their body and energy field with light. With each exhale, they release any tension or lower-vibrational energy. This meditation helps align the practitioner with higher frequencies of the universal life force.

How does mindfulness benefit Reiki practitioners during a distance healing session?

Answer: Mindfulness benefits Reiki practitioners by helping them remain fully present and focused during the healing session. This presence allows them to tune into subtle shifts in the recipient's energy field, respond intuitively, and maintain a strong, energetic connection, ensuring the universal life force flows effectively.

Which Reiki symbols are often used to enhance attunement to higher frequencies, and how do they function in a healing session?

Answer: Cho Ku Rei (power symbol) and Hon Sha Ze Sho Nen (distance symbol) are commonly used to raise the practitioner's vibrational frequency and strengthen energy flow. Cho Ku Rei amplifies the power of the energy, while Hon Sha Ze Sho Nen helps transcend time and space, allowing the practitioner to connect with the recipient's energy field during distance healing.

How can gratitude be used as an attunement technique before a distance healing session?

Answer: Gratitude is a powerful attunement technique because it raises the practitioner's vibrational frequency. By taking a few moments to express gratitude for the opportunity to serve as a channel for healing, practitioners align themselves more deeply with the universal life force, creating a positive, high-frequency energy state that enhances the session's effectiveness.

Why is mindfulness important in a Reiki distance healing session?

Answer: Mindfulness helps practitioners stay fully present during the healing session, allowing them to focus on the recipient's energy field and make intuitive adjustments to the flow of Reiki energy. It prevents distractions and helps maintain a continuous, smooth flow of healing energy.

Describe a basic mindfulness meditation technique to help practitioners stay present during a distance healing session.

Answer: Practitioners can sit comfortably in a quiet space and focus on their breath. They should notice the sensation of air entering their lungs as they inhale and let go of tension or distractions as they exhale. If their mind wanders, they gently bring their attention back to their breath, helping them stay present and focused on the healing session.

How does visualization enhance the practitioner's intention during a Reiki distance healing session?

Answer: Visualization allows the practitioner to create mental images or scenarios that align with the desired healing outcomes, helping to direct energy more effectively. For example, practitioners might visualize the recipient's body being bathed in healing light or mentally project Reiki symbols onto the recipient's energy field to amplify the healing energy.

What are affirmations, and how can they be used during Reiki distance healing?

Answer: Affirmations are positive, present-tense statements that help align the practitioner's energy with the desired healing intention. During a distance healing session, affirmations such as "Healing flows effortlessly to the recipient's highest good" reinforce the practitioner's focus and belief in the effectiveness of the Reiki energy, enhancing the healing process.

How can a practitioner maintain mindfulness throughout a distance healing session?

Answer: Practitioners can maintain mindfulness by checking in with their body and energy field through body awareness, periodically noticing sensations or tension. Additionally, gentle reminders such as silently repeating "presence" or "focus" can help the practitioner return to the present moment and stay focused on the recipient's energy field.

How does expanding consciousness enhance a Reiki practitioner's ability to channel healing energy?

Answer: Expanding consciousness allows practitioners to connect more deeply with the universal energy field, enabling them to channel higher healing energy frequencies. This expanded awareness enhances their sensitivity to subtle shifts in the recipient's energy field and allows them to address deeper, underlying causes of imbalance.

What is open-heart meditation, and how does it help expand consciousness during distance healing?

 Answer: Open-heart meditation focuses on the heart chakra, visualizing it glowing with love and compassion. This practice allows practitioners to expand their consciousness by cultivating unconditional love and connecting more deeply to the universal life force. It dissolves barriers between the practitioner and recipient, creating a space of oneness where healing can occur more effectively.

Describe cosmic consciousness meditation and its role in Reiki distance healing.

 Answer: Cosmic consciousness meditation involves visualizing oneself, merging with the infinite energy of the universe, and floating among stars and galaxies. This practice helps practitioners transcend their ego and perceive the recipient as part of the greater whole. The practitioner channels powerful, expansive healing energy beyond physical and time-bound limitations by aligning with the cosmos.

How does grounding in the Earth's energy field support the practitioner in distance healing?

 Answer: Grounding ensures that the practitioner stays centered and balanced during a healing session by connecting with the stabilizing energy of the Earth. This practice helps practitioners maintain a strong connection to the physical and spiritual planes, allowing them to channel healing energy with clarity and precision while remaining present and focused.

Why is non-attachment important in becoming an effective conduit for healing energy?

 Answer: Non-attachment allows the practitioner to release any need to control the outcome of the healing session, trusting in the flow of the universal life force. By surrendering to this process, the practitioner creates space for the energy to work naturally, guiding it where it is needed most and ensuring that healing occurs without interference from personal desires or expectations.

Chapter 5: Advanced Concepts

Multidimensionality and Parallel Universes

What does it mean to be a multidimensional being in the context of energy healing?

 Answer: A multidimensional being refers to the idea that each individual exists simultaneously on multiple planes of reality or dimensions, including the physical, emotional, mental, and spiritual. These dimensions are interconnected, and imbalances in one can affect others. In Reiki, healing can occur across these dimensions, not just the physical body.

How does Reiki healing operate across different dimensions, and what role does the Hon Sha Ze Sho Nen symbol play in this process?

Answer: Reiki operates across dimensions because it is not limited by time and space. Practitioners can use the Hon Sha Ze Sho Nen symbol to transcend these limitations and connect with the recipient's higher dimensions. This symbol allows the practitioner to access the emotional, mental, and spiritual bodies, enabling healing at a deeper level.

Why is grounding important for practitioners in multidimensional healing, and how can they maintain this balance?

Answer: Grounding is essential because it keeps the practitioner connected to the physical plane while accessing higher dimensions. This balance ensures the healing energy is fully integrated into the recipient's body. Practitioners can maintain this balance by visualizing roots extending from their feet into the Earth and remaining present during the session.

How can healing in non-physical realms, such as the emotional or mental bodies, affect the physical body in multidimensional healing?

Answer: Healing in non-physical realms can create a ripple effect that impacts the physical body. For example, emotional wounds healed in the fourth dimension can release long-held grief or trauma that manifests as physical symptoms. Similarly, clearing mental blockages in the fifth dimension can help dissolve limiting beliefs, leading to better physical and emotional health.

What is the concept of parallel realities, and how does it relate to the idea of multidimensional beings in energy healing?

Answer: Parallel realities refer to multiple versions of reality or timelines that run simultaneously, shaped by the choices and energy we hold. In the context of multidimensional beings, individuals exist on multiple planes or timelines, each influenced by different energies. These alternate versions can impact our present experience and vice versa, creating a complex web of interconnected realities.

How does Reiki healing in one timeline influence parallel realities, and what is the role of symbols like Hon Sha Ze Sho Nen in this process?

Answer: Reiki healing in one timeline or dimension creates a ripple effect that influences parallel realities because energy flows freely across dimensions. The Hon Sha Ze Sho Nen symbol allows practitioners to transcend time and space, connecting with the recipient's alternate selves in other realities. The practitioner can dissolve energetic patterns or blockages by sending healing energy to these dimensions, creating a holistic healing effect across all realities.

What is the ripple effect of healing in parallel universes, and how can this affect the recipient's current life experience?

Answer: The ripple effect occurs when healing energy in one dimension reverberates across other realities. For instance, if trauma is healed in one timeline, it can influence and alleviate the same energetic pattern in alternate realities. This creates a sense of relief and balance in the recipient's current experience as energy shifts positively across all dimensions.

How do Reiki practitioners approach healing across parallel realities, and what techniques are used to connect with the recipient's multidimensional aspects?

Answer: Reiki practitioners approach healing across parallel realities by entering a state of expanded consciousness and trusting their intuitive guidance. Techniques such as visualization, meditation, and using symbols like Hon Sha Ze Sho Nen help the practitioner connect with the recipient's energy in multiple dimensions. By visualizing the recipient's energy as overlapping layers representing parallel realities, the practitioner can send healing energy to all dimensions, ensuring alignment across timelines.

What is the quantum field, and how does it relate to the process of Reiki distance healing?

Answer: The quantum field is a space of infinite potential where all possibilities exist simultaneously. In Reiki, practitioners tap into this field to send healing energy beyond time and space constraints, allowing the energy to flow freely and reach the recipient's energy field across multiple dimensions and timelines.

How does the principle of non-locality in quantum physics support the idea of distance healing in Reiki?

Answer: Non-locality suggests that particles can remain connected across vast distances without being physically near each other. This parallels how Reiki practitioners can connect with a recipient's energy field and send healing energy across time and space, demonstrating how distance healing works beyond physical limitations.

What role does intention play in the healing process within the quantum field, and how does it affect the outcome of a Reiki session?

Answer: Intention is a guiding force in the quantum field, collapsing infinite possibilities into a specific healing outcome. When a Reiki practitioner sets a clear intention, it shapes how the healing energy flows, directing it to the areas where it is needed most, both in the recipient's current timeline and across parallel dimensions.

How can visualization techniques enhance a Reiki practitioner's ability to work within the quantum field during distance healing?

Answer: Visualization helps practitioners focus on the recipient's multidimensional aspects, allowing them to direct Reiki energy more effectively across timelines and dimensions. Techniques like visualizing the recipient's energy field within a web of light or an orb in the quantum field help strengthen the practitioner's connection to the universal life force and ensure comprehensive healing.

How does integrating quantum theory with Reiki healing bridge the gap between science and spirituality?

Answer: Quantum theory, especially concepts like non-locality and the quantum field, provides a scientific explanation for how Reiki healing works across time and space. This bridges the gap between science and spirituality, showing that both fields support the idea of interconnectedness and multidimensional healing, deepening the understanding of how Reiki energy can create transformative changes.

Collective Consciousness and Akashic Records

What is the collective consciousness, and how does it influence individual and collective well-being?

Answer: The collective consciousness is the shared energy field of thoughts, beliefs, and experiences of all beings. It influences individual well-being by shaping the energetic environment in which people exist, and individuals, in turn, influence the collective through their own energy. Collective emotions such as fear, anxiety, or love can resonate throughout society, affecting both the collective and individuals.

How can Reiki practitioners contribute to healing the collective consciousness?

Answer: Reiki practitioners can access the collective consciousness by setting intentions to send healing energy to societal, global, or collective issues. This can be done through visualizations, focusing on restoring balance to the collective field or participating in group healing sessions that amplify the healing energy directed at collective challenges, such as global trauma or fear.

What techniques can be used to access the collective consciousness for healing purposes?

Answer: Practitioners can use techniques like setting intentions, visualizing the collective as an interconnected web of light surrounding the Earth, and sending Reiki energy to dissolve imbalances. Group healing sessions, where multiple practitioners focus on a shared intention, can also be powerful for healing the collective consciousness.

How does individual healing impact the collective consciousness?

Answer: Healing at the individual level raises the person's vibrational frequency, which contributes positively to the collective consciousness. As individuals release trauma, fear, or imbalance, they help elevate the overall energetic field, benefiting society and future generations.

What are the Akashic Records, and how do they inform Reiki healing?

Answer: The Akashic Records are an energetic repository containing the history of every soul's experiences across all lifetimes, including thoughts, emotions, and actions. Reiki practitioners can access these records to gain insights into past life traumas, karmic patterns, and ancestral wounds that influence the recipient's current experience. This knowledge helps guide the healing process by addressing root causes that span lifetimes.

How do Reiki practitioners access the Akashic Records during a distance healing session?
Answer: Practitioners access the Akashic Records by setting a clear intention to connect with the recipient's records, entering a meditative state, and using Reiki symbols like Hon Sha Ze Sho Nen to transcend time and space. They may receive intuitive impressions, images, or emotions that reveal important information about the recipient's soul journey, allowing them to focus healing energy on key areas.

How can the Akashic Records help in healing past-life traumas and karmic patterns?
Answer: The Akashic Records provide insights into past-life events, unresolved traumas, or karmic lessons that continue to affect the recipient's present life. By identifying these patterns, practitioners can send Reiki energy to dissolve the blockages, allowing recipients to release burdens carried across lifetimes and align with their highest purpose.

What role does intuition play in accessing and working with the Akashic Records?
Answer: Intuition is crucial when working with the Akashic Records, as the information received is often subtle and may not follow a linear pattern. Practitioners must trust their intuitive impressions and approach the records with humility and respect, knowing that the Reiki energy will guide them to the areas that need healing for the recipient's highest good.

What are energetic imprints, and how do they affect an individual's present life?
Answer: Energetic imprints are subtle residues left behind by past experiences, trauma, or karmic patterns that become embedded in a person's energy field. These imprints influence their emotional, physical, and spiritual well-being, often manifesting as recurring patterns, fears, or physical symptoms.

How do Reiki practitioners heal past life traumas during distance healing sessions?
Answer: Reiki practitioners access the recipient's Akashic Records to identify past life experiences that created energetic imprints. By sending Reiki energy to the moments of trauma, they release the emotional, physical, and spiritual wounds carried across lifetimes, helping the recipient heal in the present.

What is the significance of ancestral and familial energy healing in Reiki?
Answer: Ancestral and familial energy healing addresses inherited imprints, such as emotional trauma, passed down through generations. Reiki practitioners can access

ancestral records in the Akashic field and send healing energy to release these imprints, freeing the recipient and future generations from the cycle of inherited emotional pain.

How can Reiki practitioners work with collective trauma and karma?

Answer: Practitioners can access the Akashic Records of the collective consciousness to identify areas affected by collective trauma or karmic patterns, such as war or social injustice. By sending Reiki energy to these imprints, practitioners help to release the collective energy that perpetuates societal imbalances, contributing to healing on a larger scale.

What is the process of integrating healing across timelines, and why is it important?

Answer: Integrating healing across timelines involves reclaiming the wisdom, strength, and resilience gained from past experiences and incorporating these insights into the present. This process empowers the recipient to move forward with greater alignment and purpose, free from the energetic burdens of the past.

Soul Contracts and Life Purpose

What is a soul contract, and how does it shape an individual's life experiences?

Answer: A soul contract is an agreement the soul makes before incarnation, outlining the key relationships, challenges, and experiences that will facilitate spiritual growth. These contracts guide individuals toward their highest potential by presenting them with opportunities for learning and evolution.

Which two chakras are most commonly associated with aligning with life purpose, and why?

Answer: The third eye (Ajna) and solar plexus (Manipura) chakras are associated with aligning with life's purpose. The third eye chakra governs intuition and higher guidance, helping individuals connect with their spiritual path. In contrast, the solar plexus chakra governs personal power and confidence, which is necessary for embracing and fulfilling one's life purpose.

How can Reiki distance healing help individuals align with their soul contracts and life purpose?

Answer: Reiki distance healing clears energetic blockages, such as limiting beliefs, fear, or unresolved trauma, that prevent individuals from fully embracing their life purpose. By working with the recipient's higher self, chakras, and Akashic Records, Reiki helps release old patterns and facilitates reconnection with the soul's deeper calling.

What role do past life experiences and karmic patterns play in creating blockages, and how can Reiki help release them?

Answer: Past life experiences and karmic patterns often create energetic blockages that manifest as emotional, mental, or physical challenges in the present life. These blockages may stem from unresolved trauma or lessons the soul needs to learn. Reiki helps release these blockages by sending healing energy to the root cause, dissolving patterns from past lifetimes.

How does distance healing provide spiritual insights that help individuals understand and embrace their life purpose?

Answer: Distance healing facilitates moments of spiritual awakening and intuitive guidance by clearing the confusion, fear, and limiting beliefs that prevent individuals from accessing their higher selves. These insights often lead to a greater understanding of the soul's path and inspire recipients to follow their true calling with clarity and purpose.

What causes energetic blockages, and how do they prevent individuals from following their life path?

Answer: Energetic blockages are caused by unresolved emotions, past trauma, limiting beliefs, or karmic patterns that disrupt the natural flow of life force energy. These blockages create stagnation and make it difficult for individuals to move forward, often manifesting as confusion, fear, or physical symptoms.

How does Reiki distance healing clear energetic blockages, and which symbols are most effective?

Answer: Reiki distance healing works by channeling universal life force energy to areas of the recipient's energy field where blockages exist. The Cho Ku Rei symbol amplifies energy to break through stagnation, while the Hon Sha Ze Sho Nen symbol accesses blockages related to past life trauma and karmic patterns by transcending time and space.

How can limiting beliefs and emotional blockages be cleared through Reiki distance healing?

Answer: Reiki helps release emotional wounds and trauma underlying limiting beliefs, such as feelings of unworthiness or fear of failure. By clearing these emotional blockages, Reiki allows individuals to reframe their beliefs and move forward with clarity and confidence.

Which chakras are often affected by mental and emotional blockages, and how does Reiki help restore balance?

Answer: Mental and emotional blockages commonly affect the third eye (Ajna) and solar plexus (Manipura) chakras. Reiki distance healing clears mental fog and emotional wounds in these chakras, helping individuals regain intuitive clarity and personal power.

How does Reiki help individuals release fear and resistance to change, and what are the key chakras involved?

Answer: Reiki helps release fear and resistance to change by dissolving energetic imprints of fear stored in the root (Muladhara) and solar plexus (Manipura) chakras. This process restores groundedness and personal empowerment, allowing individuals to align with their true path.

Chapter 6: Real-World Applications

Healing Across Generations and Ancestral Lines

What is generational trauma, and how can it manifest in a person's life?
Answer: Generational trauma refers to unresolved traumatic experiences and emotional wounds passed down from one generation to the next. It can manifest as chronic emotional distress, recurring behavior patterns, or physical symptoms like anxiety, fear, or insecurity, even if the person is not consciously aware of their family's traumatic history.

How does Reiki distance healing address ancestral karma?
Answer: Reiki distance healing addresses ancestral karma by accessing the Akashic Records and sending healing energy to unresolved karmic patterns or debts passed down through the family line. Using symbols such as Hon Sha Ze Sho Nen, the practitioner connects with and resolves the energetic imbalances created in the past, helping free the recipient from inherited karmic burdens.

Which chakra plays a crucial role in ancestral healing, and why?
Answer: The root chakra (Muladhara) is key in ancestral healing because it governs grounding, safety, and connection to one's lineage. This chakra stores much of the ancestral energy, and when it is blocked by unresolved trauma or karma, it can manifest as feelings of disconnection or insecurity. Reiki healing can clear blockages in the root chakra, restoring a sense of stability and grounding.

What is the significance of healing across time and generations in Reiki distance healing?
Answer: Healing across time and generations means that Reiki can address the root causes of trauma or karmic imbalances that occurred in the past, affecting both ancestors and future descendants. This multidimensional healing helps release inherited patterns from the recipient's family line, creating space for new, healthier patterns to emerge and benefiting future generations.

How does Reiki distance healing create a ripple effect across generations?
Answer: Reiki distance healing clears inherited energetic imprints such as trauma and unresolved emotions, creating space for healthier patterns to emerge in the individual and their descendants. This healing benefits the recipient and extends to past and future generations by breaking the cycle of inherited trauma and karma.

What types of inherited emotional patterns can be dissolved through Reiki?
Answer: Inherited emotional patterns that can be dissolved through Reiki include fear, grief, guilt, shame, anger, and abandonment. These patterns may have been passed down through family lines due to unprocessed traumatic experiences or habitual behaviors from ancestors.

How does Reiki help restore energy flow in family lines, and why is this important?
Answer: Reiki helps restore energy flow in family lines by clearing blockages in key energy centers, such as the root and heart chakras responsible for grounding and emotional healing. Restoring this flow allows the life force energy to move freely, breaking patterns of dysfunction or struggle and promoting healing throughout the family line.

What is the benefit of anchoring positive energy for future generations through Reiki?
Answer: Anchoring positive energy through Reiki helps ensure that future generations are free from the burdens of inherited trauma, allowing them to live with greater emotional freedom, joy, and alignment. This creates a foundation for healthier behaviors and relationships, positively impacting the family line for years.

Why is integrating ancestral healing into daily life following a Reiki session essential?
Answer: Integrating ancestral healing into daily life ensures that the energetic shifts created during the Reiki session are embodied and sustained. This helps to create new patterns of behavior and emotional responses, fostering healthier relationships and dynamics within the family. The ongoing integration solidifies the healing and promotes lasting change across generations.

How can individuals anchor the energetic shifts from Reiki healing into their physical and emotional bodies?
Answer: Individuals can anchor these shifts by practicing grounding techniques, body awareness exercises, and chakra balancing. Spending time in nature, deep breathing, or using visualizations can help strengthen the root chakra and keep the energy flow steady, ensuring that the new patterns remain embodied on all levels.

What role do rituals and symbols play in ancestral healing?
Answer: Rituals and symbols help anchor the energetic changes initiated through Reiki healing, solidifying the connection to the healed ancestors and reinforcing positive patterns in the family line. Rituals like creating an ancestral altar or practicing seasonal ceremonies allow families to honor the healing, while Reiki symbols continue to invite healing energy and alignment into their lives.

How can families create new behavior and thought patterns to align with ancestral healing?
Answer: Families can foster new patterns by consciously engaging in healthier communication, emotional expression, and supportive relationships. For example, they

might practice open communication, nurture emotional intimacy, or adopt mindsets more aligned with abundance and connection, reflecting the shifts that have occurred through Reiki healing.

How can the gifts of healing be passed down to future generations?

Answer: Healing can be passed down by creating an environment prioritizing emotional support, spiritual alignment, and energetic harmony. Families can teach children about energy, healing, and connection to their ancestors, equipping future generations with the tools to continue the healing journey and maintain a legacy of love and empowerment.

Empathy, Intuition, and Psychic Abilities

What is the difference between emotional empathy and energetic empathy in the context of Reiki distance healing?

Answer: Emotional empathy is the capacity to resonate emotionally with another person's feelings. In Reiki distance healing, energetic empathy goes deeper, allowing the practitioner to perceive the recipient's energy field, detect energetic imbalances, and understand their emotional or physical state at a subtle, energetic level. This allows the practitioner to direct healing energy to areas of need, even without physical presence.

How can intuition guide a Reiki practitioner in a distance healing session?

Answer: Intuition helps the practitioner understand the recipient's needs during the healing session, often providing insights through mental images, sensations, or messages. For example, intuition might guide the practitioner to use specific Reiki symbols or direct energy to certain chakras based on the recipient's energetic condition. It allows for a more personalized and effective healing session by tuning into the deeper layers of the recipient's energy field.

What are psychic abilities, and how do they contribute to Reiki distance healing?

Answer: Psychic abilities, such as clairvoyance (clear seeing), clairaudience (clear hearing), and clairsentience (clear feeling), enable the practitioner to perceive information beyond ordinary senses. In Reiki distance healing, these abilities allow the practitioner to see energy patterns, feel physical sensations related to the recipient's condition, or receive guidance from spiritual entities. Psychic abilities offer deeper insights into the recipient's energetic, emotional, and spiritual states, enhancing the healing experience.

Why is it important for Reiki practitioners to develop grounding practices alongside their empathy and psychic abilities?

Answer: Grounding practices are essential for Reiki practitioners because they help maintain emotional clarity and protect their energy field. As practitioners open themselves to sense the recipient's energy and emotions, grounding ensures they do not absorb the recipient's energy or become overwhelmed. Grounding techniques, such as meditation or visualization, help practitioners stay balanced and remain clear channels for healing energy.

Why is intuition important in Reiki distance healing, and how does it benefit the healing process?

Answer: Intuition is essential because it allows the Reiki practitioner to perceive subtle energies, identify hidden patterns, and uncover the root causes of the recipient's imbalances. By relying on intuitive insights, practitioners can direct healing energy to the areas most needed, making the session more precise and effective.

How does meditation help strengthen a practitioner's intuitive abilities during distance healing sessions?

Answer: Meditation helps quiet the mind and creates inner stillness, which makes it easier for practitioners to receive intuitive insights without interference from mental chatter. A meditative state enhances the practitioner's ability to tune into subtle energetic signals from the recipient, allowing them to guide the flow of healing energy more effectively.

What role does feedback play in developing a Reiki practitioner's intuition?

Answer: Client feedback helps practitioners validate their intuitive impressions, building trust and confidence in their abilities. When a recipient confirms the practitioner's intuitive perceptions—such as sensing an energetic blockage or emotional state—it reinforces the accuracy of the information received. It encourages the practitioner to rely more on their intuition in future sessions.

What self-care practices can help Reiki practitioners maintain balance and avoid emotional fatigue?

Answer: Reiki practitioners can engage in grounding practices such as focusing on the breath, walking in nature, or visualizing roots extending into the earth to stay connected to their energy. Additionally, setting energetic boundaries before and after healing sessions—such as visualizing a protective shield or clearing the energy field with smudging—helps protect the practitioner from absorbing the recipient's emotions or energy, preventing emotional fatigue.

How does clairvoyance benefit Reiki distance healing sessions, and what information can a practitioner receive through clairvoyant abilities?

Answer: Clairvoyance benefits distance healing by allowing practitioners to see energy, images, or symbols that provide insights into the recipient's energy field. Practitioners may perceive chakras, auric fields, or energetic blockages in the form of colors or shapes, helping them direct healing energy more precisely to areas of imbalance.

What is clairsentience, and how can it enhance a practitioner's ability to connect with the recipient during a distance healing session?

Answer: Clairsentience is the ability to feel or sense the recipient's energy or emotions within the practitioner's body. It enhances the practitioner's connection to the recipient by allowing them to experience physical sensations or emotional states corresponding to the recipient's imbalances, enabling them to offer more compassionate and precise healing.

What are some effective techniques for cultivating psychic abilities for Reiki distance healing?

Answer: Effective techniques include meditation to open the third eye chakra, psychic development exercises such as visualization and listening practices, and working with mentors or guides for feedback and guidance. These practices help practitioners refine their psychic abilities and strengthen their connection to the subtle energy realms.

Why is trusting the process important when developing psychic abilities, and how can practitioners overcome doubt during healing sessions?

Answer: Trusting the process is vital because psychic abilities often present information that transcends logic, requiring practitioners to surrender control and allow intuitive insights to flow naturally. Practitioners can overcome doubt by letting go of judgment, practicing non-attachment to outcomes, and trusting that the impressions they receive are aligned with the recipient's highest good.

Using Sound and Vibrational Healing in Distance Reiki

How does sound enhance Reiki distance healing, and what role does it play in bridging the energy between the practitioner and the recipient?

Answer: Sound enhances Reiki distance healing by acting as a carrier of vibrational energy, amplifying the practitioner's healing intentions. Sound waves resonate with the recipient's energy field, creating ripples that help clear stagnant energy, harmonize imbalances, and retune energy centers (chakras) to their natural frequency. As sound vibrations can transcend physical space, they serve as a bridge between the practitioner and recipient, strengthening the energetic connection, much like quantum entanglement.

What is the significance of Solfeggio frequencies in sound healing, and how do they correspond to different healing qualities?

Answer: Solfeggio frequencies are ancient sound frequencies that promote healing and transformation by resonating with specific parts of the body's energetic system. Each frequency has distinct healing properties: for example, 396 Hz helps release fear and guilt, while 528 Hz, known as the "miracle tone," is believed to promote DNA repair and spiritual transformation. When used in Reiki distance healing, these frequencies realign energy centers, creating a harmonious balance within the body.

How can mantras be used with Reiki distance healing, and how do they affect the healing process?

Answer: Mantras are sacred sounds or phrases that, when repeated, create a vibrational resonance that shifts the practitioner's and recipient's energy fields. In Reiki distance healing, mantras help amplify the practitioner's focus and intention, directing the flow of energy more precisely to areas of need. Repeating mantras like Om Mani Padme Hum can open energy centers like the heart chakra, allowing for deeper emotional and spiritual healing.

Describe a practical way to incorporate sound tools into a Reiki distance healing session.

Answer: A simple way to incorporate sound into a Reiki distance healing session is by using a singing bowl, tuning fork, or recorded Solfeggio frequencies. For instance, if the recipient is struggling with fear, the practitioner could play the 396 Hz frequency to encourage the release of fear and anxiety. Simultaneously, the practitioner can send Reiki energy, focusing on areas where the recipient may need grounding or emotional balance, using sound as a vibrational tool to deepen the healing process.

What role does sound play in influencing the energetic body during a Reiki healing session?

Answer: Sound generates vibrations that resonate with the energetic body, including chakras and auras. These vibrations help restore balance and clear blockages by tuning the energy centers to their natural frequencies, much like tuning a musical instrument.

Which frequency is associated with the Heart Chakra, and what is its effect?

Answer: The 639 Hz frequency is related to the Heart Chakra. It helps heal relationships, open the heart, and invite love and harmony into the recipient's life.

How do sound frequencies work with Reiki symbols in distance healing?

Answer: Sound frequencies enhance the flow of Reiki energy by creating a vibrational foundation that amplifies the healing process. When used with Reiki symbols like Hon Sha Ze Sho Nen (distance symbol) or Sei He Ki (emotional healing symbol), sound helps clear blockages, balance the energy body, and direct healing energy more effectively.

What is the benefit of using the 528 Hz frequency in a Reiki distance healing session?

Answer: The 528 Hz frequency, often called the "miracle tone," benefits the Solar Plexus Chakra. It promotes self-confidence, inner strength, and transformation, helping the recipient align with their personal power and life purpose.

Azevedo, E., & Pissolato Filho, J. (2020). Is there an information field in the life world? Empirical approach using electrophotonic analysis. Journal of Life Sciences. https://doi.org/10.17265/1934-7391/2017.04.004

Barbour, J. (1999). The end of time: The next revolution in physics. Oxford University Press.

Blakeway, J. (2019). Energy medicine: The science and mystery of healing. Harper Wave.

Bohm, D. (1980). Wholeness and the implicate order. Routledge.

Braden, G. (2007). The divine matrix: Bridging time, space, miracles, and belief. Hay House.

Brennan, B. (1988). Hands of light: A guide to healing through the human energy field. Bantam Books.

Capra, F. (1975). The Tao of physics: An exploration of the parallels between modern physics and Eastern mysticism. Shambhala Publications.

Chopra, D. (1989). Quantum healing: Exploring the frontiers of mind/body medicine. Bantam Books.

Co, S., & Robins, E. B. (2004). Your hands can heal you: Pranic healing energy remedies to boost vitality and speed recovery from common health problems. Free Press.

Dauth, M., Schulze, D., Bachmann, M., Borla Tridon, D., Kahle, R., & Maurer, E.

(2018). Flying with an umbrella: Operational strategies for the Tandem-L Mission. https://doi.org/10.2514/6.2018-2591

Dyer, W. (2004). The power of intention: Learning to co-create your world your way. Hay House.

Einstein, A., Podolsky, B., & Rosen, N. (1935). Can quantum-mechanical description of physical reality be considered complete? Physical Review, 47, 777-780.

Emoto, M. (2005). The hidden messages in water. Simon and Schuster.

Gerber, R. (2001). Vibrational medicine: The #1 handbook of subtle-energy therapies (3rd ed.). Bear & Company.

Goswami, A. (1995). The self-aware universe: How consciousness creates the material world. TarcherPerigee.

Heisenberg, W. (1927). Über den anschaulichen Inhalt der quantentheoretischen Kinematik und Mechanik. Zeitschrift für Physik, 43(3-4), 172–198.

Hicks, E., & Hicks, J. (2006). The law of attraction: The basics of the teachings of Abraham. Hay House.

Horowitz, L. G. (2012). The book of 528: Prosperity key of love. Medical Veritas International.

Judith, A. (2004). Wheels of life: A user's guide to the chakra system. Llewellyn Publications.

Kabat-Zinn, J. (1994). Wherever you go, there you are: Mindfulness meditation in everyday life. Hyperion.

Karma, B. (2012). The laws of karma: Deeper knowledge about the energy of the soul. Karma Publishing.

Kelly, M. J. (2000). Reiki and the healing Buddha. Lotus Light Publications.

Kornfield, J. (1993). A path with heart: A guide through the perils and promises of spiritual life. Bantam Books.

Laszlo, E. (2007). Science and the Akashic field: An integral theory of everything. Inner Traditions.

Lipton, B. H. (2005). The biology of belief: Unleashing the power of consciousness, matter, and miracles. Hay House.

McTaggart, L. (2008). The field: The quest for the secret force of the universe. Harper Perennial.

Petter, F. A. (2000). The original Reiki handbook of Dr. Mikao Usui. Lotus Press.

Rand, W. L. (1991). Reiki: The healing touch. Vision Publications.

Schutz, P. (1997). The Akashic records: Sacred wisdom for transformation. Hay House.

Talbot, M. (1991). The holographic universe. Harper Perennial.

Taylor, S. A. (2019). The Akashic records: Unlock the infinite power, wisdom, and energy of the universe. Hay House.

Verny, T. (2014). What cells remember: Toward a unified field theory of memory. Journal of Prenatal & Perinatal Psychology & Health, 29(1), 16-29.

Index